A HERB COOKBOOK

A
HERB
COOKBOOK

Gilian Painter

HODDER AND STOUGHTON
AUCKLAND LONDON SYDNEY TORONTO

Typeset by Glenfield Graphics Ltd, Auckland
Printed and bound in Hong Kong for Hodder & Stoughton Ltd,
44-46 View Road, Glenfield, Auckland, New Zealand.

To Betty, Bridget and John

J'ai des bouquets pour tous les gouts;
Venez choisir dans ma corbeille:
De plusieurs les parfums sont doux,
De tous, la vertu sans pareille.
La petite Corbeille de fleurs

METRIC CONVERSION GUIDE

Length
1 inch	= 25.4 millimetres (mm)	1 mm	= 0.039 inch
1 inch	= 2.54 centimetres (cm)	1 cm	= 0.394 inch

Weight (Mass)
1 ounce	= 28.3 grams (g)	1 g	= 0.035 ounce
pound	= 454 grams (g)	1 kg	= 2.20 pounds

Volume (Fluids)
1 ounce	= 28.4 millilitres (ml)	1 ml	= 0.035 ounce
1 pint	= 568 millilitres (ml)	1 l	= 1.76 pints

TEMPERATURE EQUIVALENTS

	Degrees Celsius	Degrees Fahrenheit	Gas Range Regulator
Very Cool	110-140	225-275	¼-1
Cool	150-160	300-325	2-3
Moderate	180-190	350-375	4-5
Hot	200-230	400-450	6-8
Very Hot	250-260	475-500	9-10

CONTENTS

Introduction

Cooking with herbs is an enjoyable way of using the historic natural flowerings to make food taste delicious and be more digestible. It is not difficult to do, and can become an absorbing interest. If you have not used herbs in cooking before, start with those herbs you like the taste and scent of, and add them in small quantities to food which you enjoy. Do not overdo cooking with herbs — it is not necessary to serve food with herbs at every meal; just begin gradually, adding them now and then to appropriate food, and your family and friends will soon tell you what they like or dislike. Some of the recipes in this book I have made only once or twice; others are made every few weeks, or every year in their season, and the recipes are so loved that they will become part of our children's heritage.

Cooking is both an art and a science. The science comes in balancing ingredients to make them produce the type of food you want and this is what the directions in a recipe should give you. The art comes with experience, knowing how to judge the quality, ripeness and flavour of the raw materials you are working with to get the best result. Good cooking takes time and concentration but the food is delicious. It is something everyone can share with family and friends, and in the end, time and love are the two most important things anyone has to give.

I would like to acknowledge the help and interest of one of New Zealand's leading cooks, Tui Flower, always a source of practical inspiration. My thanks to Judith Long for her beautiful cover photographs, and to Tom Beran for patient editing and guidance. Initially, I had hoped to include all the herbs used in western cookery, but this was not practical in a book of this size, so we have chosen forty of the most commonly grown herbs. However, those readers interested in obtaining a supplement of recipes using the more uncommon herbs may contact the author, c/o Post Office, Oratia, Auckland.

Gilian Painter, 1983

Using Herbs

Fresh Herbs

Herbs are not difficult to grow, so even if you have never tried before, do grow at least the nine major culinary herbs. Chives, mint and parsley, sweet marjoram, sage and thyme, sweet basil, summer savory and tarragon will give an excellent introduction to cooking with herbs.

Once you have them, look after them, and notice how to harvest them to keep them growing well. Always try to use them straight from the garden when the fragrance and flavour are at their best.

In the kitchen use a good sharp knife or pair of scissors — blunt utensils bruise more than cut. If you have only a wooden chopping board some of the flavour will be absorbed by the board, so scissors for chives, and a mouli parsmint, or similar gadget, will mince most herbs finely.

If you use a lot of garlic keep a small separate board for chopping it — its strong odour can affect other milder herbs if they are cut on the same surface.

When adding herbs to a dish add a little at a time, tasting after each addition until the food tastes right to you. It's easy to add more but often impossible to take herbs out; use a wooden spoon when tasting.

Remember that the flavour of the herb is not meant to dominate — rather it should make the whole dish taste more delicious. However, certain herbs are traditionally used with certain foods not only because they taste good, but also because they make that food more digestible. Such combinations, for example sage with pork, should therefore be respected.

Some herbs are more salty or peppery than others so taste the food before adding these seasonings — you may not need them at all or only in small quantities. Herbs are very useful in salt-free diets.

Dried Green Herbs

The flavour of dried herbs is usually stronger and slightly different so they are generally used in smaller quantities. As a rough guide, use about half the quantity that you would use of fresh herbs but, as before, add some and taste before adding more.

Dried herbs should usually be finely crumbled before being added to food. If they are only roughly chopped put them through a mouli parsmint or similar gadget. If you want their flavour and none of the bits, tie the dried herbs in a small piece of muslin, cook them with the food and remove the muslin before serving.

Do not buy dried herbs in large quantities, nor keep them more than a year, for their flavour grows less with time. Always store them in dark glass or pottery containers which are not too much larger than the quantity of herbs and which are airtight, for a large air space destroys the flavour and light fades the colour. Also, do not keep your herb jars in a hot place in the sun or near the stove in the kitchen. They may look nice, but their flavour will deteriorate.

If you wish to dry your own herbs, cut them on a dry day just as they are coming into flower and hang them in small bunches in a warm, airy place out of direct light and sun. When the leaves feel crisp, strip them off into dark glass airtight containers.

Seed Herbs
Some seeds are added whole, for example caraway seeds in cakes, but at other times a recipe calls for ground seeds. Whole seeds keep their flavour better, so if you can, try to grind just as many seeds as you need for a recipe. Traditionally a mortar and pestle was used to grind herbs, and it is still a good way to do it, if a little time-consuming. An electric coffee grinder or a small mill like a pepper mill will also grind herb seeds, but if you have none of these put the seeds between two sheets of paper and crush them with a rolling pin (or a milk bottle). In recipes where seeds are used whole, this is a good way to lightly crush the seeds to release their flavour a little more.

If the recipe calls for the flavour without the seeds they may be infused in the liquid used and strained out, or tied in muslin and removed at the end of cooking.

Garlic

Garlic is included in many recipes but, if you don't like the flavour, you can always leave it out. The dish may not taste quite the same but it will still be good.

If you like the flavour but not the texture, crush the garlic in a garlic press, or cut each clove into two or three pieces and spear each sliver on a wooden toothpick. Then the speared garlic may be fried or otherwise cooked in the dish, and easily removed before serving.

If you like the flavour but not the smell and after-taste of garlic, peel the cloves and crush them with salt before adding them to food, or use garlic-flavoured vinegar in a salad dressing, or eat plenty of parsley and/or chervil with the food.

Keep garlic utensils and boards separate and use them only for garlic so that other herbs will not be affected by its strong flavour.

Freezing Herbs

Herbs, which may be frozen in whole leaves or sprigs on their own in small bags, or with other fruit and vegetables, do not need blanching. However, I think it is more satisfactory to freeze them either in sprigs, or blended in a blender with a little water and then set them in ice-cube trays. The frozen cubes may then be tipped into plastic bags and stored in the freezer. Always label the bags because one herb puree looks just like another — which may result in some interesting mistakes — or discoveries!

Pepper, Salt and Spices with Herbs

Because herbs may taste peppery or salty it is important to taste food flavoured with herbs before adding these ingredients. That is why, in most recipes, no quantities of these seasonings are given and they should be added to individual taste.

Pepper

Both black pepper and white pepper come from the same plant, a tropical vine, *Piper nigrum*. Black pepper is produced when the berries are picked green and dried in the sun. It is aromatic and should be freshly ground and added to the food at the end of cooking so that its aroma and pungency are at their best.

White pepper results when the pepper berries are allowed to ripen to their red colour after which they are picked, stacked up and allowed to ferment. After this they are washed and dried. White pepper has a stronger flavour than black pepper and is less aromatic. It also is best freshly ground and is used in any recipe for white sauces or food where black pepper would give a speckled effect.

Cayenne pepper, chilli pepper and paprika are all derived from the *Capsicum* family. Cayenne pepper comes from a particular type of ground red chilli pepper and is very hot tasting. It is less coarse than ground chilli powder which is often a better spice to use. Chilli powder varies in flavour from relatively mild to very firey. It is used in such things as cheese straws, chilli con carne and with tomatoes, as well as to flavour many Mexican and other Central and South American dishes.

Paprika, *Capsicum tetragonum*, comes from a pepper that is bright red but does not have the pungency of the chilli pepper. Its name is Hungarian and it is the national spice of Hungary but it is also used a lot in Spain. It should taste mild and sweet and has an aroma all of its own with a little under-lying bitterness. It contains vitamin C and may be used in generous amounts.

Pepper may be combined with other herbs and spices to give a different flavour.

Herb Pepper may be made by combining 25 g each black and white peppercorns and adding about 1 tsp each dried thyme, savory and marjoram and ½ tsp dried rosemary. Grind everything small through a pepper mill and use to season savoury and meat dishes.

Spiced Pepper may be made by combining 1 tbs each ground white pepper, nutmeg and mace and adding ½-1 tsp cayenne pepper.

Lemon Pepper for use with fish and poultry, and meat like veal, may be made by grinding ¼ cup of black peppercorns and mixing them with 2 tbs grated lemon rind. Shake it together well and store in an airtight container in the refrigerator.

Pepper gives an extra fragrance to sweet dishes. Some people like to pepper and sugar their fresh strawberries before eating them and food flavoured with sweet spices is often improved by adding pepper. Experiment to taste.

Salt

Salt is an essential mineral and although some is present in the food we eat most cooks add salt to food to bring out flavour, for cooking without salt is dull. Salt should generally be added at the end of cooking, for if it is added too early, when the amount of liquid is reduced by cooking, the dish may be too salty. It is not usually possible to remedy this unless one is able to add sufficient liquid to dilute the salt. There are several varieties of salt available. Coarse salt in lumps is excellent for preserving food and it may be ground in a wooden salt mill and used as table salt. Sea salt is produced from evaporating sea water and has a fine flavour. Table salt has some salts removed from it because they attract moisture and other ingredients added to allow it to flow freely. In New Zealand we have iodized salt because there is little natural iodine in our water and lack of iodine can cause goitre.

Like pepper, salt may be flavoured with herbs, or herbs may be used separately or with salt to give varied flavours. The following combinations all taste good in various dishes and may be used as guidelines for making your own blends.

Herb Salt

Grind separately, then combine:

1 tbs dried parsley	*1 tsp dried basil*
1 tbs paprika or ½ tsp cayenne	*1 tsp dried thyme*
1 tbs onion flakes	*1 tsp dried marjoram*

When finely ground, add ½ cup sea salt, mix well and keep in an airtight container.

or

1 tsp thyme	*1 tsp celery salt*
1 tsp sweet marjoram	*1 tsp curry powder*
1 tsp summer savory	*2 tsp mustard powder*
1 tsp garlic salt	

Grind dry herbs and mix with salts and powders and sieve together several times. Add 4-6 tbs sea salt and mix well.

Salt-free Seasoning

Grind separately, combine and sieve:

3 tbs dried basil	*2 tbs dried sage*
2 tbs celery seeds	*2 tbs dried savory*
1 tbs cumin seed	*1 tbs dried thyme*
1 tbs dried sweet marjoram	

Add ground kelp to taste and store in an airtight container.

or

1 tsp each oregano, rosemary and sage   *1 tbs each basil, marjoram and thyme*

Grind each herb separately, combine and sieve. Store in an airtight container.

or

½ tsp each lavender flowers and sage   *1 tbs each oregano and thyme*
1 tsp each basil, celery seeds and parsley

Grind each dried herb separately, combine and sieve. Add 1 tsp brewer's yeast if liked, and store in an airtight container.

Herb and Spice Salt

500 g sea salt	*4-6 bay leaves*
30 g coriander seeds	*1 tsp ground cloves*
30 g peppercorns	*1 tbs basil*

Put salt in a basin and mix in finely ground seeds and dried herbs. When well combined store in an airtight container.

or

½ tsp each grated nutmeg and ground cloves   *4-6 bay leaves*
2 tsp each freshly ground allspice, mace and white peppercorns   *2 tsp each dried thyme and basil*
500 g sea salt

Mix spices and ground dried herbs into salt and store in an airtight container.

Spices with Herbs
Freshly ground or grated spices, particularly nutmeg, combine well with many different herbs. This again is a matter of taste but try combinations such as a pinch of finely grated fresh nutmeg in meat balls with a handful of sweet herbs — basil, summer savory and marjoram — and notice the difference.

Sugar
Some people prefer not to use sugar and substitute honey but this entirely alters the flavour of the dish. Sugar combines well with some herbs and helps to bring out their flavour. Sugar is essential when making herb jellies and conserves and it greatly improves fruit such as tomatoes which are used as vegetables. Some herbs such as angelica, lemon balm and sweet cicely are sweet in flavour and using them in syrups and fruit puddings may cut down the amount of sugar needed in a recipe.

Butter, Margarine or Oil
Using butter, margarine or oil in cooking is again a matter of taste. Butter of course contains animal fat and this may have an adverse effect on people with a tendency to heart disease. However, nothing else tastes quite like butter and it is an important ingredient in most cakes, biscuits, pastry and many puddings. When frying, it has a much lower burning temperature than oil and so the food must be watched carefully. A combination of butter and oil may be used to give something of the butter flavour with the hotter temperature of oil. Always make sure when frying in oil or butter that the food is quite dry, otherwise the oil will spit and may burn you. Margarine may be substituted for butter in cake recipes, etc.

Seasoned Flour
This is a mixture of flour, salt and pepper and may be spread on a plate or put in a brown paper bag and have meat rolled in it or shaken with it in the bag to coat it all over before frying.

Technical Terms and Basic Techniques

Blanch
This word has two meanings in cooking: (1) To cover a plant in the garden to prevent its leaves turning green. It is used with such herbs as dandelion and chicory because the green leaves taste more bitter than blanched leaves. (2) To cook something briefly in boiling water and then quickly cool it — a technique often used when freezing vegetables.

Bouquet Garni
This is a French term for a faggot of herbs, usually one bay leaf wrapped around a sprig of thyme and a few parsley stalks. A piece of cotton is then wound round the bay leaf and the little parcel dropped in the stock, stew or soup and cooked with it. At the end of the cooking the bouquet garni is removed before serving. Sometimes other herbs are added or substituted for thyme and parsley. Recipes using a bouquet garni are included under Bay.

Chapon
This is a small cube of bread which is rubbed all over with a cut clove of garlic and then placed in the bottom of a salad bowl to impart a garlic flavour to a lettuce salad. In France the *chapon* is often reserved for 'Papa'.

Fines Herbes
This is a mixture of equal quantities of finely chopped chervil, chives, parsley and tarragon used in salads and with egg dishes, etc. Recipes using *fines herbes* are found under Chervil. Sometimes other herbs or combinations of herbs are used in the same way.

Puree
This means to blend or sieve fruit, vegetables or soup to give a thick, smooth result. An electric blender may be used, or a vegetable mill like a mouli, or a stainless steel sieve.

17

Saute

This means to cook quickly in hot oil or butter turning the pieces of meat or vegetables quickly to brown them on all sides. It is much the same as stir frying.

Beating, Folding and Mixing

The method of beating depends on the result desired. A rotary beater such as an egg beater or an electric beater is suitable for beating eggs or whipping cream or gelatine mixtures to a stiff peak stage, but is not suitable for making salad dressings or sponge cakes. A wooden spoon or a whisk is better for beating mixtures which should have air incorporated with them to make them light and this is the reason for folding in ingredients rather than stirring them in. The action of folding is done with a wooden spoon and means to lift up the mixture and mix in the ingredients with an upward movement rather than to stir them round and round to blend them in.

Pastry and Scones

Pastry and scones are made by mixing chopped butter into flour until it is like breadcrumbs, then adding liquid to make a soft dough. A pastry cutter, a gadget with a wooden handle and a semicircle of six fine wires attached, is invaluable for cutting butter into flour because it achieves this without bringing the hands into contact with the butter which should be kept cold. It also means the mixture is mixed more lightly. Pastry should be kept cold throughout — this is why older kitchens had a marble slab for making pastry — and it is always lighter if it is allowed to rest in a cool place or in the refrigerator for 10-30 minutes before it is rolled out and used. Both scones and pastry should be baked in a hot oven.

Flour and Sugar

Most recipes in this book use plain flour and baking powder. If you wish, wholemeal flour may be substituted but the result will not taste the same, nor in the case of pastry, etc, will it be so light. You can make cakes with wholemeal flour and very nice they are too, but you cannot make a sponge cake; it is nice but not a sponge. If you wish to use self-raising flour you will not need baking powder.

Raw sugar or brown sugar may be used in place of white sugar but they are slightly moister and give a different texture. White sugar is usually better for making jams and jellies — the colour is clearer and brighter. Castor sugar is used where a fine sugar texture is needed. Icing sugar is used in sweets and icings because it is smooth.

If honey is used instead of sugar both the texture and the flavour of the dish will be altered. Honey varies in flavour and some honeys have a dominant taste so they should be used cautiously.

If, like myself, you prefer whole food to refined foods most of the recipes in this book will work well and taste good made with wholemeal flour and raw sugar, but for the occasional special dish or for something which is not made often or eaten in large quantities, I have found it better to compromise and use refined ingredients.

Bread

Bread is made from a mixture of flour, yeast, liquid, sugar and salt. Yeast is the active ingredient that makes the bread rise and taste light. It needs a little sugar or some other sweetening to help it grow, and it needs warmth and moisture to develop. If the liquid used is too hot it will kill the yeast and the bread will not rise. If the liquid is too cold the bread cannot rise either, so the liquid should be lukewarm for best results.

Kneading distributes the yeast evenly through the bread and makes it light and elastic. If the dough is sticky add a little more flour and keep your hands floured while kneading.

If you are using milk, scald it by bringing it to the boil and allow it to cool to lukewarm before adding yeast, sweetening and flour. Warm milk which has not been brought to the boil inhibits the action of the yeast. Warm water may be used in place of milk or combined with milk, and potato water strained from cooking potatoes the night before and warmed is excellent for making bread, especially rye bread as it helps it rise.

The sweetening agent helps the yeast to work. It may be 1 tsp-1 tbs of sugar or honey or malt or golden syrup and should be stirred into the liquid.

Dried yeast or a cake of yeast may be used according to taste and should be mixed with a little sugar and the liquid to start working before most of the flour is added. However, if you allow the yeast to begin to work without any flour at all the bread tastes yeasty when it is baked. Therefore I have found it better to add dried yeast to 1-2 cups flour and then pour in the sweetened liquid to make a batter. I leave this 5-10 minutes to begin working and then stir in the rest of the flour, using first a wooden spoon and finally my hands to stir and knead the bread until it is smooth and springy. Salt should be added with the last of the flour — if it is added early it, too, may inhibit the action of the yeast. 1-2 tbs of oil or melted butter helps to prevent the bread from being crumbly when it is cut.

Any type of flour may be used to make bread. White flour makes the lightest, then a mixture of white and wholemeal, then wholemeal on its own. The heaviest types are made with rye flour. A mixture of flours may be used to taste.

Once the bread has been kneaded until it is smooth and springy it should be left in a basin or on a board covered with a damp cloth, or a piece of plastic, to rise. The cloth keeps the top from drying out. It should sit at room temperature and rise gradually — if you put it somewhere hot like the hot water cupboard it will sink when you take it out. Once it has about doubled in size it is time to knock it back, which means to put it on a lightly floured surface and knead it again until it sinks to its original size and is smooth and springy. Divide it into rolls, put them on a greased tray and cover the bread with a damp cloth again, or put it into oiled bread pans, half filling the tins and allow it to rise until the bread reaches the top of the tin. Bake in a preheated oven at 220 °C according to the recipe. When done, bread sounds hollow when it is tapped on the bottom. It should be tipped out onto a wire rack to cool. If you are topping bread or rolls with seeds first brush the top with a little milk, water or egg wash and then sprinkle with seeds. Otherwise the seeds will not stick to the bread.

Jam

Jam is a mixture of fruit, sugar and sometimes liquid cooked together until it will set. Generally it should only be made of fruit which is ripe or slightly under-ripe — over-ripe fruit does not set well. The fruit should be picked when it is dry — if jam is made from fruit picked in the rain it sometimes goes mouldy.

Prepare the fruit as directed in the recipe and put it in a heavy-bottomed saucepan which is large enough not to boil over when the sugar has been added. If you are using fruit which has skins, like plums, it is helpful to rub the bottom of the saucepan with butter to stop the fruit sticking. Add water according to the recipe or, if no water is to be added, crush the fruit as it heats gently — using a wooden spoon — and boil the mixture, stirring now and then, until the fruit is cooked. Add sugar, stir until it dissolves and boil the jam until it will set. Setting depends on pectin. Some fruit, like apples and citrus fruit, contain plenty of pectin and set easily; other fruit, like strawberries, have very little and so lemon juice is added to the jam to help it set. To test for setting drop about ½ tsp jam onto a saucer and set it aside for a few minutes. Tilt the saucer and if the jam is cooked enough the little spoonful of jam will wrinkle as the saucer is tipped. If it runs all over the saucer it is not yet ready. You can also tell when the jam is ready to set by the way it drops from the spoon. If it pours off when you lift the spoon out of the jam it is still too runny, if it drops off in thick drops it is ready to set. Remove the saucepan from the heat and let the jam stand for 5-10 minutes. This allows the fruit to settle evenly through the jam, otherwise it sometimes rises to the top and leaves just liquid in the bottom of the jars. Pour the jam into clean, dry, warm jars. I usually warm the jars by filling them with hot water and dry each jar just as I am going to fill it. I use a jug to pour the jam, and the jars should be filled right up to the top of the neck, leaving a small air space. When the jam is cold, cover it with melted paraffin wax and when that is set, cover it with cellophane or plastic lids. NEVER melt the paraffin wax in a saucepan directly on the stove. It catches fire very easily. Always stand the wax in a tin or jug of its own in a saucepan of hot water and the water boiling will melt the wax so it may be poured on top of the jam. The hot jars of jam should be stood on a wooden board or on folded newspaper, not on a cold surface or they may crack. When they are cool, label them and store them in a cool, dry, dark cupboard — jam keeps better in the dark than in the light.

Because it has to cook quite a long time always watch jam carefully. It burns easily, especially after the sugar has been added; always use a wooden spoon to stir the jam.

Jelly
Jelly is made by cooking the fruit in water and straining the liquid out, combining it with sugar and sometimes herbs, and cooking it until it sets. Any fruit may be made into jelly but apples, crab apples, grapes and guavas are most often used. The fruit does not need peeling or coring — simply wash it and chop it roughly if it is large like apples, put it in a large saucepan and cover with water. Cook it steadily, stirring now and then, until the fruit is pulpy and the liquid a good colour. Take a jelly bag, i.e. a large bag of some closely woven cotton or linen — old flour bags were ideal — and tip the fruit and liquid into it holding it over a large basin. Tie a string around the top of the bag and hang it up so that the liquid drops into the basin and leave it to drain overnight. (If you have nowhere to do this tie the bag to the back of a chair and put the basin on the floor underneath.) Do not squeeze the liquid out of the bag or the jelly will be cloudy. Next day measure the liquid, pour it back into the saucepan and bring it to the boil. Add sugar according to the recipe, stir until it dissolves, then boil the syrup until it will set on a saucer. Follow the recipe as to adding herbs and/or lemon juice. Bottle, cover and store as for jam.

Marmalade
Because the skins of citrus fruits are thicker, the fruit is usually soaked before cooking, a large amount of water is added, and it is cooked a long time to soften the skin without getting too dry before the sugar is added. Otherwise it is made like jam.

Gelatine
Gelatine is a substance which is dissolved in hot liquid to

make a jelly which will set when cold. It is bought in powdered form and usually 3 tsp gelatine will set 2 cups of liquid or fruit and liquid. It is best to soften the gelatine in a little cold water so it dissolves evenly, and then stir in boiling liquid or stand the softened gelatine in a basin in a saucepan of boiling water and stir until it dissolves. The jelly is usually poured into a mould or glass dish and left in a cool place to set. It should not be put into the refrigerator until it is cold. If the jelly is to be served unmoulded, the mould should be rinsed in cold water before the jelly is poured in, and when firmly set it may be unmoulded by standing the mould in a basin of hot water briefly until it will loosen. Then hold a plate on top of the mould and turn it upside down, and the jelly will be right-side up on the plate.

Salads
Salads are made of both raw and cooked vegetables and fruit and also from cooked eggs, meat and fish. They are generally made to taste, with the food finely shredded or cut into bite-sized pieces and tossed in a salad dressing just before serving. However certain techniques make salad-making easier and more successful.

All ingredients, especially lettuce, should be handled gently, washed, and dried well in a tea towel or paper towel before using. Do not soak vegetables for a long time because they absorb water and do not taste so good. Lettuce may be stored in the refrigerator, still wrapped in the towel, for up to three hours before the salad is made, and should be kept out of the light because this causes it to wilt. Also lettuce, and other green leafy vegetables like dandelion, should be *torn* into bite-sized pieces, never cut — the metal of the knife reacts with their milky juice and causes the cut edges to turn brown.

Cucumber becomes watery when combined with salt so it should be finely sliced, sprinkled with salt and left to drain for about 30 minutes before it is added to a salad.

Tomatoes are a fruit which we use as a vegetable. Sugar sprinkled onto sliced tomato brings out their flavour as does pepper; salt, which makes them watery, is not necessary.

Beetroot is best cooked in its skin. Wash the beetroot after cutting off the leaves about 2 cm above the root and cook until tender in boiling water. Allow to cool, then slip off their skins with your hands and slice the beetroot. They may then be stored in vinegar and kept in the refrigerator, or bottled. To bottle beetroot: Cook the beetroot as usual, peel and slice it. Combine in a saucepan 1 cup each water, sugar and malt vinegar, 1 tsp each salt and cinnamon. Bring to the boil stirring to dissolve the sugar, and simmer five minutes. Add sliced beetroot and bring to the boil again. Pour into warmed jars, overflow and seal with Perfit seals. Once opened, store in the refrigerator. To serve, lift the slices of beetroot out of the vinegar with a slotted spoon and serve separately or as part of a mixed salad.

Garlic is often included in salad recipes.

Salad Dressing
Salad dressings are used, not only to give flavour to salads, but also to help preserve the vitamins in the vegetables. The classic dressing for any green salad is vinaigrette and this may be varied by adding one or more finely chopped herbs to taste. The other basic salad dressing is mayonnaise which is a creamy dressing but does not in my experience bear much resemblance to commercial salad creams. Both these dressings are easily made at home as follows:

Vinaigrette or French Dressing
In a salad bowl combine 3 tbs oil, 1 tbs vinegar, salt and pepper to taste and whisk with a wire whisk to combine thoroughly until the mixture is thick and creamy. Pile the salad on top and toss it gently with wooden salad servers to coat ingredients evenly. Serve at once. This dressing may be varied by adding more salt if it lacks body, a little mustard powder (or ground ginger) if it lacks bite, and crushed garlic if it lacks flavour. The garlic may be either crushed with salt, or added in the form of garlic vinegar or as a *chapon*. The oil is traditionally olive oil but other oils, such as safflower, may be used. The vinegar should be wine vinegar and may be a herb-flavoured vinegar to taste. Lemon juice may be used in place of vinegar.

Mayonnaise
Put 1 egg yolk in a basin, add ¼ tsp mustard powder, a pinch

of sugar, salt and pepper to taste, and stir until well combined. Add 2 tbs wine vinegar and whisk it with a wire whisk or wooden spoon until it is white and frothy. Gradually add ½ cup oil, almost drop by drop, whisking all the time until the mixture is smooth and creamy. If by any chance the mixture should curdle, put another egg yolk in a basin and slowly add the curdled mayonnaise by the teaspoonful, whisking all the time until it is smooth and creamy. Mayonnaise is the basis for other salad dressings such as Green Goddess and Thousand Islands. It is the dressing used for cole slaw.

Never try to make salad dressing with a rotary beater — the beating action is not right for the ingredients and the dressing does not have the same texture and shine.

Salads stimulate the appetite and refresh the palate. They provide fresh minerals and vitamins and really should be part of our daily food.

Vinegar

Herb vinegars are an infusion of a herb in either cider, red or white wine vinegar or honey vinegar. Malt vinegar can be used but its flavour tends to dominate the flavour of the herbs. The general method is to loosely fill a wide-mouthed glass jar with leaves or leafy sprigs of a herb just as it is coming into flower and pour in cold vinegar to cover. Cover the jar with a plastic lid and stand in a sunny place for about 10 days shaking the jar daily. Test for flavour and if it is not strong enough for your taste strain out the herbs and infuse a fresh lot in the same vinegar. When it tastes right, strain the vinegar into a clean, dry bottle and label it with a sprig of the herb. Do not use wet herbs to make vinegar, and do not heat the vinegar.

The following leafy herbs are suitable for making herb vinegar — basil, chives, dill, fennel, marjoram, mint, rosemary, salad burnet, savory and tarragon. Tarragon may be cut 2-3 times a season for vinegar, the final cutting being made just before it dies back in winter.

Coriander, dill and fennel seeds may be used to flavour vinegar in the proportion of 2 tbs lightly crushed seed to every 1 litre vinegar infused as above. Dill seed vinegar is delicious with fish.

Chive flowers, elderflowers, rose petals, violets and nasturtium flowers may be infused like leafy herbs in vinegar. Add a few finely chopped shallots to nasturtium flowers and stand 2 months.

Garlic vinegar is made by infusing 50 g chopped garlic cloves in a litre of red wine vinegar for 3-4 weeks. It may be used to mix mustards, in casseroles, to rub over meat or in salad dressings where it gives flavour with no after-taste on the breath.

Tea

Herb teas or tisanes are generally infusions of one or more herbs, but some herbs are simmered to bring out their flavour. They should be made in a warmed china pot, not a metal one, and not left too long or a bitter taste may develop. In general, a good handful of the fresh herb is enough for a pot or 1 tsp per cup of dried herbs. They may be made from leafy sprigs, flowers or seeds, and some herbs may be used with Indian or China teas too. They are usually drunk without milk, but lemon slices and/or honey may be used to taste. Because some herbs have medicinal qualities it is not wise to drink too many cups of any particular tea on the same day, though, in general they are healthy and very pleasant.

Herb teas may be served hot, warm or iced but should be strained straight after infusing. Leftover herb tea may be frozen to provide flavoured ice blocks for children.

The flowers of the following herbs are used to make tea —

Borage: Simmer 1 tsp dried or 2 tsp fresh borage flowers to every 1 cup boiling water for 5 minutes. Strain and drink.

Chamomile: Infuse 1 tsp dried, or 1-2 tsp fresh flowers in boiling water for 10 minutes. Strain and drink.

Elder: Combine equal quantities of dried elderflowers, lime flowers and chamomile, or equal quantities of elderflowers and mint, use 1 tsp per cup boiling water, infuse 5 minutes. Strain and drink.

Hyssop: Infuse 1 tbs dried hyssop flowers to every 1½ cups boiling water for 5 minutes. Strain and drink.

Marigold: Infuse 1 tsp calendula rays to every 1 cup boiling water for 5 minutes. Strain and drink.

Nasturtium: Infuse 1 nasturtium flower to 1 tsp lemon verbena leaves 5 minutes. Strain and drink. (Red flowers turn yellow.)

Rose: Simmer ½ cup rose petals in 1 cup boiling water 10 minutes. Strain and drink.

Violets: Infuse 1 tsp dried or fresh violets to every 1 cup boiling water for 5 minutes. Strain and drink.

The leaves or flowering leafy sprigs of the following herbs may be used fresh or dried. Strain before drinking.

Angelica: Infuse a small handful leaves to the pot for 5 minutes.

Bergamot: Infuse 10 fresh, chopped leaves, or 2 tsp dried leaves and flowers, in 1½ cups boiling water for 5-8 minutes.

Borage: Infuse 1 tsp dried or 1 tbs fresh chopped borage to every 1 cup boiling water for 5 minutes.

Comfrey: Infuse ½-1 tsp dried comfrey to 1 cup boiling water 5 minutes.

Hyssop: Infuse 1 tbs fresh leaves to 1½ cups boiling water 5 minutes.

Lemon balm: Infuse 1-2 sprigs fresh or 1 tsp dried balm to 1 cup boiling water for 8-10 minutes.

Lemon grass: Infuse 1 tsp chopped leaves to 1 cup boiling water for 5 minutes.

Lemon verbena: Infuse 4-6 fresh or dried leaves to 1 cup boiling water for 5 minutes.

Marjoram: Infuse 1-2 tsp flowering tops to 1 cup boiling water for 5 minutes.

Mint: Infuse 3 sprigs crushed, fresh mint to each cup boiling water 10 minutes, or 1-2 tsp dried mint.

Peppermint: Infuse 1-3 sprigs or 1 tsp dried peppermint to 1 cup boiling water 5-10 minutes.

Peppermint geranium: Infuse 1 leaf to 1 cup boiling water for 5 minutes and serve with slices of orange.

Rose geranium: Infuse 1-2 leaves to 1 cup boiling water 5-8 minutes.

Rose leaf: Wild rose leaves from dog rose or eglantine are suitable and should be picked young and green from different stems so as not to damage the plants. Spread on box lids to dry. Infuse 1 heaped tbs fresh or 2 tsp dried leaves to each 1 cup boiling water for 10 minutes.

Rosemary: Infuse 1-2 sprigs fresh or 1 tbs crushed, dried leaves to 1½ cups boiling water. Strain and drink ½ cup at a time.

Sage: Infuse 1 tsp fresh or dried sage leaves to 1 cup boiling water for 5 minutes.

Stinging nettle: Infuse 1½-2 tsp dried nettle leaves to 1 cup boiling water for 5 minutes.

Thyme: Infuse 1-2 sprigs fresh or ½-1 tsp dried thyme to 1 cup boiling water for 5 minutes.

Mixed herb teas:

Bergamot, Lemon balm and Pineapple sage: Combine equal quantities of each herb using 1-2 tsp per cup boiling water. Infuse 5 minutes.

Lemon balm (or Lemon verbena) and Mint: Combine 1 sprig balm and 2-3 sprigs mint to 1 cup boiling water. Infuse 8-10 minutes.

Lemon grass and Mint: Infuse 1 tsp chopped lemon grass and 1 sprig mint for 5 minutes.

Lemon grass and Fennel: Infuse 1 tsp chopped lemon grass and 1 tsp crushed fennel seed to each cup boiling water for 5 minutes.

Lemon grass and Ginger: Infuse 1 chopped leaf and 1 thin slice root ginger for 2-3 minutes.

Sage, Anise and Catnip: Infuse 1 tsp sage leaves, 1 tsp crushed aniseed, and 1 tsp catnip to each 1 cup boiling water 5 minutes.

Sage and Ginger: Infuse 1 tsp sage and ½ tsp ground ginger to each cup boiling water for 5 minutes.

Serenity Tea: Combine 1 cup dried peppermint leaves, 2 cups dried chamomile flowers, ½ cup dried marigold petals, ½ cup dried lime flowers, 3 tbs dried lavender flowers, 1 tsp fennel seeds, 3 dried sage leaves. Blend well and use 1 tsp to 1 cup boiling water and infuse 5-8 minutes.

Seed Teas: Lightly crush whole seeds before simmering in boiling water.

Anise: Add 1 tbs aniseeds to ½ litre boiling water. Simmer 5 minutes.

Seed tea: Combine 1 tsp each aniseed, caraway and fennel seeds and simmer 5 minutes in ½ litre boiling water.

Dill: Simmer 1 tsp dill seed in 2 cups boiling water for 10 minutes.

Fennel: Simmer 1 tsp fennel seed in 1 large cup boiling water for 5 minutes.

Herb teas with tea:

Some herbs, particularly lemon-flavoured herbs, blend well with ordinary China or Indian teas. Leafy sprigs are added with the tea in the pot and infused in boiling water.

Balm and Indian tea: Add 1 sprig fresh or 1 tsp dried balm to the tea in the pot. Add boiling water and infuse 5 minutes.

Nasturtium and Indian tea: Add 1 nasturtium seed to each cup and pour the hot tea over.

Rose geranium and Indian tea: Add 3 rose geranium leaves, 6 cloves and 2 tsp tea to the pot. Pour on boiling water and infuse 5 minutes.

Aphrodisiac tea: Mix together equal quantities of jasmine flowers, rose buds, rose hips and tea leaves. Use 2 tbs to each 1 cup boiling water and infuse 10 minutes.

Pot pourri tea: 1 cardamon pod, 2 cloves, 5cm cinnamon stick, 6-10 lemon verbena leaves, 2 tsp jasmine tea, 4 tsp Indian tea. Crush spices, crumble leaves and mix all ingredients. Infuse 1½ tsp to every 2 cups boiling water for 5 minutes.

Wine

Making wine is not difficult and only requires attention to detail, perfect cleanliness, good quality material and patience to produce a variety of delightfully different drinks.

It is essential that all equipment used in wine-making be sterilised before use and, because the wine may react with some metals, it is necessary to use only glass, wood, porcelain, enamel or stainless steel when preparing and fermenting wine. Plastic may be used but should be white, not coloured. The easiest way to sterilise equipment is to rinse everything thoroughly with a solution made by dissolving 2 camden tablets (sodium metabisulphate) in 2 cups water. This solution may be used many times to rinse previously cleaned bottles, fermentation jars, etc.

Equipment needed to make wine consists of jugs, bowls, wooden spoons, a large unchipped enamel or stainless steel preserving pan, a good new white plastic bucket or rubbish bin with a lid, and some 4-5 litre glass fermenting jars which have airlocks. A short piece of plastic hose is also needed to siphon the wine, and a sieve or jelly bag to strain out the solids. Used wine or beer bottles are quite satisfactory, as long as they are clean and have been rinsed in the sterilising solution but new corks or caps should be used. Larger wine jars may also be used as fermenting jars with their lids partially screwed down or a little cotton wool in the neck of the bottle, but airlocks are better. Wine-making equipment is available from either specialist shops or through a pharmacist.

The herbs and/or fruit should be of good quality — any damaged leaves, etc should be removed before using them. First-class wine cannot be made out of second-class material.

The raw material is usually boiled or infused in a certain amount of water, then poured onto the sugar and stirred to dissolve the sugar. The wine yeast is added when the mixture is lukewarm — if the liquid is too hot the yeast will be killed, if it is too cold the yeast is inhibited. Wine yeast is obtainable from specialist wine shops or pharmacies and directions for its use are usually on the packet. It should be started in a bottle as follows:

Put in a stainless steel or enamel saucepan 1¼ cups water, strained juice 1 lemon, and 1 tbs sugar. Stir to dissolve the sugar and bring it to the boil. Remove from the heat, allow to cool to lukewarm, then add the wine yeast according to the directions for the amount of wine you are making. Pour the mixture into a sterilised bottle, put a little clean cotton wool in the top of the bottle neck to allow air to escape but to keep bugs out, and leave it standing in a warm place. When the yeast is frothing well, usually after 24 hours, add it to the lukewarm mixture in the plastic bucket or bin. This should be covered and left according to the recipe and then the liquid should be transferred to the fermenting jars and fitted with airlocks. These are small glass gadgets which contain water and are fitted into corks which bung the neck of the jars.

They allow the air to escape from the fermenting wine but do not allow the vinegar fly to get to it. The fermenting jars should be filled right up to the neck of the bottles so that no large air space is left on the surface of the wine — or the wine will taste vinegary. If there is not quite enough wine to fill the bottles right up, use a little water which has been boiled and allowed to cool to lukewarm to top up the wine. After the wine has finished bubbling there is usually a deposit at the bottom of the jar. The wine should be siphoned off — leaving the deposit — into a clean jar or bottles by sucking it up through the plastic hose and then directing the flow into the clean container. Again any air space should be topped up with boiled cooled water. Once the wine has cleared it is bottled and corked, and should be left about six months before drinking.

Other ingredients, such as lemon or orange juice, provide vitamin C and citric acid and cold tea provides tannin. Where nutrient is listed in the recipe it means wine nutrient bought with the wine yeast which helps feed the yeast. Baker's yeast is not satisfactory to use because it makes the wine taste yeasty. There are many specialist books on wine-making and amateur wine-making societies if you wish to develop home wine-making into a fascinating hobby.

The pleasures of the table are of all times and all ages, of every country and every day: they go hand in hand with all our other pleasures, outlast them, and in the end console us for their loss.

Jean Anthelme Brillat-Savarin, 1825

Angelica

The green stalkes or young rootes being preserved or candied, are very effectuall to comfort and warme a cold and weake stomacke.

John Parkinson

Angelica, *Angelica archangelica*, is a handsome biennial plant native to the cooler regions of northern Europe. It is always grown from seed and may reach up to 2 metres high in flower. Plants should be set about 1 metre apart each way, in medium-rich, moist soil, and stems are ready to candy in the spring of its second season. After flowering the plant dies, but it readily self-sows.

Angelica is a sweet-flavoured herb generally used candied, or as a sweetener for tart fruits such as rhubarb. Young stems and leaves may be used in salads and desserts, preserves and wines, and seeds and roots are used commercially in wines and liqueurs. The ornamental *Angelica pachycarpa*, commonly grown for floral work in New Zealand, is not suitable for use in cooking. It is not poisonous but it has little flavour. It may be distinguished from *Angelica archangelica* by its shiny rather than matt green leaves, its flat rather than globular flower umbels, and it only grows about ½ metre high.

33

Angelica Cream Cheese

250 g cream cheese
30-40 g castor sugar
1 stiffly beaten egg white

*finely chopped angelica leaves
or candied stems*

Combine and mix well. Chill before serving as a spread on biscuits or as a sweet dip.

Angelica and Almond Biscuits

200 g butter
½ cup castor sugar
½ tsp vanilla essence
1½ cups flour
½ cup cornflour

½ cup chopped, candied
angelica, or ¼ cup each
candied angelica and glace
cherries
2 tbs chopped, blanched
almonds

Cream butter and sugar until light and fluffy, add essence and sift in flour and cornflour mixed. Add chopped candied angelica and almonds and knead to a soft dough. Divide into small pieces about the size of a walnut and roll into balls. Place on a greased tray and flatten with a fork or the bottom of a glass. Bake at 180 °C for 12-15 minutes. Makes 2-3 dozen biscuits.

Candied Angelica

Cut stalks when they are thick like rhubarb, cut off the leaves and stem joints and cut into 5-10cm pieces. Put the pieces in a saucepan with a little water and bring to the boil. Drain them, string stems like stringing celery, then boil in a little water until they are tender but not mushy. Drain and dry stalks, i.e. if you have 100 g angelica stalks use 100 g sugar. Cover the casserole and leave two days when the sugar will have turned to syrup. Return stems and syrup to a saucepan and boil gently until the stems are clear and the syrup mostly absorbed. Lift out the stalks quickly, dust them with a little castor sugar to frost them, and dry on a rack in a very cool oven. When quite dry store in screw-top glass jars. Any remaining syrup may be poured onto a buttered plate where it will set into delicious angelica toffee.

Uses for Candied Angelica:
To decorate any type of iced cake, or pastry such as almond roll.
To decorate any type of dessert, such as jellies, glazed fruit, etc.
In Christmas cake or fruit cake mixtures.
As a sweet with after-dinner coffee.
Candied angelica may be cut with scissors or a sharp knife into any
sized pieces suitable for the intended dish.

Angelica in Syrup

(This recipe is included by courtesy of Mrs Gertrude B. Foster). Cut
young angelica stalks into 10cm lengths and string with a knife, like
stringing celery. Soak overnight in a basin of cold water to which 1
tbs salt and 1 tbs wine vinegar have been added. Drain, put in a
saucepan with fresh water and boil until the stems are translucent.
Make a syrup of 2 cups sugar to 1 cup water and bring it to the boil.
Add drained angelica, lower the heat and cook gently until tender.
Pour into warmed jars and seal by the overflow method. Keep
opened jars in the refrigerator. Drain angelica stems before use and
lay on waxed paper to dry out before using in cakes, etc. The syrup
may be used as an ice cream topping or in punches and fruit drinks.

Angelica Cheesecake

short pastry
225 g cream or cottage cheese
75 g sugar or vanilla sugar
3 beaten eggs
50 g sultanas

1 tsp grated lemon rind
1 tbs lemon juice
1 tbs finely chopped, young
angelica leaves

Line a 30cm pie dish with short pastry and fill with mixture of
cream cheese, sugar and eggs beaten together, with sultanas, lemon
rind and juice, and angelica leaves blended in. Bake at 180 °C until
the filling is set, about 30 minutes, and serve cold. Decorate with
candied angelica.

Angelica Cassata

To your favourite plain home-made ice cream recipe add:
2 tbs finely chopped candied angelica
2 tbs finely chopped walnuts
2 tbs halved glace cherries or chopped peel

Fold into the ice cream mixture after it has been beaten, and set in trays in the freezer.

Angelica Jelly

4 tsp gelatine softened in
  cold water
¼ litre boiling water
3 tbs sugar
¼ litre apple juice

juice of 1 lemon
finely chopped fresh or
  candied angelica stalks
1 tbs finely chopped sweet
  cicely leaves

Make a jelly by dissolving the softened gelatine in boiling water and stirring well. Add sugar, apple and lemon juices, and stir until sugar is dissolved. Wet a jelly mould and put in some angelica stalks and sprinkle them with sweet cicely leaves. Pour the cooling jelly over and set in the refrigerator.

Angelica and Rhubarb Pie

short pastry
¼ cup chopped angelica stalks
4 cups chopped rhubarb

6 tbs wholemeal flour
honey or sugar to taste

Line a pie plate with short pastry and fill with the rest of the ingredients mixed together. Cover with pastry, prick to allow steam to escape and put in a hot oven, 200 °C and cook for 15 minutes. Reduce heat to 180 °C and cook for a further 20-30 minutes.

Angelica Liqueur

50 g finely chopped
  angelica stalks
1 litre brandy

2-3 drops almond essence
2 cups sugar
1 cup water

Soak angelica stalks in brandy for seven days. Add almond essence and a syrup made by boiling together sugar and water for five minutes then allowing it to cool. Filter the mixture into clean bottles and cork.

Angelica Wine

a good big bunch
   of angelica leaves   *1½ kg sugar*
4 litres boiling water   *½ kg raisins*

Place leaves in a plastic bucket and pour over boiling water. Press leaves down well with a wooden spoon, cover bucket with a cloth and leave three days. Squeeze out leaves and strain the liquid. Heat a little of it, enough to dissolve the sugar, and stir into the rest of the liquid with the raisins. Pour this mixture into 2-litre flagons, filling them to about 2cm from the top. Put a piece of cotton wool in the top of each bottle to allow air to escape but prevent bugs from entering, and leave to ferment. When the wine has finished bubbling, syphon into clean bottles and cap them. Leave six months before drinking.

Baked Fish with Angelica

Use any delicately flavoured white fish, cleaned and filleted, or left whole, and arrange it in a well-buttered casserole. Season well with salt and pepper, dot with butter and pour over it juice of a lemon. Sprinkle with 1 tbs finely chopped angelica leaves, cover and cook at 180 °C until tender, about 20-25 minutes.

Angelica Marmalade

Finely chopped, fresh or candied angelica stems may be added to any orange marmalade recipe in the proportion of 1 cup angelica to 1½ kg fruit. It should be added with the sugar after the fruit is cooked.

Rhubarb and Angelica Jam

2 kg rhubarb
½ kg angelica stems
¾ cup water

juice of 2 lemons
2 kg sugar

Trim and string rhubarb and cut into 5cm lengths. String and chop angelica stems into small pieces. Put all in a pan with water and lemon juice and cook gently until thick and tender. Stir in sugar until it is all dissolved and boil mixture until it sets when tested on a saucer. Pour into warm, dry jars and seal when cool.

Angelica in Salads

Fresh angelica stalks and/or tender, young leaves may be used in any green salad according to taste, but tender, young stems should be blanched in boiling water first, drained straight away and plunged into cold water to cool them quickly. Then they should be drained, dried and chopped finely before being added to other ingredients. Do not add more than four 10cm pieces to one lettuce or the flavour may be too strong.

Anise

The seed wasteth and consumeth winde, and is good against belchings and upbraidings of the stomacke ... Being chewed it makes the breath sweet ...   John Gerard

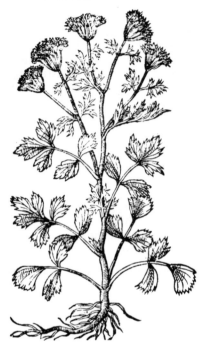

Anise, *Pimpinella anisum*, is an annual, native to the eastern Mediterranean, and will grow well only in warm climates. It must be grown from seed which should be sown early in spring in the place where it is to grow, for the small plants are difficult to transplant. Thin seedlings to 10cm apart so they give each other support. Basal leaves are rounded with toothed edges, other leaves are linear and the flowers grow in lacy white umbels. The seeds, which are ripe when they turn greenish-grey, are the part most used, but leaves may be finely chopped and used in salads, vegetable dishes and as a soup garnish.

Anise is used to flavour breads, biscuits, cakes and sweets and commercially it is important in liqueurs. It is a good digestive. Ground aniseed quickly loses its flavour so it is better to grind the whole seeds or crush them just before using them in cooking. Crush the aniseeds lightly in a mortar with a pestle, or between two sheets of paper with a rolling pin, to release the flavour.

Anise Biscuits

½ cup butter
1½ cups sugar
2 well-beaten eggs
3 cups flour
2 tsp baking powder

grated rind of 1 orange or
lemon
1 tbs aniseed
¼ cup milk or orange juice

Cream butter and sugar and mix in beaten eggs. Sift flour and baking powder together, mix in grated rind and aniseed and combine the two mixtures, adding the milk alternately with the flour. Mix thoroughly and then chill the dough in a plastic bag in the fridge. Roll out the dough on a floured board, cut into shapes with a biscuit cutter and cook at 180°C for 10 minutes or until done, the time depending on the thickness of the biscuits. Cool on a wire rack and store in an airtight container.

Anise Bread

3 cups flour
4 tsp baking powder
½ tsp salt
½ cup sugar

2 beaten eggs
2 cups milk
2 tbs melted butter
5 tsp aniseed

Sift together flour, baking powder and salt and mix in sugar. Combine beaten eggs and milk and stir them in gradually, then butter and finally aniseed. Beat well until smooth. Pour into two well-buttered loaf tins and bake at 180°C for 30-40 minutes. Turn out and cool on a wire rack.

or

2 tbs yeast
2½ cups lukewarm water, or
   2½ cups milk, scalded
   and cooled
4 cups white flour
¼ cup brown sugar
½ cup butter

½ cup brown sugar or honey
2 beaten eggs
2 tsp salt
1-2 tsp ground aniseed
additional flour to make a soft
   dough

Soften yeast in the liquid and make a batter by beating in flour and sugar. Cover and let rise while creaming the butter, brown sugar or honey, and adding the beaten eggs. Mix this thoroughly and then combine the two mixtures, adding salt and aniseed, and enough flour to make a soft dough. Knead this for five minutes, cover and rise till double in size. Knock back and divide into small rolls. Let rise for a further 10 minutes and bake 15 minutes at 200 °C. Makes about 30 rolls.

Anise Cakes

½ cup butter
3 tbs sugar
1 beaten egg
1 cup flour

1 tsp baking powder
2 tsp aniseed
milk to mix

Cream butter and sugar, add beaten egg and mix well. Fold in combined flour, baking powder and aniseed alternately with enough milk to make a stiff batter. Drop spoonfuls into greased patty tins and bake 10-15 minutes at 180 °C. Makes 12 cakes.

Dijon Spice Bread

2 beaten eggs
½ cup sugar
1 tbs baking soda dissolved
   in 1 cup hot water
1 cup honey
1½ tsp cinnamon

1½ tsp aniseed, crushed
½ tsp salt
1 tbs brandy
1½ cups rye flour
1 cup wholemeal flour
1½ tsp grated orange rind

In a large bowl, gradually beat in all ingredients, one at a time, until the mixture is smooth. Butter a bread tin thickly and shake in some raw sugar, tipping the tin back and forth to coat the bottom and sides evenly. Tip out the excess and then shake in flour to coat the tin too. This will prevent the bread sticking. Pour in the mixture and bake at 180 °C for 45 minutes. Loosen the bread in the tin with a knife before tipping it out to cool rightside up on a wire rack. Serve plain or buttered.

Peppernuts

2½ cups flour
1 tsp baking powder
½ cup brown sugar
2 tbs water
1 egg yolk

¼ tsp ground cinnamon
¼ tsp nutmeg
¼ tsp cloves
1 tsp aniseed

Knead all ingredients into a soft ball, adding a little more water if necessary. Divide the mixture into about 90 marble-sized balls and place on two greased baking trays. Flatten each ball slightly with a fork and bake about 20 minutes at 180°C. These are a traditional Dutch sweet made for 5 December, St Nicholas' Day.

Anise Shortbread

250 g butter
1 cup raw sugar

3 cups self-raising flour
2 tsp aniseed

Melt butter in a saucepan and stir in sugar and sifted flour. Turn the mixture into a greased, shallow baking dish and press it into the corners, smoothing the top with a wooden spoon. Sprinkle with aniseed and press in. Bake in a moderate oven, 180°C, for about 30 minutes and cut into squares. Leave to cool in the tin.

Anise Tablet

1 kg sugar
¼ litre milk
1 tbs golden syrup

50 g butter
2 tsp aniseed, crushed
1 tsp lemon juice

Heat sugar, milk, golden syrup and butter together, stirring until it comes to the boil. Boil rapidly, stirring with a wooden spoon till thick and creamy. Stir the aniseed into the mixture with the lemon juice and mix well. Pour onto a greased tin or plate, and cut into shapes when almost cold.

Anisette

Infuse 25 g aniseed in ½ litre brandy. Cork and stand until you judge the flavour to be strong enough. Then filter and bottle the aniseed.

or

1 tbs fennel seed
2 tbs coriander seed
4 tbs aniseed

½ litre vodka
½ cup castor sugar

Crush seeds and add to vodka and sugar. Shake well and stand for one week, shaking every day. Then filter out seeds and bottle in clean, dry bottles. Use as an after-dinner liqueur.

Anise Milk

Infuse 1 tsp aniseed in 1 cup hot milk until the flavour is strong enough, 5-10 minutes. Strain and drink.

Chinese Tea Eggs or Spicy Eggs

12 hard-boiled eggs
3 tbs tea
2 pieces of stick cinnamon
1 tsp aniseed, or 3 pieces of
    star anise

4 tbs soya sauce
1½ tbs salt
2 tsp sugar

Either peel the hard-boiled eggs, or crack them all over by tapping them with the back of a heavy spoon. Put them in a pot with just enough water to cover them, add remaining ingredients and boil gently for 1-2 hours. Drain and cool the eggs, if they are to be used straight away, or leave them in a jar covered with the liquid in the refrigerator where they should keep indefinitely. To serve, peel and/or cut them lengthways into six pieces, and serve with salad or fish dishes.

Figs in Anise Rum

½ kg dried figs
2 cups water
½ tsp aniseed

3 tbs sugar
4 tbs rum
whipped cream

Soak dried figs in water for 3-4 hours. Then add aniseed and sugar and cook gently until tender. When cold add rum, and serve with whipped cream. Fresh figs may be used and do not need to be soaked.

Spiced Mandarins

1 cup cider vinegar
2 cups raw sugar
5cm cinnamon stick

1 tsp aniseed
2-6 whole cloves per mandarin
6-10 mandarins

Bring vinegar, sugar, cinnamon and aniseed to the boil in an enamel or stainless steel saucepan. Stick several cloves in each mandarin, add to syrup and simmer 10-15 minutes. Pour into hot jars, and overflow and seal. More vinegar or a little boiling water may be needed to overflow the jar. Make a few weeks in advance of using, and serve one with each helping of roast duck.

Anise Raisins

Use large muscatel raisins and remove any seeds with a sharp-pointed knife. Insert 1-2 aniseeds in each raisin. Wrap the raisins up in parcels of about 6-8 in two grape leaves, one each way, and fasten with toothpicks or raffia. Put in the oven at about 160-180 °C and leave until the leaves are brittle. Serve cold as an after-dinner sweetmeat with coffee.

Anise Beef

2 tbs oil
1½ kg topside
1cm root ginger, crushed
1½ cups water
3 tbs soya sauce

½-1 tsp crushed aniseed
1 tbs brown or raw sugar
1 tsp salt
3cm cinnamon stick
2 tbs sherry

Heat oil in a heavy-bottomed saucepan and brown the topside on all sides. Add crushed ginger, water, soya sauce and all other ingredients, except sherry, and bring to the boil. Cover, reduce heat and allow meat to simmer gently for about 1½ hours. Add sherry and cook a further 10 minutes. Serve hot or cold, and use the strained liquid as a gravy to accompany the meat.

Anise Pork

1 kg pork fingers
½ cup sherry
½ cup raw sugar
2cm peeled, sliced root ginger
3 finely sliced shallots
½ cup soya sauce
1 tsp aniseed
1 tsp salt
1 crushed clove garlic
pinch pepper
oil for frying

Marinate pork in all ingredients, except the oil. Leave for six hours, basting frequently, and then drain the pork. Heat oil in a large pan and cook pork on all sides until browned. Add the marinade and enough water to cover the meat, bring to the boil, and then lower the heat and simmer until meat is tender. Do not cover the pan, and add more water as necessary. Serve with rice and salad.

Anise Veal Casserole

thin slices of veal
1 beaten egg
breadcrumbs
melted butter for frying
1 cup wine or sherry
1 tsp lemon juice
1 tbs aniseed

Dip slices of veal in beaten egg, then in breadcrumbs and brown in melted butter in a frying pan. Transfer to a casserole and cover with a sauce made from sherry, lemon juice and aniseed, previously cooked together for five minutes. Cover and cook at 180 °C for about 1½ hours, until meat is tender.

Topside Casserole with Anise

Make a marinade by combining:

1 peeled, sliced onion	*6 black peppercorns*
4 cloves peeled, sliced garlic	*1 tsp aniseed*
1 tsp salt	*2 cups dry red wine*

Add 1-1½ kg topside and leave to marinate for 4-5 hours turning from time to time. Remove meat, drain and dry thoroughly. Heat 3 tbs oil in a pan and brown meat on all sides. Place in a casserole and add 125 g chopped bacon. Strain the marinade over the meat, add ½ cup water, cover and cook at 180°C for 2-3 hours, until meat is tender. Remove to a hot plate and transfer the liquid to a saucepan. Boil, uncovered, until it is reduced to 1½-2 cups. Serve as a sauce with the sliced meat.

Glazed Carrots with Anise

Slice carrots into straws, and cook gently in a covered saucepan with 25 g butter, 2 tbs water, 1 tbs brown or raw sugar and 1 tsp aniseed, until tender (about 10 minutes). Shake the saucepan to glaze the carrots all over and serve hot.

Instead of cooking aniseed with the carrots, finely chopped anise leaves can be sprinkled onto the cooked carrots just before serving.

Red Cabbage and Anise

1 red cabbage	*2 tbs cider vinegar*
3 peeled, sliced onions	*½ cup chicken stock*
3 peeled, cored, sliced apples	*2-3 tsp aniseed*
3 tbs raw sugar	*salt and pepper*

Wash cabbage and remove the very hard stalks. Slice finely and layer it in a casserole with onion and apple slices, sprinkling sugar over the layers. Pour in cider vinegar and stock, and sprinkle with aniseed and salt and pepper to taste. Cover and cook at 150°C for 2-3 hours. Serve hot.

Basil

*Basil is a small Herb, Native of warmer Countries,
but not uncommon in our Gardens ... The whole
Plant has a very fragrant Smell.*   Sir John Hill

Basil or sweet basil, *Ocimum basilicum*, is a comparatively recent herb in Western cooking, for it was not introduced into England until 1573 and was considered only a medicinal herb at that time. Basil, an annual grown from seed, does not germinate or thrive in cold weather. However, if started late in spring the plants are easy to grow and will give plenty of fresh leaves to use throughout summer and autumn.

There are many types of basil varying in growth habit, colour, size and flavour of leaves. Sweet basil and the larger-leafed Lettuce leaf basil are most commonly used, although Bush basil, Lemon basil and the Purple or Dark Opal basil are also popular. The leaves are the part used and are best used fresh. Larger leaves should be hand-picked round the plant allowing smaller leaves to grow on. If flowerheads are pinched out when they begin to form the plant will be more bushy and last longer. Basil may be dried or frozen for winter use but the flavour is then different. It is used with cheese, eggs, rice, tomatoes and many mild-flavoured vegetables, and is indispensable in many Mediterranean-type dishes.

47

Egg and Basil Tartlets

2 cups flour
pinch salt
125 g butter
cold water to mix

1 cup mayonnaise
1 crushed clove garlic
3 tbs chopped basil
3 hard-boiled eggs

Mix flour and salt in a basin and rub in butter until mixture resembles breadcrumbs. Stir in enough cold water to make a pliable dough, and knead. Allow to rest a few minutes, then roll out thinly and cut into circles and line greased patty tins with the pastry. Prick cases and bake at 200-220 °C until crisp and golden. Remove from patty tins and cool.

Blend mayonnaise, garlic and basil together until well mixed. Chop hard-boiled eggs and put a little in each pastry case. Pour over enough mayonnaise mixture to fill, and serve. This filling may be used in vol-au-vent cases too.

Camembert Bread with Basil

Heat gently together until blended:
1 packet camembert cheese
100 g butter

½-1 tsp finely chopped basil
½ tsp onion or garlic salt

Stir to mix thoroughly and allow to cool 10 minutes. Cut a long French loaf in half longways and spread it with some of the cheese mixture. Replace the top and spread it with the rest. Wrap the loaf in foil and bake 20 minutes in a hot oven until well heated through. Turn back the foil for the last five minutes to brown the crust. Cut in chunks and serve hot with soup or as an appetiser.

Tomato and Basil Bread

4-6 cups flour
1 tbs dried yeast
2 tbs sugar or honey
1 tsp salt
1 cup warmed tomato juice

4 tbs oil
3 skinned, de-seeded tomatoes
2 beaten eggs
4 tbs finely chopped basil
50 g melted butter

Put 2 cups flour in a basin with yeast and sugar and mix well. Add salt, tomato juice, oil, tomatoes, beaten eggs and make a batter.

Leave a few minutes at room temperature to allow yeast to begin to work. Combine basil with 2 more cups of flour and stir in, add more flour as necessary to form a dough which is not sticky. Turn out on a floured surface and knead until the bread is smooth and springy. Roll a little melted butter round a large basin, put the dough in it and brush the top with butter. Cover with a cloth and leave to rise until double in size. Knock the dough back and divide in half, placing each half in a buttered loaf tin. Brush tops with melted butter and leave to rise to the tops of the tins. Bake at 200 °C for about 30 minutes. Turn out on a rack to cool.

Fruit and Basil Loaf

1½ cups flour
1 tsp baking powder
½ tsp salt
50 g butter
125 g mixed dried fruit

2 tbs sugar
1-2 tsp minced basil
1 beaten egg
½ cup milk

Sift together flour, baking powder and salt and rub in butter. Stir in fruit, sugar and basil, and mix well. Combine beaten egg and milk and stir into the flour mixture, making a well in the middle and beating until smooth. Place in a greased loaf tin and bake at 180 °C for about one hour, until the loaf is firm and comes away from the sides of the tin. Turn out on a rack to cool and keep a day before cutting.

Hot Tomato Punch with Basil

2 cups chicken stock
4 tsp finely chopped basil

1½ kg tomato juice, fresh or canned

Simmer basil in the broth for 10 minutes. Add tomato juice and reheat.

49

Basil Baked Tomato Eggs

6 tomatoes
6 tbs breadcrumbs
1½ tbs finely chopped basil
1 tbs chopped chives

salt and pepper to taste
6 eggs
6 slices buttered toast
basil sprigs to garnish

Cut tops off tomatoes and carefully scoop pulp out into a basin with a spoon. Mix pulp with soft breadcrumbs, basil and chives, and season to taste. Set tomato cases in a buttered ovenproof dish, break an egg into each, top with some of the breadcrumb mixture and bake at 180 °C for 30-40 minutes, until eggs are set and tomato cases soft. The remaining breadcrumb mixture may be baked in the dish too, and all served on hot, buttered toast garnished with basil sprigs.

Pea and Basil Frittata

4 tbs oil
2 cloves garlic
1 onion, peeled and sliced
9 eggs
1 cup dry breadcrumbs

salt and pepper
⅓ cup finely chopped parsley
1-2 tsp finely chopped basil
½ cup grated cheese
500 g cooked green peas

Heat 2 tbs oil in a frying pan. Halve garlic cloves, spear them with toothpicks and add them, and peeled, sliced onion, to the oil and cook slowly until onion is soft and golden. Remove and discard garlic. Allow onion to cool. Beat eggs lightly in a bowl and add cooled onion and all other ingredients. Mix well and return to frying pan. Cover and cook over a low heat until sides of frittata shrink away from the pan. If the middle puffs up, prick it with a knife. Place the whole dish under a grill in the pan to finish cooking. Cut into pieces and serve.

Basil Omelette

2 eggs
salt and freshly ground pepper
1 tsp butter

1 tsp finely chopped basil
grated cheese

Beat eggs moderately and season with salt and pepper. Heat butter in a frying pan and pour in the eggs. Cook on a hot element, tipping and shaking the pan to ensure that the omelette is cooked evenly. Sprinkle with chopped basil and a little grated cheese, fold over and serve on a hot plate.

Sweet Omelette with Basil

2-3 large basil leaves
2 tsp sugar
2 eggs

2 tsp sugar
knob butter

Pound basil leaves in a mortar with 2 tsp sugar and set aside. Separate eggs and beat the whites stiff. Beat the yolks with 2 tsp sugar and fold in the whites. Melt butter in a pan and cook the omelette gently until it sets. Do not turn or fold it. When firm, slide onto a warm plate and sprinkle with basil sugar.

Scrambled Eggs with Basil

Beat 2 eggs for each person and add sliced tomato, with a pinch of salt and finely chopped basil to taste. Heat butter in a heavy frying pan, add the egg mixture and cook gently, lifting the mixture to let the uncooked egg run onto the hot pan until it is all set and the tomato heated through. Serve with buttered toast.

Jellied Tuna with Basil

500 g tinned tuna
500 g tomato pulp
2 tbs finely chopped basil
1 tbs grated onion

¼ cup cold water
2 tbs gelatine
salt and pepper
250 g plain yoghurt

Empty tuna onto a plate and remove skin and bones. Pour tomato pulp into a saucepan with basil and onion, and heat gently. Soften gelatine in cold water and dissolve by standing the cup in a basin of hot water and stirring the mixture. Add dissolved gelatine to tomato mixture and stir well. Flake tuna with a fork and blend into the tomato. Taste and season with salt and pepper and finally fold in the yoghurt. Pour into a wet mould and set in the refrigerator. Serve unmoulded, garnished with basil sprigs, with a green salad.

Dolmas with Basil

3-4 cabbage leaves for each
  person
50 g butter
2 cloves garlic
1 sliced onion
1 sliced capsicum

500 g minced steak or liver
1 cup cooked rice
1-1½ tbs finely chopped basil
rashers of bacon
2 tbs wine/stock/water
salt and pepper

Wash large cabbage leaves, remove tough stalks and blanch for a few minutes in boiling water. Drain. Melt butter and cook crushed garlic, sliced onion and capsicum until soft. Add meat and cook gently, stirring often. When well browned add rice and basil. Mix well, taste and season. Spread out blanched cabbage leaves and place a small mound of the meat mixture on each one and then wrap to make a parcel. Layer the parcels in a casserole with slices of bacon, add liquid, cover, and cook at 140 °C for 1½-2 hours. Add more liquid if necessary.

Lamb's Fry with Basil

250 g sliced bacon
2 tbs flour
salt and pepper
500 g lamb's fry

2 tbs butter
1 cup stock
2 tbs chopped basil

Fry bacon in a pan, and when cooked, remove to a serving dish and keep warm. Combine flour, salt and pepper, and toss sliced lamb's fry in the mixture. Add butter to bacon fat in the pan and cook lamb's fry until tender, about 8-10 minutes. Remove and place on the serving dish with the bacon. Add stock to the juices in the pan, bring to boil, stirring all the time. Add basil and cook a minute more. Taste and add salt and pepper if necessary, then pour over lamb's fry and serve.

Herb Luncheon Sausage

500 g minced beef
1 tbs dry red wine
¾ tsp dried basil or 1½ tsp
  fresh basil
¾ tsp dried oregano

2 tbs parmesan cheese
2 tsp garlic salt
½ tsp freshly ground black
  pepper

Mix all ingredients together well to distribute seasonings, cover and chill 24 hours. Shape into a sausage about 20cm long and place in an oven bag with no holes. Shape oven bag around sausage, gather up and secure ends of bag with string or wire twists to give cracker effect. Make several holes in top of the bag. Stand the sausage in a baking dish on a rack in the oven. Bake at 110 °C for 3½-4 hours. Cool. Wrap in foil and store in fridge 24 hours before using.

Basil Jelly

crab or windfall apples   sugar
water   basil

Place crab or chopped windfall apples in a preserving pan and cover with water. Boil gently until fruit is tender and liquid is a good colour. Strain overnight through a jelly bag but do not squeeze out the liquid or it will be cloudy, not clear. Next day, measure the liquid and bring it to the boil. For every cup of liquid add a cup of sugar, stir till dissolved and boil till the mixture jells. Put a sprig of basil in each clean, warm jar and pour the jelly over. Cover when cold. If preferred, the basil may be finely chopped to taste and added to the jelly at the end of cooking, but do not cook it too long — not more than five minutes — or it may taste bitter.

Zucchini Pickle

For each litre preserving jar:
3-6 small zucchini   1 cup water
1 tsp salt   1 cup vinegar
¼ tsp cayenne pepper   1 sprig of fresh basil, or dill,
2 cloves garlic   or tarragon
1 tsp olive oil

Slice zucchini into chunks and combine all ingredients except basil in a saucepan, bring to boil and simmer five minutes. Pour into the jar containing sprig of basil, overflow and seal. When open keep in the refrigerator.

Basil Rice

½ cup oil
1 cup rice (brown)
½ cup chopped onions
½ cup chopped celery
4-6 mushrooms (optional)

1 tsp salt or kelp powder
chicken stock
½ cup walnuts or cashews
2 tsp fresh or 1 tsp dried basil

Heat oil, add rice and brown gently. Stir in onions and celery and brown. Add all other ingredients and pour into a casserole using sufficient stock to cover the rice mixture by about 2cm. Cover the dish and cook in the oven at 180 °C for an hour.

Hot Rice Ring

4 tbs oil
1 cup rice
2 cups hot water
1 tsp salt
2 tbs butter
1 peeled, sliced onion
1 clove garlic
1 cup mushrooms

1 green pepper
2 eggs
1 tbs minced basil and/or
    marjoram and thyme
½ cup chopped parsley
½ cup grated cheese
salt to taste

Heat 2 tbs oil and fry washed rice, browning and stirring it. Add water and salt and cover tightly. Cook on a low heat about 20 minutes. Heat remaining oil with butter and slowly cook onion, garlic and chopped mushrooms for about 10 minutes. Add cooked rice and finely chopped green pepper and mix well. Stand several hours. Half an hour before the meal add eggs, herbs and cheese and season to taste. Mix well, press into a buttered ring mould and bake 30 minutes at 180 °C. To serve, unmould onto a hot dish and fill the centre with some hot, cooked green vegetables.

Savoury Rice Balls

1½ cups long grain rice
2½ cups water
1 tsp salt
½ cup grated cheese
1 beaten egg
1½ cups tomato puree

50 g cooked ham, or bacon, or
    salami
¾ cup breadcrumbs
oil for frying
20-30 basil leaves

Place rice in a saucepan with water and salt, cover and cook until water is absorbed and rice is tender. Turn rice into a bowl and stir in cheese, beaten egg and 2 tbs tomato puree. Leave until cold. Dice meat and mix with 2 more tbs tomato puree. With wet or floured hands, pick up about 1 tbs of the rice mixture at a time and shape it into a ball. Make a hollow in the centre and add 1 tsp of the meat mixture as a stuffing. Cover with a little more rice and remould into the ball shape. Continue until all the rice and meat mixtures are used. Then roll each ball in breadcrumbs and fry till crisp and golden in hot oil. Drain on brown paper and garnish with 2 basil leaves to each ball. Heat remaining tomato puree and serve as a sauce.

Macaroni Cheese with Basil

2 cups macaroni, cooked as usual	1 tbs fresh, chopped basil
1 cup grated cheese	2 tbs butter
1/3 cup grated onion	1 tbs flour
250 g skinned, chopped tomatoes	1½ cups milk
3 rashers bacon, chopped	salt and pepper to taste
	breadcrumbs
	grated cheese for topping

Layer a buttered casserole with macaroni, cheese, onion, tomato and bacon, garnished with basil. Make a white sauce by melting butter, stirring in flour and adding milk gradually, stirring all the time. Cook the smooth sauce for 2-3 minutes, add salt and pepper to taste, and pour over the macaroni mixture in the dish. Top with breadcrumbs and grated cheese and bake in a moderate oven, 180 °C, for 30-40 minutes.

Basil and Tomato Salad

10 ripe tomatoes, sliced	freshly ground pepper
1 (red) onion, peeled and sliced	basil vinegar
1 tbs sugar	finely chopped basil

Layer tomatoes and onion in a serving dish sprinkling with sugar and pepper. Add a little basil vinegar and finely chopped fresh basil to taste and mix gently.

Bean and Tomato Salad with Basil

250 g cooked, sliced green
    beans
400 g sliced tomatoes
1 small clove garlic
½ tsp salt

2 tbs vinegar
2 tbs lemon juice
6 tbs oil
½ tsp pepper
1 tbs chopped basil

Arrange the sliced vegetables in a bowl. Crush the garlic in salt and then combine with other dressing ingredients in a screw-top jar and shake well. Pour over the tomatoes and beans and leave in a cool place about an hour before serving.

White Bean and Basil Salad

2 cups fresh white beans
1 tsp salt
100 g cooked ham
3 tbs oil

1½ tbs lemon juice or vinegar
pepper and salt to taste
1 tbs fresh, finely chopped
    basil

Cook beans in boiling water with 1 tsp salt until tender, but not mushy. Drain and tip into a salad bowl. Add finely chopped cooked ham. Combine oil and lemon juice to make a salad dressing and pour over the beans and ham. Mix well, allow to cool and then chill. Toss with fresh basil just before serving. A clove of garlic may be rubbed around the salad bowl before the beans are added.

Green Salad with Basil Dressing

Combine in a screw-top jar and shake well:
4 tbs oil
2 tbs vinegar

1½ tbs finely chopped basil
grated rind 1 lemon

Wash, dry and tear into bite-sized pieces:
1 small lettuce
100 g spinach or silverbeet
    leaves (no stalks)

6-8 sliced radishes
6-8 spring onions or shallots

Arrange in a salad bowl and just before serving pour over the dressing and toss well.

Leek and Basil Salad

3 leeks
1 tomato
½-1 lettuce

1 tsp finely chopped basil
1 tsp finely chopped chervil
French dressing

Slice white part of washed leeks and cut tomato into sections. Arrange in a bowl of lettuce torn into bite-sized pieces. Sprinkle with herbs and toss with French dressing just before serving. A *chapon* rubbed with garlic may be added.

Mushroom Salad with Basil

Combine:
2 cups sliced raw mushrooms   2 sliced tomatoes

Combine in a casserole and marinate in Basil Dressing. Chill in the refrigerator for an hour, then drain and serve on crisp lettuce torn into bite-sized pieces. 1 tsp Worcestershire sauce may be added to the dressing.

Basil and Tomato Sandwiches

Make sandwiches using Basil Butter or sprinkling sliced tomato with finely chopped fresh basil. Add pepper and sugar to taste.

Basil Butter

Combine finely chopped basil and butter in proportion of 1 tbs basil to every 50 g butter, mixing them together thoroughly with a fork. Add a little lemon juice. The butter may then be patted into balls and should be chilled, covered, in the refrigerator before serving with jacket potatoes and/or grilled meat. It can also be used at room temperature as a spread on biscuits, in tomato sandwiches, etc.

57

Basil and Eggplant Spread

1-2 eggplants
1 minced onion
1 crushed garlic clove
1 tomato
½ finely chopped green pepper

½ cup tomato sauce
¼ cup finely chopped basil
  and parsley
3 tbs each vinegar and oil
salt and pepper to taste

Boil unpeeled eggplant until tender. Cool, peel and mash. Add remaining ingredients and blend or stir well until thoroughly mixed. Chill 24 hours before using as a spread or with cold meat.

Herb Sauce for Pasta

6 tbs olive oil
1 minced onion
1 minced garlic clove
1 cup finely chopped parsley
1 cup minced fresh basil,
  marjoram and thyme, mixed
  together

½ cup dry white wine
1 cup mushrooms
2 cups stock or water
2 cups tomato puree
pinch each allspice, cloves,
  nutmeg, salt, pepper

Heat oil in a pan and gently fry onion and garlic for 10 minutes. Add herbs, stir well and add wine. Continue to cook a further 10 minutes. Chop mushrooms and soak in the hot stock or water for 10 minutes, then add all ingredients, tomato puree and seasonings to the pan, stir well and continue to cook gently for about an hour until the sauce is thick. Use with any type of hot cooked pasta.

Herb and Spice Sauce for Mixed Vegetables

2 cloves garlic
½ tsp salt
½ tsp each caraway seeds,
  cinnamon, pepper and
  thyme
3 tbs oil

1 bayleaf
1 tsp lemon juice
½ cup vegetable water
cooked mixed vegetables to
  taste

Crush garlic with salt and put all ingredients except lemon juice in a saucepan with ½ cup liquid saved from cooking the vegetables. Cover and simmer very gently about 10 minutes before adding the cooked mixed vegetables and heating gently until thoroughly warmed through. Remove bay leaf, sprinkle with lemon juice and serve with rice.

Basil Mayonnaise

Stir finely chopped basil into prepared mayonnaise, in the proportion of 1 tbs basil to every cup of mayonnaise. Mix well and serve with potatoes, salads, cold chicken.

Basil Mustard

2 tbs mustard powder
2 tbs white flour
½ tsp salt

2 tsp sugar
vinegar to mix
1 tbs finely chopped basil

Make the mustard by combining the first four ingredients and mix to a smooth paste with vinegar. Add basil and mix well. Store in a covered pot to allow flavour to develop, for 2-4 weeks before using. This mustard will keep well in small screw-top jars in a cool, dark cupboard.

Basil Spaghetti Sauce

6 kg tomatoes
¼ cup oil
1 kg onions
3-4 cloves garlic
2 stalks celery
2 tbs sugar

2 tbs salt
1 tsp pepper
2 tbs parsley
1½ tbs marjoram
2 tbs basil (if dry, use half
    quantity)

Cook tomatoes gently in a buttered pan until thoroughly soft and strain them through a sieve to remove skins and seeds. Heat oil and cook finely chopped vegetables and garlic. Combine vegetables and sieved tomato and cook a further 30-45 minutes. (Long cooking is necessary when bottling vegetables.) Add seasonings and herbs and cook a further 10 minutes. Pour into hot jars, overflow while boiling, and seal. Use with cooked spaghetti as a sauce, or thin with stock and reheat as a soup.

Pesto or Pistou

Pesto Genovese is a sauce first made in Genoa. Its popularity spread along the Riviera to Provence where it is known as Pistou. The name 'pesto' comes from the original method of preparing the basil by pounding it with a pestle in a mortar. Pound 2 cloves of garlic in a mortar with several basil leaves. Add, still pounding in the mortar, 2 tbs oil and a little salt. When completely pureed, add 4 tbs grated parmesan cheese and blend all together. A modern version is:

2 cups fresh basil leaves	*2 tbs of pinenuts or walnuts*
½ cup olive oil	*1 tsp salt*
2 cloves of garlic, minced	*½ cup grated parmesan cheese*

Blend chopped basil, oil, garlic and nuts at high speed until pureed. Pour mixture into a bowl and mix in salt and cheese thoroughly. Parsley can be added in equal quantity to the basil. Serve with hot, drained pasta, or with baked pumpkin or hot jacket potatoes, or in Pistou soup. Pesto can be kept in a screw-top jar in the refrigerator.

Variations on Pesto:
1. Use equal quantities of parsley and marjoram instead of basil and pinenuts.
2. Use parsley and walnuts instead of basil and pinenuts.
3. Use ground almonds with basil instead of pinenuts.
4. Use equal quantities of parsley and basil.

Basil Soup

⅓ cup minced fresh basil leaves	*2 cups heated tomato juice*
1 clove garlic, minced	*2 cups hot chicken stock*
1 tsp minced fresh tarragon	*salt and freshly ground pepper*
3 tbs butter	*3 egg yolks or 2 eggs*
	finely chopped basil to garnish

Saute basil, garlic and tarragon in heated butter over a low heat for a few minutes. Add heated tomato juice and stock and simmer gently for 10 minutes. Add seasonings. Beat the eggs or egg yolks in the serving bowl, and pour the hot soup into them, lightly beating it with a fork or whisk, to blend it. Garnish with basil and serve.

Cold Carrot and Basil Soup

500 g carrots, peeled and
  sliced
2-4 chopped tomatoes
4 cups chicken stock

salt and pepper to taste
2 tbs gelatine
2 tbs cold water
1 tbs finely chopped basil

Cook carrots and tomatoes in the stock gently until tender. Season to taste and allow to cool a little. Puree vegetables through a mouli or in a blender and set aside in a bowl. Combine gelatine with the cold water in a bowl and stand this in hot water until gelatine dissolves. Add this to the soup before it cools too much and stir well, adding basil at the same time. Cover and leave in the refrigerator until the soup is lightly set. Serve in chilled bowls.

Pistou Soup

1 tbs butter
1 onion, peeled and sliced
1 leek, sliced
2 tomatoes, peeled and sliced
1½ litres stock

250 g sliced green beans
3 small potatoes, peeled and
  sliced
salt and pepper
3 tbs pesto

Melt butter and cook onion, leek and tomatoes gently. Add stock, beans and potatoes, season with salt and pepper and cook till the vegetables are tender. Finally add pesto and serve. About 100 g of spaghetti can be added about 5-8 minutes before the end of cooking as a variation.

Choko and Basil Savoury

3-4 chokos
boiling water
1 tbs butter
1 tsp salt

½ tsp pepper
2 tomatoes
1 tsp finely chopped basil

Peel chokos, quarter and remove pips. Cut into 8 pieces and cook in a little boiling water in a covered saucepan for about 20 minutes until tender. Drain them, return to the saucepan with butter, salt, pepper and peeled, chopped tomatoes. Sprinkle with finely chopped basil, cover and cook very gently for a further five minutes.

Green Bean and Basil Savoury

500 g cooked, sliced green	2 tbs flour
beans	salt and pepper
2 onions, peeled and sliced	1 tsp mustard powder
3 tbs butter	1 cup milk
3-4 basil leaves	¾ cup grated cheese
4 tomatoes, skinned and sliced	breadcrumbs

Place cooked beans in an ovenproof dish. Cook sliced onions in butter gently until golden. Drain and mix into the beans with chopped basil. Arrange sliced tomatoes on top. Reheat butter, stir in flour and season with salt and pepper to taste. Add mustard powder and cook until frothy. Remove from the heat and gradually stir in milk, bring it back to the boil and cook, stirring, for three minutes. Remove from the heat, add grated cheese and mix well before pouring the sauce over the vegetables in the dish. Sprinkle with breadcrumbs and bake until heated through, about 20 minutes at 180 °C.

Peas with Basil

1 tbs butter and 1 tsp fresh, finely chopped basil to every 500 g peas. Melt butter and add green peas, shake gently to coat peas with butter. Add about 1 tbs hot water to stop peas sticking to the pan, cover tightly and cook over a low heat till tender. Add basil and mix thoroughly, remove the pan from the heat and stand in a warm place for 5-10 minutes before serving.

Basil Potatoes

1 kg small new potatoes	1 beaten egg
3 tbs flour	3 tbs breadcrumbs
2 tsp finely chopped basil	1 tbs oil
salt and pepper	2 tbs butter

Scrub potatoes and cook in a little boiling water until just done — they must still be firm. Combine flour, basil and seasonings in a bag and shake drained potatoes in it to coat them. Beat egg in a basin and roll potatoes in the egg and then in breadcrumbs. Combine oil and butter and heat and fry potatoes until brown on all sides.

Tomato Casserole

Grease an ovenproof dish and arrange layers of sliced onions alternately with layers of sliced tomatoes sprinkled with salt, pepper and a little finely chopped basil until the dish is full. Top with torn pieces of white bread and a sprinkling of grated cheese and bake about 30 minutes at 180 °C.

Vegetable Casserole with Basil

2 zucchini
1 eggplant
4 tbs butter
1 clove of garlic, minced
4 tomatoes, skinned and sliced
salt and pepper

1 tsp oregano
1 tbs fresh basil
1 cup parmesan cheese
1 cup cheddar cheese, grated
breadcrumbs and butter

Slice zucchini, peel and slice eggplant, sprinkle with salt, toss well and leave ½ hour. Drain, rinse in cold water and drain again. Melt butter and cook zucchini, eggplant, garlic and tomatoes gently but do not brown. Season, stir in herbs, pour into a casserole, top with cheese and breadcrumbs. Bake at 180 °C for 30-40 minutes.

Bay

*The later Physitions doe oftentimes use to boyle
the leaves of Laurell with divers meats, especially
fishes, and by so doing there happeneth no desire
of vomiting; but the meat seasoned herewith
becometh more savory and better for the stomake.*

John Gerard

The bay or sweet bay tree, *Laurus nobilis*, is a tall-growing evergreen, with shiny green leaves which are aromatic when broken or crushed. There are both male and female trees and only the female trees produce dark purplish-black berries after the small creamy flowers, though the leaves of both have the same scent and flavour. Bay leaves may be used both fresh or dried and, as a general rule, only 1-2 leaves are cooked in any dish because of their very strong flavour.

Bay is traditionally part of the bouquet garni — a sprig of thyme and a few stems of parsley are placed on a bay leaf which is folded over to enclose them and tied up with cotton wound around it. This parcel is cooked in any soup or stew, the tail of cotton being left over the handle of the saucepan so that it may be easily removed before serving. Bay is also added to court bouillon for cooking fish, to milk puddings in place of nutmeg or other spices, and to pickling spice mixtures and vinegars. It may be used when cooking vegetables such as cabbage, cauliflower, beans or potatoes, to improve the flavour and reduce the smell of cooking. It tenderises meat, and meat may be flambeed on bay leaves.

To Dry Bay Leaves

Gather mature bay leaves on a dry day and layer them between sheets of thin linen or brown paper and press them flat under a board or heavy books until they are dry. When quite dry store them in a dark glass container. Do not dry bay leaves in the sun as it will fade the colour and the flavour will evaporate.

Pickling Spice

2 tbs each allspice, crushed bay
  leaves
2 tsp each dill seeds, fennel
  seeds, small chillis

1 tbs each mustard seed, black
  peppercorns
1 tsp whole cloves
5-7cm cinnamon bark, crushed

Mix together and keep in an airtight container. To use, spoon some of the mixture into a muslin bag and simmer in the liquid for cooking fish, meat, chutneys, sauces and pickling vinegars. For pickling fruit omit chillis. For making spiced vinegar use 2 tbs pickling spice to every 1 litre vinegar, bring it to the boil, cover and infuse until cold. Remove pickling spice in the bag before using vinegar.

Mackerel with Apple Sauce

2 filleted mackerel
cider
1 tbs cider vinegar
1 bay leaf
juice ½ lemon
salt and pepper

50 g butter
75 g sugar
1 kg cooking apples, peeled
  and quartered
lemon slices

Arrange mackerel fillets in a casserole and pour in enough cider to cover half the fish. Add vinegar, bay leaf and lemon juice and season with salt and pepper. Cover and cook at 190 °C until fish is tender, about 15-20 minutes. While fish is cooking make sauce by melting butter in a heavy saucepan and adding sugar. Cook until sugar turns golden before adding quartered apples and a little cider. Cover and simmer until soft. Sieve or mouli apples and serve separately with the fish, garnished with slices of lemon.

Fish in Aspic

1-1½ cups cooked fish pieces
1¼ cups white wine
¼ cup white vinegar
1 cup water
1 finely chopped onion

4 whole allspice
2 tbs sugar
2 bay leaves
1 tsp salt
1½ tbs gelatine

Arrange fish in a 4-cup mould. Combine all other ingredients except gelatine in a saucepan and bring to the boil. Simmer 10 minutes and strain. Soften gelatine in a little cold water and pour on the hot liquid, stirring to dissolve it. Cool slightly, then pour over fish in the mould and allow to set. Store in refrigerator and unmould onto a bed of lettuce leaves before serving.

Baked Fish with Bay

When baking whole fish which have previously been cleaned and scaled, place a bay leaf in the cavity of each fish and pour over 1 tbs each white wine and olive oil. Place 2 slices of lemon on top of each fish and season with salt and pepper. Bake at 190°C for 30-45 minutes, basting with the liquid.

Court Bouillon for Cooking Fish

Sufficient for 500 g fish:
½ cup finely chopped onion
¾ cup each olive oil, white
   wine, water
juice 1 lemon
1 clove garlic
1 bouquet garni

branch fresh fennel
10 coriander seeds
2 sweet red peppers
¾ tsp salt
pinch freshly ground pepper

Simmer onion in oil without allowing it to brown. Add liquids, crush unpeeled clove garlic and add with herbs and seasonings and red peppers cut in strips. Boil gently for 15 minutes and strain and use liquid for cooking or marinating fish.

Mussels Cooked with a Bouquet Garni

1 litre mussels

2 crushed cloves garlic

½ cup cold water
½ cup white wine
1 sliced carrot
1 sliced onion

50 g butter
bouquet garni
salt and pepper
chopped parsley to garnish

Wash and scrub mussel shells. Put all ingredients except the mussels and parsley in a saucepan, bring to the boil and simmer about ½ hour. Strain liquid into a large pan and add mussels. Cook over a hot element, shaking constantly, for about five minutes, then turn the mussels and cook again for a further five minutes by which time the mussel shells should be open. Discard any that have not opened. Remove mussels from their shells, remove their beards and put them in a dish and strain the cooking liquid over them. Garnish with parsley.

Soused Herrings

6 herring fillets
salt and pepper
¾ cup vinegar
½ cup water

1 tbs mixed pickling spice
4 bay leaves
1-2 sliced onions

Season herring fillets with pepper and salt and roll them up, skin outwards. Place them in an ovenproof dish and cover with a mixture of vinegar and water to which has been added the pickling spice, bay leaves and onions. Cover and cook in a slow oven, about 160°C, for 1½ hours. Serve hot or cold.

Bay Marinade for Hogget

2 cups red wine
½ cup red wine vinegar
¼ cup oil

12 bay leaves
¼ tsp each salt and pepper
2 kg leg hogget

Combine all marinade ingredients and pour over hogget in an enamel, glass, porcélain or stainless steel dish. Turn meat and baste with the marinade 3-4 times a day for three days, keeping it covered between times. Then drain meat thoroughly, place on a rack in a roasting dish and put in a hot oven, 220°C, for 15-20 minutes, basting three or four times. Lower the temperature to 180°C and continue to cook 2-2½ hours more.

Breton Lamb with Bay

1 cup haricot beans, soaked overnight	1-1½ kg leg lamb
1 onion	1 sliced clove garlic
salt and pepper	50 g butter
bouquet garni	1 shallot, chopped
	1 tomato, peeled and sliced

Combine soaked beans, whole peeled onion, salt and pepper and bouquet garni in a pan and cover with water. Bring to the boil and simmer until beans are tender. Skim mixture as needed. When beans are cooked, after about one hour, drain them and keep them and the onion warm.

Slit skin of lamb in several places and insert slivers of garlic, pressing them in close to the bone. Sprinkle meat with salt and pepper and rub with 25 g butter. Roast at 190°C until meat is tender, about 40 minutes to each kg, then lift onto a serving dish and keep warm. In a small pan melt remaining butter and cook shallot and tomato with the boiled onion until all are soft. Add cooked beans and reheat. Pour over meat and serve.

Chicken Fricassee

1 chicken cut in bite-sized pieces	1 tsp finely chopped savory
seasoned flour	¼ cup chopped parsley
3 tbs oil or butter	2 shallots, chopped
boiling water to cover	50 g butter
1 bay leaf	3-4 tbs flour
½ tsp freshly ground pepper	1 beaten egg or 2 egg yolks
	1 cup hot top milk

Roll chicken pieces in seasoned flour and cook in hot oil or butter, turning to brown all sides. Pour on boiling water to cover meat, add bay, pepper, savory, parsley and shallots, cover pot and simmer until chicken is tender, 1-1½ hours. Lift chicken into a serving casserole and keep hot. Measure stock and bring quantity up to 3 cups with boiling water. In a small pan melt butter and stir in flour to make a smooth paste. Gradually add 1 cup stock, stirring all the time to keep mixture smooth. Simmer a minute and stir in rest of stock. Combine beaten egg in a bowl with hot top milk, stirring all the time. Remove stock from the heat and stir in egg and cream mixture, add chicken and reheat but do not boil or sauce will curdle. Serve with mashed potatoes or over hot toast.

Braised Beef with Bay

For the marinade:

2 wine glasses red wine	4 cloves
1 tbs wine vinegar	1 bay leaf
1 sliced onion	sprig thyme
1 sliced carrot	6 peppercorns

1½ kg topside beef	2-4 tbs flour
butter	½ cup cream
½ cup stock	salt and pepper

Put all marinade ingredients in a bowl and mix well. Add beef and marinate for 48 hours turning from time to time. Drain meat and put in a pan with hot butter and brown it on all sides. Transfer to a casserole and add stock and marinade. Cover and cook at 160 °C for three hours. Strain pan juices and discard solids. Mix flour with a little water in a small saucepan, stir in the hot pan liquids, bring to boil and simmer 3-5 minutes. Remove from the heat, stir in cream and keep hot. Slice meat, pour sauce over and serve.

Egg Noodles with Bay

1½ litres water	250 g egg noodles
1-2 bay leaves	25 g butter
1 tsp salt	

Combine water, bay leaves and salt in a large saucepan and bring to the boil. Add noodles and boil rapidly, uncovered, until they are just tender. Remove bay leaves and drain noodles. Toss with about 25 g butter and serve.

Rice Cooked with Bay

Wash brown or white rice till clean and put in a saucepan with 1 bay leaf, 3 cloves, a little sliced onion, ½-1 tsp salt and a knob of butter. Add water to cover about 1cm above rice and bring to the boil. Stir quickly with a fork, cover with a tight-fitting lid, turn down the heat and leave rice to cook gently in its own steam. When water is absorbed rice should be tender and grains separated. If rice is not cooked, add a little more water and cook with the lid on again.

Liver Casserole with Bay

50 g butter
500 g calves' liver
1 sliced onion
1 crushed clove garlic
100 g mushrooms
2 carrots, peeled and sliced
salt and pepper

1 tsp each basil, parsley and
   thyme
2 tsp flour
¼ cup each wine and
   water or ½ cup water
1 bay leaf

Heat butter in a pan and saute thinly sliced liver, onions and garlic until browned. Arrange this in layers in a casserole alternately with chopped mushrooms, carrots, seasoning and herbs. Sprinkle with flour, blend in water and wine, top with bay leaf and bake, covered, about 30 minutes at 180 °C.

Potted Pork with Bay

350 g lean pork
100 g fresh pork fat
1 tsp salt
½ tsp pepper

¾ cup water
2 bay leaves
2 cloves
strip lemon rind

Cut pork and fat into very small pieces and place with all other ingredients in a casserole. Cover and cook at 130 °C for 3-4 hours. Remove from oven, discard bay, cloves and lemon rind and remove meat with a slotted spoon. Mince meat finely, mix with cooking liquid and pack into a small pot. Cover and refrigerate for a day before using as an entree or a spread on toast.

Rabbit Stew with Bay

1 dressed rabbit cut in pieces
4 tbs seasoned flour
50 g butter
500 g carrots, peeled and sliced
1 onion, peeled and sliced
500 g potatoes, peeled and
   diced

500 g tomatoes, skinned and
   chopped
500 g turnips, peeled and sliced
1 wine glass red wine
1 bay leaf
1 tsp thyme

Roll rabbit pieces in seasoned flour and fry in hot butter until browned on all sides. Transfer to a casserole, layering with all the vegetables. Add wine, bay and thyme, cover and cook at 180 °C for about 1½ hours or until meat and vegetables are tender.

Steak with Bay

Marinate each steak with a bay leaf and 1 tbs red wine vinegar for an hour. Drain and place on a rack for grilling, breaking bay leaf into small pieces over the steak, and grill to your taste, turning once. Strain pan juices over the steak with a little melted butter and salt and pepper to taste.

Baked Custard with Bay

½ litre milk
1 bay leaf

4 tbs sugar
2 eggs and 2 egg yolks

Put milk, bay leaf and sugar in a saucepan and bring very slowly to simmer, stirring to dissolve sugar. Remove from the heat, cover and allow to cool slightly. Beat eggs and egg yolks in a large basin and pour strained milk over them, whisking at the same time to blend the mixture evenly. Set custard cups or individual ramekins in a baking pan and pour in boiling water to cover three-quarters of the cups. Take them out and strain the custard into them, cover with foil and set the cups back in the pan of water. Set in a cool oven, 160 °C, until the custards are set, about 1-1¼ hours, remove from pan and serve warm.

Rice Pudding with Bay

2 tbs rice
½ litre water

2 tbs sugar
1 bay leaf

Soak rice in milk with sugar most of the day. Pour mixture into a greased ovenproof dish and add bay leaf. Cook in a slow oven, 160 °C, until milk is absorbed. Remove bay leaf and serve.

71

Sago Pudding with Bay

¼ cup sago
1¼ cups milk
3 slices white bread
½ cup sultanas

strip lemon rind
25 g melted butter
½ cup sugar
1 bay leaf

Simmer sago in milk for 15 minutes. Add all other ingredients except bay leaf, mix well and pour into a buttered pie dish. Place bay leaf on top and bake at 140 °C for 1½-2 hours. Remove lemon rind and bay leaf before serving.

Beetroot Salad with Bay and Marjoram

6 beetroot, cooked, peeled and
  sliced
1 onion
1 tsp finely chopped marjoram
2 bay leaves
1 clove garlic

nutmeg
salt and pepper
oil
red wine vinegar
dry red wine

Arrange a layer of sliced beetroot in a shallow dish and cover with a layer of finely sliced onion. Sprinkle with a little marjoram, pieces of bay, slivers of garlic, freshly grated nutmeg and salt and pepper. Repeat layers until all is in the dish. Combine equal quantities of oil, vinegar and wine, pour over the beetroot mixture and stand an hour or two before serving.

Brown Lentil Salad

1 cup lentils
1 bay leaf
2 onions
pepper and salt

4 tbs oil
2 tbs vinegar or lemon juice
¼ tsp dry mustard powder
chopped parsley for garnish

Place lentils in a saucepan and cover with water. Add bay, 1 chopped onion and seasoning and bring to the boil. Cover and simmer until lentils are tender but not mushy, about one hour. Drain and remove bay leaf. Chop remaining onion finely and add to lentils with oil, vinegar and mustard. Chop parsley finely and add, mix all together and leave until cold before serving.

Finnish Fish Soup

potatoes	mixed fish in whole chunks
onions	butter
1 bay leaf	rye flour
½-1 tsp whole allspice	chopped dill and chives

Peel and dice potatoes and onions, put in a large saucepan with bay leaf and whole allspice tied in a piece of muslin, and cover with water. Simmer until vegetables are almost done, then add pieces of fish and several dabs of butter. Continue to cook until fish is tender. Thicken by stirring in a little rye flour mixed with cold water and stir for a further five minutes as it boils. Serve sprinkled with chopped chives and dill leaves.

Haricot Bean Soup

500 g haricot beans	2 diced carrots
bouquet garni	500 g tomatoes
25 g butter	salt, sugar and pepper
2 onions, peeled and sliced	parsley or chives to garnish

Soak haricot beans overnight and then boil in the same water with bouquet garni until soft. Saute onions and carrots in melted butter until soft, add peeled, sliced tomatoes and cook 20 minutes. Combine with beans and reheat, simmering 10 minutes before removing bouquet garni, and sieve to form a puree. Season with salt, sugar and pepper and garnish with finely chopped parsley or chives.

Hotch Potch Soup

1 cabbage, sliced	250 g bacon
3 potatoes, peeled and sliced	bouquet garni
3 carrots	1 litre cold water
250 g cooked white beans	salt and pepper to taste

Put all ingredients in a large saucepan and bring to the boil. Simmer about one hour, remove bouquet garni and season to taste with salt and pepper. Remove bacon, chop it up and return to the soup. Mash vegetables slightly and serve very hot.

Bechamel Sauce

slice of onion
6 peppercorns
½ tsp grated nutmeg
1 bay leaf
3 cups hot milk

25 g butter
25 g plain flour
salt and pepper
1 tbs cream

Infuse onion, spices and bay in milk for five minutes but do not boil. Melt butter in another pan, remove from the heat and stir in flour. Gradually stir in strained milk, blending carefully with a wooden spoon. Season to taste and boil gently for two minutes, then remove from heat and add cream.

Bearnaise Sauce

Combine in a saucepan:
6 tbs wine vinegar
12 peppercorns
1 bay leaf

a blade of mace (or pinch of mace)
2 slices of onion

Boil until quantity is reduced to 2 tbs and set pan aside. Beat 4 egg yolks in a small basin with a pinch salt and 25 g butter. Strain vinegar mixture onto this, set basin in a pan of boiling water, turn off the heat and stir till the mixture begins to thicken. Then add 100 g butter in small pieces, stirring all the time and season with pepper. Add 2 tbs meat jelly and 2 tsp of chopped chervil, parsley and tarragon and a pinch of chives. Keep warm and serve over steak or chops.

Mushroom Sauce with Bouquet Garni

1 finely chopped onion
1 clove garlic, crushed with
   ½ tsp salt
1 tbs butter

50 g mushrooms
1 cup cold gravy
½ cup red wine
bouquet garni

Combine onion and garlic and fry gently in hot butter until onion is transparent. Add peeled, sliced mushrooms and cook 3-4 minutes. Remove from the heat. Combine gravy, wine and bouquet garni in a saucepan, bring to the boil and simmer 10 minutes. Remove bouquet garni and add mushroom mixture. Cook until heated through, taste and season as necessary with pepper. Serve with rissoles, fritters or meat loaf.

Potatoes with Bay

When cooking potatoes peel them and add 1 bay leaf to the boiling water with the potatoes. Cook as usual and serve either hot, mashed, or slice and toss with French dressing to make a potato salad. Garnish with finely chopped chives. Cauliflower may be cooked in the same way.

Borage

Those of our time do use the floures in sallads, to exhilerate and make the mind glad. There be also many things made of them, used every where for the comfort of the heart, for the driving away of sorrow, and encreasing the joy of the minde.

John Gerard

Borage, *Borago officinalis*, is a sturdy and upright annual with hairy stems and leaves and generally beautiful blue flowers, though there are white and pink flowered forms. It is always grown from seed and self-sows very easily because it is a favourite plant of the bees. Borage has little scent but the leaves have a slight cucumber flavour and may be used raw, finely chopped to mask their hairyness, or cooked before the plant flowers. The flowers are edible and may be used in salads or crystallised, and whole flowering sprays, leaves included, are used in wines and fruit cups for their cooling effect and their beauty. If left in any drink the acid present gradually turns the flowers from blue to pink.

76

Cottage Cheese with Borage

Combine and mix well:
250 g cottage cheese   *salt and pepper to taste*
½ cup young, finely chopped
   borage leaves

Spread the mixture on biscuits or bread and garnish with a few
fresh borage flowers.

To Candy Borage Flowers

Pick the borage flowers, each with a small stem, when they are
quite dry and paint each one with lightly beaten white of egg, using
a watercolour paintbrush. Dust them lightly with castor sugar and
set to dry on waxed paper in a warm place like an airing cupboard
or in a very cool oven.

or

Make a mixture of an equal quantity of acacia powder (from a
chemist) and rose water and leave to stand 24 hours. Paint this mixture onto both sides of the borage flowers, dust with castor sugar
and leave to dry as above.

When quite dry, store the candied flowers in layers in an airtight
container, such as a plastic ice cream container, with sheets of
waxed paper between the layers. Use to decorate cakes, desserts,
etc.

Fruit Punch

1 large handful lemon balm   *1 litre cold tea*
1½ litres boiling water   *syrup of 1 cup sugar boiled*
2 large handfuls borage   *with ½ cup water*
1 large handful mint   *3 litres ginger ale*
juice 6 lemons and 2 oranges   *ice*
1 cup apple or pineapple juice   *borage flowers to garnish*

Put lemon balm in a bucket and pour boiling water over it. Steep
about 20 minutes then strain onto borage and mint. Add fruit
juices, tea and syrup and stand 12 hours. Strain and discard herbs
and serve punch, chilled, with added ginger ale, crushed ice or ice
blocks, and borage flowers to decorate.

Borage Ice Blocks

Half fill ice block trays with cold water and freeze solid. Remove from freezer and tip out the half blocks. Put a borage flower into each division, replace the half blocks and top them up with water. The flower is then trapped between the water and the ice and when the tray is returned to the freezer the borage flower will be set in the middle of the ice block. Otherwise the flowers tend to float to the top.

Borage Flower Syrup

2 cups borage flowers   *sugar*
boiling water to cover

Place 1 cup of flowers in a bowl and cover with boiling water. Cover the bowl and leave to stand overnight. Next day strain out flowers and discard them. Heat liquid to boiling point in a small saucepan, then pour it over remaining cup of borage flowers. Cover and steep 10 hours. Strain out the flowers, discard them and measure the liquid. Add an equal quantity of sugar and heat slowly, stirring until the sugar dissolves, then boil for five minutes. Skim and bottle when cold. Store in refrigerator and use as a pick-me-up (1 tbs at a time), to add to fruit salad, or as a syrup to poach fruit in.

Borage in Wine

Individual borage flowers scattered in a wine or punch bowl are very attractive, or sprigs of leafy, flowering borage may be steeped in any wine before serving to cool it and add to its flavour and appeal.

Borage with Salads and Vegetable Dishes

Borage flowers, which made an attractive edible garnish, may be added to any green or fruit salad to taste. Young, finely chopped borage leaves may be added to any green salad, but do not add too much because of their hairy texture.

Borage Fritters

1 cup flour	*½-1 cup cooked, chopped*
1½ tsp baking powder	*borage leaves*
½ tsp salt	*1 tbs grated onion*
½ cup milk	*oil or butter to fry*
1 beaten egg	

Sift together flour, baking powder and salt into a basin. Make a well in the centre and stir in combined milk and egg to make a stiff batter. Add chopped, cooked borage leaves and grated onion. Heat oil in a frying pan and fry the mixture in tablespoonfuls, turning to brown both sides. Drain on brown paper and eat hot with mashed potatoes and grilled tomatoes.

Borage Leaves as a Vegetable

Wash young borage leaves and remove stalks. Chop finely and cook in a little butter in a covered saucepan over a very low heat. Season to taste. The dampness of the washed leaves should be enough to keep them from sticking to the bottom; they should soon be tender and their hairy texture disappears with cooking.

I prefer to combine the borage leaves with cabbage or silverbeet using about one-third borage leaves to two-thirds cabbage or silverbeet and cooking in the same way.

Borage in Sandwiches

Spread buttered bread with a mixture of Vegemite and finely chopped young borage leaves and sprinkle with pepper and salt.

or

Mix finely chopped borage leaves with mashed hard-boiled egg, seasoned with salt and pepper and blended with a little butter, and spread on buttered bread.

Caraway

Caraway confects, once only dipped in sugar, and
a spoonful of them eaten in the morning fasting,
and as many after each meal, is a most admirable
remedy for those that are troubled with wind.

Nicholas Culpeper

Caraway, *Carum carvi*, is an annual or biennial native to the Mediterranean. It must be grown from seed and if planted in the autumn it will flower the following spring-summer, but if planted in the spring it will not flower until its second summer. While the leaves and roots of the plants, which resemble carrots, may be eaten, the most important part for food is the fruit, or seeds, which have been used for hundreds of years for their digestive properties.

The seeds may be harvested when they are brown and will come away from their umbels easily. The whole plant may be cut off at ground level and hung upside down in brown paper bags to dry, or individual umbels may be cut off into a basin and dried. If the seeds are to be kept for a long time it is a good idea to dip umbels into boiling water and let them drip dry over a muslin screen, for tiny insects often lie hidden in the seeds and will eat them in the storage jars. When the seeds are really dry store them in dark glass containers.

Caraway seeds are traditionally used in cakes and rye bread, with meat dishes and to flavour cabbage and beetroot.

They are also used in pickles, soups, cheese, and some liqueurs, and are valuable in preventing flatulence. However caraway is a flavour which people feel strongly about — they either love it or hate it — so make sure it is liked before using it in your cooking.

Caraway and Cheese Tart

pastry to line a pie plate
1 tbs butter
2 chopped rashers bacon
1 finely sliced onion
3 beaten eggs

3 tbs milk
1-2 tsp caraway seeds
½-1 cup grated cheese
salt and pepper to taste

Line a pie plate with pastry. Melt butter in a frying pan and cook bacon and onions until tender but not brown. Drain and arrange evenly on the pastry. Cover with a mixture of beaten eggs and milk with 1 tsp caraway seeds mixed in. Sprinkle cheese on top and another 1 tsp caraway seeds over that. Bake at 180°C for 30-40 minutes until pastry is cooked and the filling firm.

Caraway and Cheese Frites

3 tbs butter
2 cups flour
pinch salt
1 beaten egg
water to mix

2 hard-boiled eggs, mashed
¾ cup grated cheese
1 tbs caraway seeds
salt, paprika to taste
poppyseeds

Make a dough by cutting butter into flour and salt and when mixture is like breadcrumbs stir in beaten egg and enough water to make a soft dough. Knead it lightly, roll out thinly and cut into small squares. Mix together the mashed, hard-boiled eggs, cheese, caraway seeds and seasoning to taste and put 1 tsp of this filling into each square. Damp the edges of the dough and fold each square into a triangle. Fry until golden in deep oil or fat, drain, sprinkle with poppyseeds and serve very hot.

Caraway Cheese and Beer Spread

Combine in a saucepan:

500 g grated cheese
½ cup beer
2 tbs butter

2 cloves crushed garlic
1 tbs caraway seeds
½ tsp salt

Cook over a gentle heat until blended and then beat till smooth. Store in refrigerator and serve with biscuits.

Liptauer Cheese

250 g cottage cheese
little cream to mix
2 tbs sour cream
100 g butter
pinch salt

1 tsp grated onion
2-3 tsp caraway seeds
chopped parsley and capers
    (optional)
paprika

Sieve cottage cheese and a little cream with butter and sour cream until smooth. Add salt, onion and caraway seeds, according to taste. Add finely chopped parsley or capers to taste and finally mix in 2-3 tsp of paprika, according to taste. Press mixture into a dish and use with biscuits or bread. The paprika may be sprinkled over the cheese rather than mixed through it.

Cottage Cheese and Caraway

1 cup cottage cheese
little cream to mix
1 tsp caraway seeds

½ tsp finely chopped chives
salt and pepper to taste

Blend cottage cheese with a little cream until smooth. Mix in other ingredients and turn into a serving dish. Cover and leave at least 30 minutes for flavour to develop before using.

Toasted Caraway and Cheese Sandwiches

Spread mustard on a slice of bread, sprinkle with caraway seeds, cover with a thin slice of cheese and another slice of bread. Cook in the oven or fry in butter until bread is toasted and cheese melted.

Caraway Soup Breads

2 cups flour
2 tsp baking powder
½ tsp salt
25 g butter

100 g grated cheese
¾ cup milk
1½ tbs caraway seeds
1½ tsp salt

Make a scone dough by sifting together flour, baking powder and salt, rubbing in butter and mixing in cheese. Stir in milk to make a firm dough and roll out on a floured board to form thin round strips. Cut these into 10-15cm sticks and brush with milk, then dip them in a mixture of caraway seeds and salt. Cook on a greased tray at 200 °C for about 10 minutes, till crisp and brown, and serve with soup.

or

1 cup mashed potato
1 cup flour
½ cup butter

1 tbs caraway seeds
coarse salt
milk

Combine potato, flour, butter and caraway seeds and mix well with a fork. Set aside in the refrigerator to chill for 30 minutes. Roll out thinly on a floured surface, brush with milk and sprinkle with salt and more caraway seeds. Cut into strips with a hot knife and place on a buttered tray. Bake at 200 °C until crisp and brown, about 10 minutes. Cool on a rack and serve with soup or stews.

or

1 cup each rye, wholemeal and
    white flour
1 tsp salt
3 tsp baking powder
2 tbs caraway seeds

2 cups grated cheese
6 tbs oil
2 beaten eggs
milk to mix

Combine flours, salt, baking powder, caraway seeds and cheese. Add oil and eggs and mix to a dough with milk so that it can be rolled out about 1½-2cm thick. Place on a greased tray and cut into fingers. Bake at 220 °C for 15-20 minutes. Serve with soup.

Caraway Snaps

1 cup flour
1 tsp celery salt
1 tsp mustard powder
pinch cayenne pepper
75 g butter

75 g grated cheese
water to make dough
milk
caraway seeds

Combine flour and seasonings, rub in butter, add cheese and enough water to make a firm dough. Roll out thinly, brush with milk and sprinkle with seeds. Bake at 180°C for 15 minutes.

Rye Bread with Caraway

1 tbs dried yeast
1 tsp sugar
600 ml warm potato water
1 cup mashed potato

2 cups wholemeal flour
4 cups rye flour
1 tbs caraway seed
1 tsp salt

Add yeast and sugar to warm potato water and gradually add mashed potato and wholemeal flour to make a batter. When this begins to froth, stir in rye flour, caraway and salt, and knead well. Allow to rise in a covered basin in a warm place till about double in size, knock back and place in a greased loaf tin and allow to rise again for ½ hour. Bake about an hour at 180°C.

Caraway Cakes

½ cup butter
½ cup sugar
1 beaten egg
1 cup flour

1 tsp baking powder
2 tsp caraway seeds
milk to mix

Cream butter and sugar, add beaten egg and mix well. Add sifted flour and baking powder alternately with milk and caraway seeds to form a fairly wet dough. Grease 12-18 patty tins and put a tablespoon of the mixture in each. Bake at 180°C for 10-15 minutes. Cool on a rack.

Caraway and Fruit Loaf

2 tbs butter
2 tbs brown sugar
1 beaten egg
1 cup wholemeal flour
1 tsp baking powder
1 cup dates

1 cup walnuts
½ cup sultanas
pinch salt
2 tsp caraway seeds
½ cup milk

Cream butter and sugar and add beaten egg. Combine flour and baking powder with chopped fruit and nuts, salt and caraway seeds and add to the mixture alternately with milk. Pour into a greased, lined tin and bake about one hour at 180 °C.

Caraway and Lemon Ring

100 g soft butter
2 tbs golden syrup
75 g castor sugar
2 beaten eggs
1 ½ cups flour

2 tsp baking powder
3 tsp caraway seeds
50 g chopped peel
1 tbs lemon juice
1 tbs milk

Cream butter, syrup and sugar. Add beaten eggs, sifted flour and baking powder combined with caraway seeds and peel. Add lemon juice and milk and stir well. Bake in a greased ring tin for about an hour at 180 °C. When cold, ice with lemon icing, and decorate with grated, fresh lemon peel.

Wholemeal Crumble for Fruit Pies

50 g wholemeal flour
50 g sugar
50 g butter
1-2 tbs coconut

1-2 tbs wheatgerm
1 tbs caraway seeds or ground
    coriander

Combine flour and sugar and rub in butter cut into small pieces until it resembles breadcrumbs. Mix in coconut, wheatgerm and seeds and blend well. Use as a topping to cover approximately 500 g prepared fruit in an ovenproof dish and bake at 180 °C for 30-45 minutes until fruit is cooked and topping crisp.

Beef Stew with Caraway

750 g chuck, rump or sirloin
   steak
4 tbs flour
1 tsp salt
1-2 tsp paprika
2 tbs oil or butter
1 onion, peeled and chopped

500 g tomatoes, skinned and
   chopped
2 cups beef stock
1 tsp caraway seeds
500 g potatoes, peeled and
   sliced

Cut beef into cubes and toss in a mixture of flour, salt and paprika.
Melt butter in a pan, add onion and fry gently for a few minutes.
Add meat and cook five minutes, stirring until evenly browned.
Add tomatoes and stir in stock. Bring to the boil, stirring, add
caraway seeds and sliced potatoes, cover and simmer for about 2½
hours, until meat is tender.

Caraway Dumplings

1 cup flour
1 tsp baking powder
½ tsp salt
pepper to taste

½ tsp caraway seeds
3 tbs butter
cold water to mix

Combine all dry ingredients and mix well. Rub in butter until
mixture is like fine breadcrumbs, then add enough water to make a
soft but not sticky dough. Roll into small balls, about the size of a
walnut, and cook in boiling water or stock until light and fluffy,
about 20-30 minutes. Serve with any casserole or soup.

Roast Beef with Caraway

1 kg boned, rolled beef
2 onions, finely chopped
2 tbs caraway seeds
pinch salt

2 tbs dripping or oil
2 tbs vinegar
pepper to taste
2 tbs flour

Unroll beef and spread out flat. Sprinkle with 2 tbs finely chopped
onion, 1 tbs caraway seeds and a pinch of salt, roll it up again and
tie with string. Heat dripping or oil in a roasting pan, add
remaining onion and place meat in the centre. Sprinkle with 1 tbs

caraway seeds, vinegar and season to taste. Add enough water to cover quarter of meat and roast for an hour, basting from time to time. When meat is tender place in a hot dish and skim off 2 tbs fat from the top of the pan juices. Heat fat in a pan, stir in flour and cook over a low heat until a good brown colour. Gradually stir in liquid from the pan with onions and bring to the boil, stirring all the time. Taste, season and serve this gravy with the meat.

Veal with Caraway Rice

2 tbs oil
750 g cubed veal steak
1 sliced onion
½ cup chopped celery
1 tbs sugar
1 cup tomato puree

1 tbs Worcestershire sauce
1½ cups rice
1½ tsp caraway seeds
1 tbs chopped parsley
1 cup pineapple pieces

Heat oil and brown meat gently on all sides. Add onion and celery and cook gently for a few minutes. Add sugar, tomato puree and sauce, cover and simmer until meat is tender, about 1½-2 hours. In the meantime cook rice in boiling, salted water, simmering it gently in a covered pot until liquid is absorbed and rice tender. Toss caraway seeds through rice. Add parsley and pineapple to the meat, mix well and serve over the caraway rice.

Pickled Beetroot with Caraway

4 cups cold, cooked beetroot
2 tsp salt
2 tsp brown sugar

3 tsp caraway seeds
2 cups cider vinegar

Peel and slice cold, cooked beetroot and put into glass jars or an earthware crock. Combine all other ingredients and bring to the boil. Simmer 10 minutes, cover and cool. When cold, strain the cold vinegar over to cover the beetroot and cover the containers with corks or plastic lids.

Courgette Relish with Caraway

1 kg courgettes, sliced	2 cups sugar
2 onions, peeled and sliced	1 tsp caraway seeds
1/3 cup salt	1 tsp turmeric
2 cups white vinegar	1-2 tsp mustard

Cover courgettes and onions with water and dissolve salt in it. Stand 2-4 hours then drain well. Bring all other ingredients to boil, stirring to dissolve sugar and pour this over courgettes and onions in a bowl. Stand two hours. Return everything to the large container on the stove, bring to the boil and boil 15 minutes. Pour into warm, dry jars and seal when cold.

Coleslaw and Caraway Dressing

1 small or 1/2 large cabbage	6 tbs oil
1/4 red cabbage	2 tbs pineapple juice
2 carrots	2 tbs lemon juice
1 green and 1 red pepper	1/2 tsp salt
3-6 stalks celery	1/2 tsp soya sauce
1 onion or bunch of chives	1 1/2 tsp caraway seeds

Wash and shred the cabbage finely, wash and grate the carrots, deseed and slice the peppers, slice the washed celery and peel and grate the onion or finely chop the chives. Arrange all in a salad bowl. Combine remaining ingredients for the dressing and shake well in a screw-top jar. Pour over salad in the bowl and toss to blend.

Scandinavian Dressing

Infuse 1 dessertspoon of crushed caraway or dill seeds in 1/2 cup boiling water. Cool and strain. Mix together 2 tbs caraway liquid, 1 1/2 tbs vinegar, 1 tsp salt and 2 tsp castor sugar, and use as a dressing for beetroot. Store remaining caraway seed liquid in a screw-top jar in the refrigerator where it should keep at least two weeks.

Hot Beetroot with Caraway

Peel and slice several large beetroot while hot and toss them in a dressing made by combining 1 tsp caraway seeds with ¼ cup of melted butter. Garnish with chopped parsley.

or

Combine in a saucepan, heat gently but do not boil, and serve hot:

2 cups cooked, sliced beetroot	*¾-1 tsp caraway seeds*
2 tbs butter	*⅓ cup sour cream*
1-2 tbs lemon juice	*salt and pepper to taste*

Caraway Cabbage

Cook chopped cabbage gently in a little butter with 3 rashers of chopped bacon and ½ tsp caraway seeds. Drain and serve.

Caraway Baked Potatoes

Scrub large potatoes and cut them in half. Dip the cut side into a saucer of mixed caraway seeds and salt. Place on an oiled tray, cut side down, brush with oil or melted butter and bake at 180°C for 45-60 minutes.

Potatoes and Caraway

500 g potatoes	*1 tsp salt*
boiling water	*pepper to taste*
25 g butter	*1 cup hot milk*
1 tsp caraway seeds	*chopped parsley*

Put washed whole potatoes into a saucepan and cook in boiling water until nearly done but still firm. Peel and slice them into thick chunks. Melt butter in a heavy pan, add potato slices and brown them carefully on both sides. Season with caraway seeds, salt and pepper and pour in hot milk. Cover and cook gently about 15 minutes. Serve garnished with finely chopped parsley. This is nice with fritters, meat loaf or sausages, or, if an egg is added with the milk, can be a main dish.

Caraway Salad

Combine, mix well and serve hot or cold:

2 cups of cooked, peeled,
   sliced beetroot
1 cup sliced apple
1 cup cooked, sliced potato

1 tsp grated horse radish
1 tsp caraway seeds (or more
   to taste)

Red Cabbage and Caraway

1 kg red cabbage
3 tbs butter
½ cup brown sugar

¾ cup vinegar cider
1 tbs caraway seeds

Shred cabbage, removing hard stalks. Melt butter in a heavy pan, add sugar and vinegar and stir well. Add cabbage and caraway seeds and cook about 25 minutes, stirring often until cabbage is tender. Serve with roast pork.

Cream of Rye with Caraway

1 cup whole rye grains
2 tbs oil
1 sliced onion
1 cup shredded cabbage

1 tbs caraway seeds
3 cups boiling water
salt to taste

Roast rye grains until light brown in a moderate oven, cool and crack them in a grinder. Heat a little oil in a frying pan and gently cook the cracked rye, stirring, until it smells sweet. Remove from the heat. Put the remaining oil into a large, heavy saucepan and heat. Add onion and saute until just golden, add cabbage and caraway seeds and cook stirring until just tender. Add rye, boiling water and salt and continue to cook until rye is soft and thick. Serve in flattish bowls with Lebanese bread or chupatties and pickles.

Sauerkraut with Caraway and Frankfurters

500 g sauerkraut

1 tsp caraway seed

1 cooking apple	pepper to taste
2 carrots	4 thick slices bacon
4 tbs melted butter	8 frankfurters

Soak sauerkraut in cold water for 15 minutes and then drain and squeeze it dry with your hands. Peel, core and grate apple, peel and grate carrot and mix with sauerkraut, melted butter and caraway seeds. Turn into a casserole and season to taste. Top with slices of bacon, cover and cook 45 minutes at 180 °C. Remove the cover, arrange frankfurters on top and bake uncovered for a further 15 minutes.

Caraway Leaf Soup

25 g butter	1 egg
25 g flour	2 tbs cream
1 litre chicken stock	
1 cup finely chopped caraway	
leaves	

Melt butter, stir in flour and gradually add chicken stock stirring all the time, and simmer five minutes. Add caraway leaves. Beat egg with cream or top milk, pour soup over this, return to saucepan and reheat but do not boil.

Potato Soup with Caraway

2 kg potatoes	1 litre milk
2 litres water	2 tsp marjoram
2 tbs caraway seed	1 tsp salt
1 tsp salt	1 tsp paprika
6 leeks	cream and parsley to garnish

Peel and slice potatoes and cook 30 minutes in boiling water to which caraway seeds and 1 tsp salt have been added. Slice white part of leeks and add to potato mixture with green leek tops left whole. Cook 30 minutes, remove leek tops and mouli or mash vegetables. Add milk, marjoram, salt and paprika and stir and cook another 15 minutes. Serve with a little cream added and a garnish of finely chopped parsley.

Caraway Beef Broth

6 beef stock cubes
3 cups boiling water
¾ tsp caraway seeds

1 tsp arrowroot
1 tbs cold water

Dissolve stock cubes in boiling water in a saucepan and add seeds. Simmer gently for 10-15 minutes. Strain. Mix arrowroot with cold water and stir in a little stock. Return to pan and cook, stirring until slightly thick.

Seed Cake

125 g butter
125 g sugar
2 eggs
1 tsp brandy or whisky (optional)

1½ cups flour
1 tsp baking powder
1 tbs caraway seeds

Cream butter and sugar and add well beaten eggs and brandy. Sift together flour and baking powder, add caraway seeds and stir into the butter mixture. Mix well, pour into a greased tin and bake at 180 °C for 30-45 minutes.

Chervil

Chervill is held to be one of the pot herbes, it is pleasant to the stomacke and taste ..John Gerard

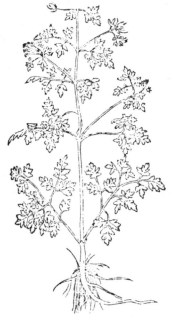

Chervil, *Anthriscus cerefolium*, is an annual native to South-East Europe and introduced to England by the Romans. It is always grown from seed and does better in cooler climates or seasons, tending to be small and pink with sunburn in hotter situations. Chervil has a mild flavour and pleasant scent and is generally used fresh and raw, the leaves being picked around the plant like parsley, for if the centre of the plant is picked it dies. If a few plants are left to flower and seed, chervil will come up every year without trouble and provide plenty of leaves for garnishing from late autumn through the winter and well on into spring.

Chervil may be used to flavour cream and cottage cheeses, eggs and egg dishes. It goes well with different meats, poultry and fish as a garnish or in butter or sauces. It may be used in all types of salads, with soups and different vegetables, and because it has a mild flavour it may be used generously. With chives, parsley and tarragon it forms part of the famous *fines herbes* combination much used in French cuisine, and chervil seems to enhance other flavours. The whole sprigs are best picked, then the smaller leaflets picked off and finely chopped and added to the food just before serving. Chervil does not retain its flavour when dried but may be blended with water and frozen in ice blocks like basil.

93

Chervil with Avocado

For each avocado use:
1 tbs lemon juice
2 tbs cream

1 tbs chopped chervil
pinch salt and pepper

Halve avocados and remove stone. Scoop out flesh without damaging skin and mash it with lemon juice. Blend in cream and season with salt and pepper to taste. Stir in chervil and pile back into avocado skins reserving a little chervil to sprinkle on top. Wrap in foil and chill in refrigerator before serving with crisp bread. A little crushed garlic may be added and blended in.

Cheese Boneks

Filling:
200 g cottage cheese
100 g grated cheese
1 tbs chopped onion
½ clove garlic

1 tbs each parsley and chervil
salt, pepper, sesame seed and
    chopped mint
1 beaten egg

Puff pastry

Combine filling ingredients and mix well with egg. Roll pastry out thinly and cut into small rounds. Place a teaspoon of filling in each round and fold in half to make a crescent. Brush with egg and bake at 220 °C for 10-15 minutes.

Chervil Rolls

3-4 cups flour
1 tbs dried yeast
1 tsp sugar

1 cup lukewarm water
1 tsp salt
2 tbs finely chopped chervil

Mix in a basin 1 cup flour, yeast and sugar. Stir in water to make a batter and leave to begin to bubble. Add enough flour to make a soft dough, then salt, and mix well, turning and kneading until dough is smooth. Leave in a warm place, covered with a cloth, to rise for 30 minutes. Knead again, mixing in the chervil, and divide into small rolls. Cover with the cloth again and leave to prove 15 minutes. Heat the baking tray at 200 °C and grease it. Place rolls quickly on it and bake at 200 °C for about 10 minutes. If you brush the tops with milk or water just before the rolls are put in the oven they will be browner.

Chervil and Egg Spread

2 beaten eggs
1 tbs milk
1 tsp salt

1 tbs butter
1 tbs finely chopped chervil

Combine beaten eggs, milk and salt and scramble in hot butter in a pan. When creamy, sprinkle in chervil and mix gently. Allow to cool completely and use as a spread for sandwiches or on biscuits.

Stuffed Eggs with Chervil

1 hard-boiled egg per person
salt and pepper

cream
½-1 sprig chervil per egg

Cut hard-boiled eggs in half lengthways and remove yolks to a basin. Mash them with a fork using a little cream to moisten them and snipping in chervil leaves to taste. When well mixed, pile the filling back into the egg whites and serve cold with salad.

To serve hot — place the filled eggs in an ovenproof dish, cover with a little white sauce flavoured with a pinch of nutmeg and heat gently at 180 °C for 15-20 minutes.

Omelette aux Fines Herbes

For two people:
4 eggs
1 tbs butter
salt and pepper to taste

2 tbs finely chopped chervil,
chives, parsley and tarragon
mixed

Heat butter in the omelette pan and pour in eggs slightly beaten with a fork. Season quickly and add enough fines herbes to colour the omelette green. Cook, tipping the pan so that the uncooked egg runs under the cooked egg as the omelette is lifted. When set, tip the omelette onto a warm plate.

Chervil and Asparagus Quiche

250 g pastry
4 slices bacon
1 tbs chopped onion
400-500 g cooked asparagus
2 beaten eggs
½ cup top milk

50 g grated cheese
1 tsp sugar
½ tsp salt
pepper to taste
1 tbs finely chopped chervil

Roll out pastry and line a pie plate with it. Leave in refrigerator until filling is ready. Cut up bacon and cook gently in a pan with onion, until bacon is crisp and onion tender. Leave to cool. Drain tinned or cooked asparagus and slice into small pieces. Combine all other ingredients and mix well. Fill the chilled pastry with a layer of bacon and onion, a thick layer of asparagus and then pour egg mixture over it. Cook at 200 °C for 10 minutes and then reduce heat to 180 °C and continue cooking 20-30 minutes more, until pastry is crisp and filling is set. Serve warm or cold.

Cheese and Chervil Souffle

3 tbs butter
4 tbs flour
1 cup milk
salt and pepper to taste

60 g cheese
3 eggs, separated
2 tbs finely chopped chervil

Melt butter in a pan, stir in flour and gradually blend in milk. Season with salt and pepper and bring to the boil, stirring all the time. Remove from the heat and add grated cheese (gruyere is nice). Beat in egg yolks one at a time and add chervil. Finally fold in stiffly beaten egg whites and pour mixture into a buttered souffle dish. Cook at 180 °C for 30 minutes and serve at once. 2-4 tbs finely chopped watercress may be used in place of chervil.

Fish Fillets aux Fines Herbes

Use one fillet of flounder per person and dip in melted butter both sides and then in breadcrumbs. Place in a well-buttered ovenproof dish and sprinkle each fillet with 1 tsp chopped onion and 1 tsp finely chopped mixed chervil, parsley and thyme **or** 1 tsp finely chopped mixed marjoram, parsley and rosemary, and add 1 tbs sherry or vermouth. Bake at 220 °C until tender and golden brown.

Tomato Baked Eggs aux Fines Herbes

Use ½ large firm tomato per person and remove enough pulp from each half to hold a raw egg. Break in egg and sprinkle with salt and pepper to taste and a mixture of finely chopped chives, chervil or parsley, basil, and tarragon and thyme. Place in a buttered dish and bake at 180 °C for about 20 minutes until the tomato is tender and egg is set.

Cauliflower and Chervil Salad

1 cauliflower cut into florets	1 tsp coriander
2 cups water	12 peppercorns
1 cup oil	1 tsp chervil
juice 3 lemons	1 sprig thyme
1 sliced stalk celery	½ bay leaf
1 crushed clove garlic	pinch salt
1 tsp fennel seeds	

Place cauliflower florets in a large saucepan and add liquids, celery and garlic. Crush fennel, coriander and peppercorns lightly and thyme and bay. Tie them in a piece of muslin and add to the pan. Finely chop chervil and add with salt. Bring all to the boil, reduce heat and simmer five minutes stirring now and then. Pour into a bowl, cool, cover and marinate in the refrigerator overnight. Remove the muslin spice bag and serve as a salad or entree.

Chervil and Nasturtium Flower Salad

1 small lettuce, washed and dried	3 tbs oil
1 cup nasturtium flowers, stamens removed	1½ tbs lemon juice
	1 tbs finely chopped chervil

Arrange washed, dried lettuce leaves in a salad bowl and top with washed, dried nasturtium flowers. Combine oil and lemon juice in a screw-top jar and shake well. Pour over salad, sprinkle with chervil, toss and serve.

Orange Salad with Chervil

4 oranges	*finely chopped chervil and*
2 tbs oil	*tarragon*
2 tsp lemon juice	*watercress to garnish*

Peel oranges, slice thinly in rounds and remove pips. Combine oil and lemon juice and toss orange slices in the dressing, with finely chopped chervil and tarragon sprinkled between. Arrange on a glass serving dish and garnish with watercress.

Chervil Salad Dressing

Combine and shake well in a small container:

6 tbs oil	*1 tsp finely chopped onion*
3 tbs tarragon vinegar	*3 tbs finely chopped chervil*
salt and pepper to taste	

Chervil and Cheese Dressing for Cauliflower Salad

125 g cottage cheese	*½ tsp mixed mustard*
2 egg yolks	*salt and pepper*
3 tbs oil	*pinch sugar*
2 tsp lemon juice	*2-3 tbs finely chopped chervil*

Beat cottage cheese and egg yolks together (with a wooden spoon in a basin) until blended. Gradually beat in oil until mixture is like mayonnaise. Stir in lemon juice and other seasonings and combine well. Keep covered in refrigerator until ready to serve over sprigs of just-cooked cauliflower that has been drained and cooled in a serving dish.

Chervil Sauce

1 tbs butter	*1-2 tbs cold water*
1 small onion	*1 cup hot vegetable stock*
2 tbs finely chopped chervil	*salt to taste*
1 tbs flour	*2 tsp sweet or sour cream*

Melt butter in a pan and gently cook onion until tender. Add chervil, then flour and cook 1 minute, before stirring in the cold water and removing from the heat to blend. When smooth gradually stir in hot stock and cook another 15-20 minutes. Taste and add salt as needed, adding cream just before serving.

or

50 g butter
15 g flour
1 bunch chopped chervil
1 sliced spring onion

½ tsp grated lemon rind
1 cup cream
lemon juice
salt and pepper

Melt butter in a basin over water or in the top of a double boiler. Stir in flour and blend well. Then add chervil, spring onion, lemon rind and cream and continue stirring over the hot water until mixture is smooth and slightly thick. Season to taste with a little lemon juice, salt and pepper and serve with chicken or fish.

Chervil Sauce for Shellfish

4 tbs butter
4 tbs flour
1¼ cups milk or chicken stock
2 tsp finely grated onion
cooked shellfish

2-3 tbs finely chopped chervil
salt and pepper
½-1 cup grated mild cheese
2-3 tbs breadcrumbs

Melt butter in a pan and stir in flour. Cook one minute and gradually stir in milk or stock. Bring to the boil, stirring all the time and add onion, cooked shellfish and chervil. Taste and season. Pour into a large or several small buttered ovenproof dishes and sprinkle a mixture of mild-flavoured grated cheese and breadcrumbs over the top. Bake at 200 °C for about 10 minutes and serve when golden brown.

Cold Cucumber Soup with Chervil

Peel cucumbers, cut into chunks and cook gently until tender in a little boiling water. Drain, puree and cook a little longer with 2 tbs butter and a little flour blended with cold water added to thicken the soup. Stir constantly until it comes to the boil and cook a few minutes. Cool, add a little cream until texture is quite smooth. Add 1 tbs finely chopped chervil and chill before serving.

Chervil Soup

2 tbs butter	5 tbs finely chopped chervil
2 tbs flour	salt and pepper to taste
½ litre chicken stock	1 tbs cream

Melt butter in a saucepan and stir in flour. Cook one minute and then stir in stock gradually and bring to the boil stirring all the time. Add 3 tbs finely chopped chervil, cover and simmer gently for 15-20 minutes. Taste and add salt and pepper as needed, and remove from the heat. Add cream and serve with 2 tbs chopped chervil as a garnish.

or

3-6 leeks	salt and pepper to taste
1½ litres chicken stock	3-4 tbs finely chopped chervil

Slice leeks and cook gently in stock until tender. Add pepper and salt to taste and chervil, and serve at once. If a thicker soup is wanted combine 2 tbs flour with 3-4 tbs cold milk and blend well. Thin with a little of the hot soup and pour back gradually into the soup, stirring all the time and cook gently until it thickens.

Beetroot Soup with Chervil

3 beetroot	1 tsp salt
1 onion	1 tsp sugar
1 small head celery	6 cups chicken stock
50 g butter	fresh chervil to garnish

Peel beetroot and onion and slice in long thin strips. String celery and chop small. Cook gently in a covered saucepan with the butter, salt and sugar. When tender add chicken stock and simmer a further 20-30 minutes. Add finely chopped chervil to taste and serve.

Parsnips with Chervil

Cook parsnips in a little boiling water until tender. Drain and add a little butter and hot milk or cream before mashing. Season to taste with salt and pepper and sprinkle with finely chopped chervil or a mixture of chervil and thyme.

Chervil and Potato Soup

2 tbs butter
500 g potatoes, peeled and
   sliced
4 onions, peeled and sliced
1 litre chicken stock

¼ tsp freshly grated nutmeg
1 bay leaf
½ cup top milk
salt and pepper
6 tbs finely chopped chervil

In a saucepan melt butter and add potatoes and onions. Cover and cook gently for 10 minutes, then add stock, nutmeg and bay leaf, cover and simmer 30 minutes until vegetables are tender. Remove bay leaf and cream mixture by processing in a blender or mouli. Return to the saucepan, add top milk and season to taste. Reheat but do not boil, then stir in chervil and serve at once.

Lima Beans with Chervil Butter

2-3 cups fresh lima beans
2 tbs butter

1 tbs chervil, finely chopped
freshly ground pepper

Cook beans in boiling salted water until tender then drain. Cream butter and chervil together with a fork and season with freshly ground pepper. Pour the hot drained beans into a serving dish and dot with small pieces of chervil butter. Crisp fried bacon may be added.

Chervil Cassoulet

½ kg dried beans or peas
4 shallots, or 2 onions, or
   2 leeks
100 g butter

2 cloves garlic crushed
2 cups tomato puree
salt, pepper and sugar to taste
2-4 tbs chopped chervil

Pour boiling water over beans and leave overnight. Drain and simmer in fresh water until tender, about 1½ hours. Drain and place in a warm serving dish and keep hot. Cook finely chopped shallots in butter with garlic and add tomato puree. Season to taste and pour over beans. Mix well and just before serving garnish with chervil. Pieces of crisp fried bacon may be added.

Chervil with Peas

4 tbs butter
4-6 shallots or spring onions
2 cups fresh or frozen peas

salt and freshly ground pepper
½ cup chicken stock
1-2 tbs finely chopped chervil

Melt butter in a saucepan and add finely chopped shallots or spring onions. Cover and cook gently but do not allow to brown. Then add peas, seasonings and chicken stock, and cover and cook gently for about 10 minutes. Remove the lid and continue to cook until peas are tender and liquid mostly evaporated. Sprinkle in chervil and toss to blend well before pouring into a serving dish.

Chervil and Egg Soup

25 g butter
1½ tbs flour
1 litre chicken stock
1-2 tbs finely chopped chervil

2 tbs finely grated carrot
salt and pepper
an egg for each person

Melt butter in a saucepan and stir in flour. Cook gently for a minute before gradually adding stock, while stirring all the time to keep it smooth. Bring to the boil and boil gently for 15 minutes. Add chervil and carrot, taste and season as needed, and pour immediately into bowls each containing a raw, lightly beaten egg. Stir while adding the hot soup to the egg so that the egg cooks by contact with the liquid, and serve at once.

Chervil Potatoes

Combine 2 tbs chopped chervil and 1 tbs chopped chives with 2-4 cups mashed potatoes. Top with grated cheese and bake 10-20 minutes at 180 °C.

Chicory and Endive

These herbes eaten in sallades or other wise... doth comfort the weake and feeble stomacke, and cooleth and refresheth the stomacke overmuch heated.
John Gerard

Chicory, *Chichorium intybus,* was formerly called succory, and is sometimes confused with its annual or biennial cousin endive, *Chicorium endivia.* Both are more pot herbs than flavouring herbs and both have been grown from ancient times as salad plants. Chicory has become better known since it has been grown commercially and blanched. This type of chicory is called Belgium endive or witloof and is available as a winter salad. It is a tonic and digestive herb and loses its bitterness when blanched.

Both chicory and endive are grown from seeds and are easy plants in the garden. In flower they both have beautiful blue flowers which open early and close about noon. Their green leaves may be used in salad but are bitter and the blanched 'chicons' are generally preferred. The root of chicory is also used, washed, dried and roasted to mix with coffee. This counteracts some of the caffeine and so is beneficial to health.

Chicory is used both cooked and as a raw salad herb or vegetable. It is a valuable food containing calcium, copper and iron as well as vitamins B and C.

To Prepare Witloof

Always keep witloof away from direct light and sun because it will turn green and taste bitter in the light. Discard any damaged leaves, trim the stalk end and cut a small cone of the stalk out 1-2cm deep but leave enough stem to hold the leaves together. Then when the witloof is cooked it will not taste bitter. Prepared witloof may be sprinkled with lemon juice to keep it white.

Chicory Salads

Almost any combination of finely sliced blanched witloof and other salad greens or vegetables may be used according to taste and depending on what is available. Chives, marjoram, parsley and tarragon are aromatic herbs which combine well with chicory. Apples and nuts also taste well with chicory and the salads may be dressed with French dressing, lemon juice, mayonnaise, yoghurt, cottage cheese or horseradish.

2 heads blanched chicory
1 red and 1 green apple
1 green pepper
walnuts to taste

French dressing to which has
been added 1 tsp each finely
chopped chervil, lemon
balm, mint and salad burnet

Finely slice chicory and core and slice apples. Combine with deseeded, sliced green pepper and mix well. Pour over French dressing mixed with chopped herbs, toss and serve.

Avocado and Witloof Salad

2 cups finely sliced witloof
1 cup torn lettuce leaves
1 finely sliced orange
¾ cup finely sliced onion rings
½-1 avocado, peeled and diced

1 clove crushed garlic
½ tsp salt
1 tbs lemon juice
2 tbs oil

Combine vegetables and fruit and toss well in a salad bowl. Crush garlic with salt, stir in lemon juice and oil, pour over salad; mix well and serve.

Beetroot and Witloof Salad

½ kg finely sliced witloof
2-3 cooked, peeled, diced
  beetroot
1 peeled, cored, diced apple
1 tbs lemon juice

1 tbs oil
salt and pepper
mayonnaise
finely chopped parsley

Combine witloof, beetroot and apple in a salad bowl and mix well.
Combine lemon juice, oil, salt and pepper to taste, pour over salad
and toss through. Add mayonnaise to taste, garnish with parsley
and serve.

Savoury Fruit and Witloof Salad

2-3 heads witloof
1 banana
1 lemon
small bunch grapes
walnuts

French dressing made with oil,
  lemon juice, and seasoned
  with mustard, pepper and
  salt
celery to garnish

Slice witloof finely and arrange in a bowl. Peel and slice banana
and soak in lemon juice to keep it white. De-seed grapes and
combine with banana and witloof. Add chopped walnuts to taste.
Combine dressing ingredients and shake well in a screw-top jar.
Pour over salad, toss well and garnish with finely chopped celery.

Potato and Witloof or Endive Salad

3-4 heads witloof, or 1 head
  endive
2 cooked, diced potatoes
1 finely chopped onion
1-2 tbs each raisins and
  walnuts
250 g yoghurt or cottage
  cheese

2 tbs lemon juice
1 tsp horseradish or mustard
salt and pepper to taste
hard-boiled egg and parsley to
  garnish

Combine finely chopped witloof or endive, potatoes, onion, raisins
and nuts. Combine yoghurt or cottage cheese with lemon juice and
horseradish or mustard and season to taste. Pour dressing over
salad and serve garnished with sliced hard-boiled egg and parsley.

Chicken and Witloof Salad

2 heads chicory
250 g cold, cooked, diced
   chicken
125 g cottage cheese
lemon juice

salt and pepper
cream as necessary
1 peeled, sliced orange
finely chopped tarragon

Take off large leaves of chicory and dice the rest finely. Combine with chicken, cottage cheese, lemon juice and seasonings and make to the desired consistency by adding cream. Arrange whole chicory leaves in a bowl and pile chicken-chicory mixture into them. Decorate with slices of orange sprinkled with tarragon.

Poached Eggs with Chicory or Endive

½ head chicory per person
½-1 cup stock
1 bay leaf or bouquet garni

1 egg per person
salt and pepper

Quarter chicory heads and blanch in boiling water for 5 minutes. Drain and squeeze out moisture and put in a saucepan with a little stock and a bouquet garni. Cook covered, over a low heat until tender. Remove bouquet garni, drain chicory and keep hot while poaching 1 egg per person. Chop chicory finely and arrange on warmed plates. Serve with poached egg on top.

or

Allow 1 small head of endive and 1 poached egg per person. Cook the endive gently in a little water until tender. Drain and keep hot. Make a sauce by combining 3 tbs melted butter and 2 tbs flour in a saucepan and stirring in a little milk until the sauce is moderately thick. Add salt and pepper and boil stirring 3 minutes. Add 1 tbs cream per endive, and the chopped endive and remove from the heat while the eggs are poaching. Serve each egg on an individual plate on a bed of endive in sauce. Toast may be served with it if liked.

Witloof Quiche

250 g pastry

1 cup cream

2-3 heads witloof
pepper and lemon juice
2 beaten eggs

½ tsp salt
pinch freshly ground nutmeg
knob butter

Roll out pastry and line a shallow pie plate. Finely slice witloof and toss with a little lemon juice and pepper to taste and arrange it on the pastry. Combine beaten eggs and cream and stir well, adding salt. Pour this over witloof and sprinkle with a pinch of nutmeg. Dot with small pieces butter and bake at 180 °C for 25-35 minutes until the pastry is crisp and the filling set.

Witloof with Beans

1 kg cooked mashed potatoes
3 heads witloof, blanched and
  chopped
1-2 cups cooked dried beans or
  chick peas

1 cup white sauce
salt and pepper
grated cheese

In a large ovenproof dish arrange a layer of half the mashed potato. Cover this with a layer of witloof and then add the beans or chick peas. Pour in white sauce, season with salt and pepper and top with the remaining mashed potato. Sprinkle with grated cheese and bake in the oven until heated through and golden brown and crunchy on top.

Chicory and Dandelion

Cook chopped bacon in a pan until crisp. Add 3 tbs wine vinegar, and 1 tbs grated onion. Then add sliced chicory and torn dandelion leaves and cook gently, mixing all together. Serve with toast.

Chicory au Gratin

Cook 4 heads of chicory in a little water and the juice of a lemon until they are tender, and drain well. Wrap each cooked chicory head in a slice of cooked ham and arrange in a casserole. Cover with 1 cup cheese sauce, sprinkle with breadcrumbs and dot with butter. Cook in the oven at 180 °C until brown, 10-15 minutes.

Stir-Fried Chicken and Witloof

500 g sliced chicken
1 tbs cornflour
1 tbs soya sauce
2 tbs oil
2 heads sliced witloof

juice 1 lemon
50 g mushrooms
¼ cup stock
salt and pepper to taste

Roll sliced chicken meat in cornflour, then in soya sauce. Heat oil and gently fry chicken for about 5 minutes. Sprinkle sliced witloof with lemon juice, add to chicken and stir fry. Add sliced mushrooms and stock and continue to stir and cook until meat and vegetables are tender. Season to taste and serve with boiled rice or noodles, or allow to cool and use as a spread on biscuits or sandwiches.

Chicory Flower Syrup

1 cup chicory flowers
water

1 cup sugar
1 cup icing sugar

Soak flowers in water for 5 minutes then drain and dry on paper towels. Combine sugars and ¾ cup water in a saucepan and cook gently for 10 minutes, stirring until sugar is dissolved. Boil for 5 minutes, remove from the heat and stir in flowers, cover and leave 3-5 minutes. Lift flowers out carefully, drain them and put onto a plate sprinkled with castor sugar, sprinkling them with more sugar to crystallise them. Set them in a warm place to dry. Strain the syrup into a jar and use like Borage Syrup in fruit salad or compotes.

Pickled Chicory Flowers

2 cups chicory flowers or buds
3 cups cider vinegar
½ tsp ground ginger, or
  cloves, or cinnamon

½ tsp salt
½ cup honey

Wash and dry chicory flowers. Bring vinegar, ginger and salt to the boil and simmer 5 minutes. Stir in honey, add flowers and bring to the boil, overflow and seal. Store a week before using.

Endive Salad Fan

Wash endive in cold water and leave to soak until leaves open out. Drain and dry leaves and arrange on a large flat dish in a fan shape. Cover with peeled, sliced avocado, watercress, and carrots cut in julienne strips. Ingredients may be varied to suit.

Braised Chicory or Endive

3-4 endive or chicory
1 tbs lemon juice for each
  endive
½ cup chicken stock

1 tsp salt
1 tbs sugar
3 tbs butter
1 tbs flour

Blanch endive or chicory in boiling water for 10 minutes. Drain, cut in quarters and put in a well-greased casserole. Add lemon juice, stock, salt and sugar and 2 tbs butter. Cover and cook at 180 °C until tender, about 25 minutes. Remove vegetables to a serving dish and reduce the pan liquid by boiling it down. Melt remaining butter in a small saucepan and stir in flour. Gradually add pan liquid, bring to boil and stir until thick. Pour over chicory or endive and serve.

Endive Salads

Wash, dry and tear into bite-sized pieces 1 head endive, 1 lettuce and a bunch of corn salad. Add 1 sliced green pepper and 1 peeled, sliced avocado. Season with salt and pepper and toss in French dressing.

or

Mix together washed, dried and torn endive leaves, chopped walnuts and a dressing made by combining and shaking well 3 parts oil to 1 part wine vinegar and 1 part grape juice. Toss well and serve.

Chives

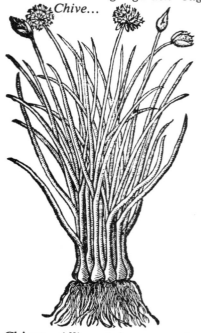

No cottage garden ought to be without the Chive...

J.C. Loudon

Chives, *Allium schoenoprasum,* are a member of the onion family and are grown for the foliage and flowers. They are the smallest and most delicately flavoured of their family, their smooth, green hollow leaves growing up from a clump of small bulbs ready to pick most of the year. Chives may be grown from seed or division of the clumps and are hardy perennials as long as they are grown in any reasonable garden soil with adequate sun and moisture. They die back in winter, but their cousin, Chinese or Garlic Chives, *Allium tuberosum,* does not and provides long, flat not hollow, leaves with a slightly more garlicy flavour to take their place.

Chives should be picked carefully. If you take them by their green hair and cut them off low down you will cut all the young growing leaves which would have provided you with garnish for the next few weeks. It is better to hand pick the largest leaves, which is quite quick to do, and leave the smaller ones for next time.

Chives are best used raw, washed and finely snipped with scissors, and added to a dish just before serving. They have a delicious flavour and leave no onion smell on the breath. However they are sometimes cooked in bread and scones and in sauces. The beautiful purple flowers may be used in salads and to make a pink herb vinegar.

Cottage Cheese and Chives

Snip chives with scissors into small pieces and add to taste to a carton of cottage or cream cheese. Leave 5-10 minutes for the flavour to blend and serve on biscuits or bread.

Cheese, Date and Chive Ball

1 cup dates
juice ½ orange
500 g cottage cheese

2 tbs finely chopped chives
sunflower seeds or walnuts

Soak dates in orange juice and blend well. Add cottage cheese and chives and stir until all are combined. Shape into a ball and roll in sunflower seeds or walnuts. Chill slightly and serve with biscuits.

Chive and Vegetable Spread

1 small onion
1 carrot
2 sticks celery

2-3 stalks parsley
chives to taste
grated cheese to bind

Mince, finely grate or chop onion, carrot and celery. Add minced parsley and finely chopped chives to taste and combine with enough soft grated cheese to bind to a spreading consistency. Use as a sandwich spread or on biscuits, or make with cottage cheese and use as a dip.

Cheese and Chive Bread

1 clove crushed garlic
50 g butter

1 tbs chopped chives
bread or a French loaf

Combine garlic, butter and chives and mix well. Spread on slices of bread, or butter a French loaf that has been sliced nearly to the bottom. Sprinkle grated cheese to taste on the sliced bread and heat it under the grill until cheese has melted or put the French loaf, also sprinkled with cheese, in the oven to heat until warmed through and the cheese melted.

Baked Eggs with Chives

For each egg use 1 tbs butter or cream, and 1 tsp finely chopped chives, salt and pepper to taste. Breadcrumbs optional. Butter an individual ramekin for each egg and stand them in a pan of water in a moderate oven to warm for about 10 minutes. Remove from the oven, break an egg into each ramekin on top of either 1 tbs melted butter or warmed cream and sprinkle with the finely chopped chives. Season with salt and pepper to taste and either cover with foil or top each egg with fresh breadcrumbs. Return to the oven and bake until the egg white is firm and the yolk still soft. Serve with buttered toast or bread.

With potatoes

For each person:
1 hot potato baked in its skin
1 tbs butter
1 tsp chopped chives
pinch salt and pepper

a little cooked, chopped bacon
1 egg
grated cheese (optional)

Scoop out cooked potato carefully leaving skin whole. Mix potato with butter, chives, seasoning and bacon, and stuff this back into the skin. Make a hollow in the centre and carefully break an egg into this. Sprinkle with cheese if liked, and bake at 180 °C until egg is set and cheese melted.

In tomatoes

For each egg:
1 large tomato
1 tbs breadcrumbs

1 tsp finely chopped basil
and chives
salt and pepper to taste

Cut tops off tomatoes and scoop out pulp without breaking the shell. Mix pulp with breadcrumbs and herbs and season to taste. Spoon a little of this mixture into each case, break an egg carefully on top, and then add rest of the breadcrumb mixture on top of that without breaking the egg yolk. Place them in a buttered dish and bake in a moderate oven at 180 °C for about 30 minutes. The tomatoes should be soft but firm enough to hold their shape. Serve on or with hot toast.

Cheese and Chive Scones

2 cups flour
2 heaped tsp baking powder
pinch salt and cayenne pepper

6 tbs grated cheese
2-3 tbs chopped chives
approximately 200 ml milk

Sift dry ingredients, add cheese and chives and stir in milk. Pat out
lightly on a floured board and cut into circles with a ring cutter or a
floured glass. Put close together on a tray and bake at 230 °C for
10-15 minutes.

Boiled Eggs with Chives

1-2 eggs per person
salt and pepper

1-2 tsp finely chopped chives
per egg

Bring a pan of water to the boil. Lower eggs carefully into water,
cover, remove pan from heat and leave 10 minutes. Spoon egg out
of the shells into a glass, season, sprinkle with chives and serve with
hot buttered toast.

Omelette with Chives

Mix about 1 tbs finely chopped chives into a 2-3 egg omelette and
cook in the usual way, or sprinkle the chives onto the cooked
omelette before folding it over.

Courgette Salad with Chives

500 g courgettes
boiling water
salt
2 tbs oil

juice ½ lemon
freshly ground pepper
2 tbs finely chopped chives

Cook courgettes in boiling, salted water for 5 minutes and drain.
Cool them quickly in cold water and drain again. Cut courgettes
into small slices and arrange in a serving dish. Combine oil, lemon
juice and pepper and mix well. Pour over courgettes, add chopped
chives, toss together to blend the flavours and serve.

Cucumber and Chive Salad

1 long green cucumber or
   several apple cucumbers
salt
1 tsp each tarragon vinegar
   and sugar

2 tbs cream or yoghurt
white pepper to taste
2 tbs salad oil
1 tbs chopped chives

Peel and slice cucumber, put in a colander and sprinkle with salt to bring out the moisture. Leave to drain for ½ hour and then arrange in a serving dish. Mix the dressing in order of listing and blend well. Pour over cucumber and serve at once.

Green Salad with Tomatoes and Chives

1 bowl mixed green salad
2 tbs finely chopped chives
6 sprigs thyme

French dressing
slices of large, firm tomatoes
chives to garnish

Add chives and thyme leaves to green salad, dress with French dressing and toss well. Arrange slices of tomato over salad and sprinkle liberally with more finely chopped chives. A little more olive oil may be added, with salt and pepper to taste.

Lettuce Salad with Chives

1 lettuce torn in bite-sized
   pieces
¼ cup each red wine vinegar
   and olive oil

salt and pepper to taste
¼ cup finely chopped chives

Arrange lettuce in a bowl. Combine vinegar, oil, salt and pepper in a screw-top jar, shake to blend well and pour over lettuce. Toss lightly to coat lettuce and sprinkle with chives, toss again and serve.

Potato Salad with Chives

750 g hot, cooked, diced
   potatoes
1 bunch celery
½ cup chopped nuts

1 cup mayonnaise
salt and pepper to taste
1 small lettuce or chicory
2 tbs chopped chives

Combine potatoes, chopped celery, walnuts and mayonnaise. Season with salt and pepper to taste and allow to cool. Wash and dry chicory or lettuce and tear into pieces. Pile potato mixture into middle of a salad bowl, arrange chicory or lettuce around it, and sprinkle potatoes with chopped chives.

Rice Salad with Chives

1½ cups long grain brown rice
1 tsp salt
1 bay leaf
knob of butter
2 tbs wine vinegar
4 tbs oil

1 onion, grated
cooked or raw vegetables as
  available — celery, peppers,
  tomatoes, peas
2 tbs chopped nuts
2 tbs chopped chives

Cook rice in a saucepan with salt, bay leaf and butter, added to water to just cover the rice. Bring to the boil, stir, then cover and turn heat down to cook gently. When water is all absorbed the rice should be tender. Combine vinegar and oil and toss through the rice with grated onion, while rice is still warm. Add sliced, cooked or raw vegetables, nuts and chives when the rice is cold, and toss to mix well. Diced cold meat may also be added.

Blue Cheese and Chive Dressing

75 g mashed blue vein cheese
3 tbs finely chopped chives

½ cup oil
½-1 cup buttermilk

Combine all ingredients, blending and mixing thoroughly to get a smooth texture. Chill and serve with any green salad.

Sour Cream and Chive Dressing

1 cup sour cream
½ tsp salt
1 tbs sugar
2 tbs herb vinegar

2 tbs chopped chives
1 tsp dill seed
prepared cucumber
paprika

Combine all dressing ingredients and pour over sliced cucumber which has been salted, left an hour and then drained. Chill slightly and sprinkle with paprika before serving.

115

Yoghurt and Chive Salad Dressing

To 1 carton plain yoghurt add:

1 tbs chopped chives
¼ tsp dry mustard
¼ tsp plain or garlic salt

1 tsp lemon juice
pepper to taste

Mix well and keep chilled. Use as a dressing with any salad.

Chive Salt

Put a layer of plain salt in a baking dish and cover with a layer of washed, dried and chopped chives. Cover with more salt and put in the oven at 150 °C for 10 minutes. Then stir the mixture, respread it and cook 10 minutes more. Crumble herbs and cool before bottling. The chives can be sifted out or left in, but the mixture must be quite dry or the salt will go mouldy later.

Chive Sauce for Fish

For 4 pieces of fish:

3 hard-boiled egg yolks
3 tbs oil
1 tbs vinegar

2 tsp chopped chives
salt and pepper

Sieve the egg yolks and add the oil drop by drop blending well. Then stir in vinegar and chives, season to taste and serve.

Chive Sauce for Hot Corned Beef

3 large slices white bread with
* crusts removed*
milk
2 hard-boiled egg yolks
salt and pepper

½ tsp mixed mustard
pinch of sugar
juice ½ lemon
3 tbs oil
1 tbs chopped chives

Soak bread in milk for 5 minutes, then squeeze dry and put into a bowl. Sieve in egg yolks and blend well with the bread, using a fork. Stir in salt, pepper, mustard and sugar. Add lemon juice and blend until smooth. Gradually add oil, drop by drop until it is absorbed, and just before serving, add chives and blend well through the mixture. Serve with hot boiled beef.

116

Roquefort Butter

Beat together:

¼ cup softened butter
¼ cup blue vein cheese,
   crumbled
1 tbs lemon juice

3 tbs finely chopped chives
a pinch of pepper
a dash of Worcestershire sauce
1 tsp brandy

When all ingredients are well blended, cover and store in refrigerator, but allow to soften at room temperature before serving with steak, chops or fish.

Sweet and Sour Chive Sauce

1 egg
1 tbs water
2 tsp barley flour
½ cup water
2 tbs wine vinegar

2 tsp sugar
salt and pepper
2 tbs oil
3 tbs chopped chives

Beat egg with 1 tbs water and add to flour to make a smooth paste. Heat in a small pan ½ cup water, 1 tbs vinegar, sugar and seasonings. Pour into the egg mixture, stirring all the time, return to the saucepan and boil gently until mixture thickens. Remove from the heat, stir in oil, 1 tbs wine vinegar and chopped chives and serve warm.

Artichoke and Chive Soup

500 g Jerusalem artichokes
1 onion
1-2 potatoes
4 sticks celery
2 tbs butter

½ litre chicken stock
1 bay leaf
salt and pepper
2 tbs finely chopped chives

Peel and slice vegetables and cook them gently in butter for a few minutes. Add chicken stock and bay leaf and simmer covered until vegetables are tender. Blend till smooth or put through a mouli, and reheat. Season with salt and pepper to taste and serve garnished with chives.

Chicken Soup with Chives

Just before serving any chicken soup garnish it with finely chopped chives to taste.

Vichyssoise

3 leeks
1 onion
2 tbs butter
4 potatoes

4 cups chicken stock
salt and white pepper
1 cup cream
chopped chives

Cook sliced leeks and peeled, sliced onion in butter until tender. Add peeled, sliced potatoes and chicken stock and simmer until potatoes are cooked. Put through a sieve, add salt and pepper and cool. Stir in cream, garnish with chives and serve.

Hot Beetroot with Chives

Cook washed, unpeeled beetroot whole in gently boiling water until tender, drain and slip off skins. Leave small beetroot whole and slice larger ones into a hot vegetable dish. Melt 50 g butter in a small pan, add 1 tbs finely chopped chives, pour over beetroot and serve.

Hot Cucumber with Chives

2 cucumbers
boiling water
1 cup hot white sauce

salt and pepper
1 tbs finely chopped chives

Peel cucumbers and cut into cubes. Cook in boiling water for a few minutes, but do not allow to get mushy. Drain well and put into hot white sauce. Taste, season, stir in finely chopped chives and serve.

Stuffed Cucumbers

4 medium-sized green
  cucumbers
100-150 g cream cheese

1 tbs chopped chives
pinch of paprika or to taste

Cut ends off unpeeled cucumbers and remove centres longways with an apple corer. Drain cucumbers and dry the insides by pushing a paper towel through the middle of each. Then fill with a mixture of cream cheese and chives seasoned with paprika — a little cream may be added if mixture is not smooth enough. Wrap each cucumber in foil and store in refrigerator until well chilled and the filling is firm. Serve sliced thinly with a little thick mayonnaise on each slice.

Baked Potatoes in their Jackets with Chives

Wash 4-6 old potatoes, put them in cold water in a saucepan and bring to the boil. Drain them and place in the oven with a meat skewer through the centre of each potato. Bake at 180°C until tender, about one hour.
About 15 minutes before serving combine:

¾ cup sour cream or yoghurt
1-2 tbs chopped chives
1 small clove garlic, crushed

salt and pepper
grated cheese or crumbled blue
  vein cheese (optional)

Cut potatoes in half and top with this chive dressing.

Potato Cakes

750 g hot, cooked potatoes
salt and pepper to taste
4 tbs butter
2 tbs chopped chives

1 beaten egg
flour
butter or oil for frying

Mash hot, cooked potatoes with salt and pepper, then blend in butter, chives and beaten egg. Allow mixture to cool, shape into flat cakes, roll in a little flour and fry in hot butter or oil until both sides are lightly brown.

Comfrey

... we have plenty of good green vegetables, so for most people it can be useful only as a 'spinach' to use in early spring, but Comfrey has the distinction of being the only land plant so far known to extract vitamin B 12 from the soil.

Lawrence D. Hills

Comfrey, *Symphytum* species, is a rough, hairy perennial which has been known and used for hundreds of years as a medicinal plant and a pot herb. In New Zealand the hybrid known as Russian comfrey is grown and can be used for food and medicine, to feed animals and as a compost plant or green manure. It grows vigorously, and although it dies down in winter it provides masses of leaves to use for most of the year. The young leaves are the part most used, and if it is kept cut back and older leaves added to the compost or used as a mulch, a supply is always ready for the picking.

Because it is deep rooted, comfrey contains many minerals and vitamins as well as vitamin B 12 which is very important for vegetarians and vegans. It also contains allantoin in the roots which stimulates tissue formation and promotes healing, including healing fractured bones, hence its old name of knitbone. If you wish to use it but do not find it palatable it may be infused as a tea or used in soups, stews, stocks or mixed with other vegetables.

120

Comfrey Leaf Fritters or 'Green Fish'

Pick young comfrey leaves, wash them in cold water, shake dry, and dip in batter. Fry gently in hot butter, browning on both sides. Eat immediately with a squeeze of lemon, and a sprinkle of sugar.

Comfrey au Gratin

Arrange in an ovenproof dish alternate layers of cooked rice, finely chopped raw comfrey, grated cheese and onion (optional) and a sprinkle of salt and pepper. Add a little milk to keep the dish moist, top dish with a last layer of rice and dot it with a little butter. Cook at 180°C for about 30 minutes.

Comfrey Soup

1 sliced onion
1 tbs butter
1 peeled, diced potato
12 leaves comfrey
gloveful of nettle tops if
    available

1 cup stock or water
1 tsp Marmite or Vegemite
    (optional)
1 cup top milk
salt and pepper to taste
chopped parsley to garnish

Cook sliced onion gently in butter in a large saucepan until soft. Add potato and saute. Fold comfrey leaves in half and cut out stems, then chop them finely and add to potato. Saute all together for several minutes with nettles, also washed and with stalks removed. Then add stock or water and bring to the boil and simmer gently until vegetables are tender. Stir soup through a sieve or blend in a food mill or mouli, add Marmite and milk. Taste, season and reheat but do not boil. Garnish with chopped parsley and serve.

Comfrey Stock for Soups or Stews

Boil 6-8 large comfrey leaves in 1 litre water for 10 minutes. Allow to cool with lid on. Strain and add to soups or stews.

Comfrey and Courgette Egg Pie

¼ cup finely chopped onion
1-2 sliced courgettes
1 tbs oil
1 cup finely chopped comfrey
pinch each finely chopped
   sage, rosemary and/or
   thyme

2 tbs finely chopped parsley
2 beaten eggs
3-4 tbs grated cheese
salt and pepper to taste

Fry onion and courgettes in heated oil, turning lightly until tender but not soggy. Add comfrey and cook until limp. Season with herbs and parsley and set aside to cool. Combine beaten eggs and cheese and season to taste. Combine egg mixture with vegetables and pour into a buttered ovenproof dish. Bake at 180°C for about 30 minutes, until set. Serve hot or warm, cut in squares.

Comfrey as a Vegetable

Pick young leaves, fold them in half and cut out their stalks. Wash them and put them damp into an enamel or stainless steel pan with a little butter, cover and cook gently in their own steam over a low heat for 8-10 minutes. Chop, drain and season to taste with salt and pepper.

Comfrey leaves may be combined with any cabbage, silverbeet or spinach leaves and cooked in the same way. Comfrey may be served with a white or cheese sauce or with breadcrumbs toasted in a little butter.

Comfrey Wine

1 kg comfrey leaves
4 litres water
1½ kg sugar

2 lemons
wine yeast and nutrient

Boil comfrey leaves in water in a large saucepan for 30 minutes. Strain out leaves, press all moisture out of them and make liquid up to 4 litres by adding boiled water if necessary. Pour the liquid over sugar and stir until it is dissolved. Add strained lemon juice. When liquid is lukewarm add wine yeast and nutrient and stir well. Cover and leave 1-3 days before pouring into jars fitted with fermentation locks. When fermentation ceases, siphon into clean dry bottles, cap and store at least 6 months before drinking.

Candied Comfrey Roots

Dig roots in autumn, wash and cut them up into 5-10cm lengths. Boil in water until tender, strain and reserve liquid. Make a syrup by combining 500 g sugar with 2½ cups of the cooking liquid and bring to the boil in a saucepan. Add juice of 1 lemon and cooked comfrey roots and simmer slowly until liquid is largely absorbed. Lift roots out with a slotted spoon, drain and roll them in a little sugar, and dry thoroughly in a cool oven.

Comfrey Root Chutney

500 g young comfrey roots
cider vinegar to cover
500 g peeled sliced onions
500 g peeled chopped apples
½-1 cup sugar

½-1 cup sultanas
1 tsp sea salt
1 tsp ground ginger or a piece
  of bruised ginger root

Wash and chop up comfrey roots and cook them for 30 minutes in cider vinegar. Add onion and apple and continue to cook until soft. Add sugar, sultanas, salt and ginger and simmer until thick. Pour into warm dry jars and cover when cold.

Comfrey Root Jam or Marmalade

Grated comfrey root may be added to any jam — 250 g comfrey to 500 g fruit — and cooked with the fruit before the sugar is added, and the jam made in the usual way.

For marmalade, the grated root should be soaked with the fruit in water for 12-24 hours before making the recipe.

Comfrey Root Sweets

Combine:
2 tbs sugar or honey
2 tbs grated comfrey root
pinch salt
2 tsp cocoa

2 tbs grated or desiccated
  coconut
aditional coconut to roll

Let mixture stand and when gluey roll into small balls and roll in additional coconut. Stand in a warm place to dry.

Comfrey Root Wine

4-6 comfrey roots, washed,
   peeled and chopped
4 litres water

1½ kg sugar
juice 1 orange or 1 lemon
wine yeast and nutrient

Boil comfrey roots in water in a large pan until tender. Strain liquid onto sugar and stir to dissolve it. Make quantity up to 4 litres with boiled water and add strained fruit juice. When it has cooled to blood heat add wine yeast and nutrient and stir well. Cover with a cloth and leave about 7-10 days, stirring daily. Pour into a fermentation jar fitted with an air lock. When fermentation ceases, leave tightly capped for 6 months before bottling and then leave a further 6 months before drinking.

Coriander

The whole Plant when fresh has a bad Smell, but as the Seeds dry, they become sweet and fragrant. They are excellent to dispel Wind; they warm and strengthen the Stomach and assist Digestion.

Sir John Hill

Coriander, *Coriandrum sativum,* is an annual native to the Mediterranean, and can only be grown from seed. It is an erect, slender plant, up to ½ metre high, with pretty pinkish white flowers. The lower leaves are stalked and pinnate but the upper leaves are linear and much divided, and the fresh herb has a strange smell which accounts for its name — coriander is derived from *koris,* a bug. However the lower pinnate leaves are used as parsley in both Chinese and Mexican dishes and are sometimes called Chinese parsley or cilantro. The seeds are the part most used, and form an important ingredient in curry as well as being used in bread and cakes, desserts, meat and vegetable dishes.

Coriander is easy to grow, the seeds germinate well and the plants prefer a light, fertile soil and a sunny situation where the seed will ripen quickly. When it turns light brown, the seed may be snipped or picked off and dried in the sun. The fragrance develops as the seed dries and it may then be used whole or ground. Whole seeds should always be slightly crushed to release the essential oils before being added to cooking. The fresh leaves finely chopped may be used as a parsley substitute, or added to fresh chutneys for accompanying curry or to salads and sauces.

125

Coriander Avocado Dip

Combine and blend well:
pulp 2 large avocados
1 skinned, chopped tomato
½ tsp salt
2 tbs lemon juice

1 crushed clove garlic
2 tbs finely minced coriander
leaves

Pour into a bowl and serve with crackers.

Coriander and Garlic Chicken

1 roasting fowl
4 whole plants fresh coriander
6 cloves garlic crushed with
  2 tsp salt

1 tbs crushed peppercorns
2 tbs lemon juice

Cut fowl into serving pieces. Combine finely chopped coriander
with other ingredients and rub into the fowl. Marinate, covered,
for at least an hour. Grill 15cm from heat, turning every 5 minutes
until tender and crisp.

Lebanese Lamb

1 cup water
1 tbs olive oil
750 g lean lamb
3 sliced onions
2 crushed cloves garlic
parsley stalks
1 tbs cornflour

1 tbs water
½ litre yoghurt
1 tsp grated lemon rind
salt and pepper
1 tbs each chopped parsley and
coriander leaves

Heat water and oil and add lamb, cut in small cubes, with onion
and garlic. Add parsley stalks, cover and simmer gently until lamb
is tender, 1-1½ hours. Combine cornflour with 1 tbs water and mix
it into yoghurt and lemon rind. Put this mixture into a saucepan,
bring to the boil, stirring all the time, and simmer 10 minutes. Add
yoghurt mixture to lamb and simmer a further 10 minutes before
removing from the heat and tasting. Add salt and pepper as
necessary and pour into a serving dish. Sprinkle with finely
chopped parsley and coriander leaves.

Pork Pieces with Coriander

¾ kg pork pieces
oil for frying
200 g firm tomatoes

3 serrano chillies
finely chopped coriander
leaves

Fry pork pieces in hot oil until browned on all sides. Cook tomatoes gently in salted water and then combine with chillies, deseeded and sliced, and coriander leaves in a blender. Add this to pork pieces and fry a little longer. Then cover and cook gently until meat is tender. A little extra warm water may be added if necessary.

Cucumber and Coriander Salad

1-2 long green cucumbers
salt
1 cup plain yoghurt
1 tbs chopped cress or chives

1 tbs finely chopped
coriander leaves
salt and pepper

Peel and chop cucumbers into bite-sized pieces and sprinkle with salt. Leave ½ hour then drain. Combine yoghurt and herbs and pour over cucumbers in a serving dish. Toss gently to combine, and season with salt and pepper to taste.

Sauce for Cold Meat

Blend until smooth:
½ cup grated fresh coconut
1 green pepper, deseeded, or
    2 small green chillies
salt to taste

2 tbs minced onion
1 tbs lemon juice
bunch finely chopped
    coriander leaves

Serve in a bowl with cold meat and salads.

Coriander Leaves in Soups

Finely chopped leaves may be added to any soup to taste as a garnish. If you do not know if every one enjoys the flavour a small bowl of leaves may be served separately for guests to add their own garnish to taste.

Meat Balls in Curry Sauce

½ green pepper
1 onion
1 garlic clove
500 g minced raw meat
2 tbs chopped coriander leaves
2 tsp garam masala
pinch nutmeg
1 beaten egg
¼ cup plain yoghurt

For sauce:
2 tbs butter
1 onion, sliced
2 skinned, chopped tomatoes
2 crushed cloves garlic
2 tsp curry powder
2 cm green ginger
¼ litre plain yoghurt
¼ litre hot water

Make meat balls by chopping green pepper and onion finely, crushing garlic and combining all ingredients, binding them with beaten egg and yoghurt. Form into balls about 3 cm in diameter and simmer in sauce for ½ hour.

For the sauce: Melt butter and fry onions until light gold. Add tomatoes, garlic and curry powder and continue to fry gently for 2-3 minutes. Stir in ginger and yoghurt and cook 15 minutes. If sauce is too thick add hot water, and season with salt and a little cayenne to taste.

Banana Rayta

1½ tbs butter
1 tsp black mustard seeds
50 g freshly grated coconut
1 cup plain yoghurt

1 tsp salt
1-2 bananas sliced in rounds
1 tsp finely chopped coriander
    leaves

Heat butter in a frying pan and add mustard seeds. When they begin to crackle and burst with the heat add coconut, stir well and remove from the heat. Cool, add yoghurt, salt and sliced bananas. Finally add finely chopped coriander leaves and mix well. Chill in a covered container in the refrigerator for an hour before serving with any curry.

Spicy Cauliflower

5 tbs oil
1 tsp mustard seed
2 cm root ginger, peeled
    and crushed

1 cauliflower, broken into
    florets, and chopped stems
salt to taste
juice ½ lemon

1 onion, peeled and sliced
1 tsp turmeric

1-2 tbs finely chopped
   coriander leaves

Heat oil, add mustard seed, cover and cook 2 minutes. Add ginger, onion and turmeric and fry a further 3 minutes, stirring. Add cauliflower, and salt to taste and mix well before sprinkling with lemon juice. Cover and cook very gently for about 20 minutes until cauliflower is tender. Arrange in a serving dish and sprinkle with coriander leaves.

Coriander Apple Cake

50 g butter
1 cup flour
1 tsp baking powder
2-4 tbs sugar

2-3 tsp ground coriander
1-2 peeled, thinly sliced apples
milk to mix

Rub chopped butter into flour until mixture is like breadcrumbs. Sift in baking powder, add sugar and coriander and mix well. Add sliced apples and enough milk to make a light, soft, scone-type dough. Pat out into a round and place on a greased tray or in a buttered shallow tin and bake at 180 °C for 30-45 minutes. Eat warm or cold.

Coriander Cake

125 g butter
125 g sugar
rind and juice of 1 lemon
   or orange
2 beaten eggs

250 g flour
1 tsp baking powder
1-2 tsp ground coriander
milk if necessary

Cream butter and sugar and add grated fruit rind and juice. Stir in beaten eggs, gradually add flour and baking powder, and blend well. If mixture seems too stiff add a little milk. Pour mixture into a buttered cake tin and sprinkle ground coriander on top. Bake at 180 °C for 30-45 minutes.

Variations:
1. Replace fruit juice with 2 tbs milk, and combine coriander with sifted flour.
2. Add 1 cup crystallized cherries with flour.

Apricot Nut Bread

1 cup chopped, dried apricots
¾ cup orange juice
1 tbs butter
1 cup sugar
1 beaten egg
¾ cup milk

1 tbs grated orange rind
3 cups flour
3 tsp baking powder
1 tsp salt
1 tsp ground coriander
¾ cup chopped nuts

Soak chopped apricots in orange juice until they soften. Cream butter and sugar and beat in egg until mixture is fluffy. Beat in milk, orange juice and apricots, and orange rind. Sift flour, baking powder, salt and coriander together and gradually stir into mixture with chopped nuts. Pour into a greased loaf pan and bake at 180 °C until done, about an hour.

Coriander Butter Biscuits

2 cups flour
2 tsp baking powder
2 tbs ground coriander
1 cup sugar

¾ cup butter
1 beaten egg
1 tsp vanilla essence
1 tbs milk

Sift flour, baking powder and coriander into a bowl and stir in sugar. Cut in butter with a pastry blender. Combine beaten egg, vanilla and milk and stir into the butter-flour mixture to make a dough. Knead well and form into small balls. Place 5cm apart on an ungreased baking tray and flatten with the bottom of a glass. Bake at 200 °C for 6-8 minutes, until pale brown. Cool on a rack, and store in an airtight container.

Gingerbread

250 g butter
2 cups molasses or golden syrup
2 cups raisins
2 cups chopped peel
1½ cups brown sugar
3 tsp baking soda

1 tbs ground coriander
1 tbs ground cloves
2 tsp caraway seeds
2 tsp ground ginger
2 beaten eggs
5 cups flour

Put butter and molasses in a saucepan and warm gently until butter

130

is melted. Combine remaining ingredients except eggs and flour in a large bowl and pour in butter molasses mixture and stir until blended. Beat in eggs and gradually add flour beating with a wooden spoon until the whole is thoroughly blended. Turn into a greased and lined 25cm square tin and bake in a slow oven, 150 °C, for about 2-3 hours. Cool on a rack and keep a week before using.

Coriander Honey Bread

1 cup hot coffee
1 tbs butter
1 cup honey
2 cups white flour
1 cup rye flour

3 tsp baking powder
1 tsp cinnamon
1 tsp ground coriander
pinch salt

Pour coffee over honey and butter and stir until dissolved. Add dry ingredients and mix well. Bake in a greased, lined tin for about an hour at 180 °C.

Coriander Cornbread

1 cup milk
½ cup oil
1 beaten egg
1 cup wholemeal flour
1 cup fine cornmeal

2 tsp baking powder
1 tbs sugar
½ tsp salt
1-2 tsp ground coriander

Beat milk, oil and egg together until well blended in a basin. Combine all other ingredients in a large bowl and stir the liquid into a well in the middle of the dry mixture, blending thoroughly with a wooden spoon. Pour into a greased, wide loaf tin and bake at 180 °C for 25-30 minutes. This bread may be served hot with meat dishes or cold with butter.

Coffee with Coriander

Place 1-3 whole coriander seeds, depending on the size of the cup, in the bottom of the coffee cup and crush them. Pour the hot coffee over and infuse a minute or two before drinking.

Coriander in Curry

Coriander seed is one of the most important spices used in curry. The seeds are lightly roasted whole, then ground and blended with the other ingredients, but coriander is used to control the basic flavour and a greater quantity of it is usually used than of any other spice. The 'hot' flavour of curry depends on the amount of chilli added, so that if a really hot curry is wanted chilli can be added in a larger quantity than the coriander. Curries in Asia vary and are usually especially blended for the dish they are to flavour. The following recipe is for a mild spicy curry.

Coriander Curry Powder

6 tbs coriander seeds
1½ tbs turmeric
1½ tbs cumin
1½ tbs fenugreek

½ tbs cardamon
½ tbs ground cloves
⅛ tsp cayenne pepper

Mix well and grind finely before use. Keep in an airtight jar.

The desired quantity of this blend should be fried in oil, butter or ghee with the onion and/or garlic to bring out its flavour before liquid is added to the curry.

Curry Paste

Some dishes are flavoured with curry paste rather than curry powder. Again there are many variations on the basic recipe but the following is fairly typical.

125 g coriander seeds
25 g mustard seed
25 g cumin seed
25 g peppercorns
15 g ground ginger
25 g ground turmeric

2 dried chillies
2 tbs salt
25 g crushed garlic
¼ cup butter or ghee
2 tbs vinegar

Grind all the seeds, add ground ginger, turmeric, chillies and salt and mix well. Sieve to remove chaff and mix with crushed garlic, butter and vinegar to make a paste. Store in a covered container and use to taste like a curry powder, in Vindaloo.

Garum Masala

Garum masala, literally 'hot mixture', is a combination of spices including coriander which in India is usually made at home or bought at the bazaar. It is used as a basic flavouring for many dishes.

3 tbs whole coriander seeds	*6 tbs whole cumin seeds*
3 tbs whole cloves	*¾ cup cardamon pods*
3 tbs black peppercorns	*4 8cm cinnamon sticks*

Roast whole mixture in a pan in a hot oven for 20 minutes, shaking frequently to keep it from browning. Cool and then discard cardamon pods. Crush cinnamon with a rolling pin and grind all the mixture in an electric blender or coffee mill.

Ratatouille

2 eggplants	*3 courgettes*
salt	*2 crushed cloves garlic*
2 finely sliced onions	*1 tsp crushed coriander seeds*
4 tbs oil	*fresly ground black pepper*
2 peppers	*4 skinned, chopped tomatoes*

Chop eggplants, without peeling them, into small pieces, place in a colander, sprinkle with salt and leave to drain about 20 minutes. Cook onions gently in hot oil until tender, then add sliced, deseeded peppers and drained eggplant. Cover and simmer about 20 minutes before adding the remaining ingredients and cooking a further 15 minutes. Remove from the heat, taste and add more salt and/or pepper as necessary, and serve at once. Ratatouille may also be cooled and then served chilled.

Baked Chops with Coriander

2 cloves crushed garlic	*flour*
2 tsp ground coriander	*beaten egg*
breadcrumbs	*rind and juice ½ lemon*
chops	

Crush garlic and mix with coriander and breadcrumbs until well blended. Dip chops in flour, then in beaten egg, and in breadcrumb mixture. Put in an oiled baking dish, sprinkle with lemon rind and juice and cook at 180 °C until crisp and tender.

133

Chicken Tandoori

4 skinned chicken pieces
1 tbs finely chopped root ginger
1½ tsp ground coriander
½ tsp ground cardamon
¼ tsp ground cloves
salt and pepper
25 g melted butter

2 peeled sliced onions
25 g butter
10-12 blanched almonds
¼ tsp turmeric
½ cup plain yoghurt
¼ cup raisins

Prick chicken portions with a fork. Combine root ginger, coriander, cardamon, cloves and salt and pepper in a bowl. Brush chicken with melted butter and rub with mixed spices. Set under a pre-heated grill and cook, basting with remaining butter and turning frequently. Melt 25 g butter in a pan and fry sliced onion gently until soft. Add almonds and turmeric and stir fry 3-4 minutes. Add yoghurt and raisins and heat through but do not boil. Pour into a serving dish and pile grilled chicken pieces on top.

Pork and Coriander

500 g pork pieces
1 tbs oil
½-¾ cup white wine
2 tsp ground cumin

1 crushed clove garlic
salt and pepper
3-6 slices lemon
1-2 tsp crushed coriander seeds

Fry pork pieces in hot oil until meat is sealed. Add ½ cup wine, cumin and garlic and season to taste with salt and pepper. Cover and simmer gently until the pork is tender. Add a little more wine, the lemon slices cut in quarters and crushed coriander seeds. Cook, uncovered for 5 minutes and serve with rice and a green salad.

Peach and Coriander Jam

1½ kg peeled, chopped peaches
¾ cup water
6 cups sugar

1 tbs butter
juice 1 lemon
1 tbs freshly ground coriander

Put peaches and water in a heavy saucepan and cook, stirring gently until peaches are soft. Stir in sugar until it dissolves, add butter and lemon juice and boil hard until it sets when tested on a saucer. Stir in coriander and boil 5 more minutes. Pour into hot jars and allow to cool completely before topping with melted paraffin wax and covering with a cellophane or plastic lid.

Orange and Coriander Marmalade

4 oranges   2 kg sugar
2 lemons   1 tbs coriander seeds
6 cups water

Slice fruit finely and soak in water for 12 hours. Pour into a preserving pan, bring to the boil and cook until fruit peel is tender. Stir in sugar and add crushed coriander seeds tied in a muslin bag. Boil until marmalade jells when tested on a saucer. Remove and discard the bag and pour marmalade into hot jars. Allow to become quite cold before topping with melted paraffin wax and covering with cellophane or plastic lids.

Pickled Quinces

firm quinces   wine vinegar
water   coriander seeds
sugar

Peel, quarter and core quinces, put in a saucepan, cover with water and bring to the boil. Cook 10 minutes, strain out fruit and measure the liquid. For every cup of liquid add 1¼ cups sugar, ¼ cup wine vinegar and 1 tsp coriander seeds. Bring this mixture to the boil in a large saucepan, add quinces and cook gently until tender. Remove fruit with a slotted spoon and pack into warm jars. Bring syrup back to the boil for 2-3 minutes and pour over fruit. Overflow and seal, or cover when cold and store in a cool, dry place.

Fresh Fruit Salad with Coriander

To any fruit salad made with fresh fruit add ½-1 tsp freshly ground coriander seeds and ¼-½ cup wine. Mix well and chill in refrigerator about an hour before serving.

Coriander Biscuit Pie

250 g plain wholemeal biscuits
250 g butter
3-4 tsp ground coriander
250 g cream cheese
½ cup castor sugar
½ cup orange juice

1 tsp grated orange rind
3 tsp gelatine
1 cup evaporated milk, chilled
1 tbs lemon juice
orange slices to decorate

Crush biscuits with a rolling pin between two sheets of paper. Melt butter, combine with biscuits and coriander and press into a 25cm pie dish. Chill in refrigerator while making filling. Beat together cream cheese and castor sugar until smooth and continue to beat while adding orange juice and rind. Soften gelatine in cold water and stand over boiling water until dissolved. Beat evaporated milk with lemon juice until stiff, fold into cream cheese mixture and lastly add gelatine and blend thoroughly. Pour into prepared crumb crust and chill till firm. Decorate with thin slices of sweet orange before serving.

Coriander Crumble

1 cup flour
50 g butter

50 g sugar
2 tsp ground coriander

Sift flour into a bowl and cut in butter, rubbing mixture between the fingertips until it is like breadcrumbs. Add sugar and coriander and mix well. Use as a topping on apple or any other fruit, baking at 180 °C for about an hour, until fruit is cooked and crumble topping is brown. Serve with custard, cream or ice cream.

Lemon and Coriander Jelly

2 lemons
½ litre cold water
3 tsp gelatine

6 tbs sugar
2 tsp coriander seeds
1-2 tbs sherry

Peel lemon rind thinly and place in a saucepan with most of the water. Soften gelatine in rest of cold water and gradually add to saucepan as it heats. Stir in sugar and crush and add coriander seeds. Stir until mixture comes to the boil. Cover and remove from the heat and leave to infuse 10-15 minutes. Add lemon juice and sherry and strain into a wet mould. Cool, then place in the refrigerator to set. Serve unmoulded with cream or custard.

Coriander Butterscotch

250 g butter
500 g brown sugar

juice ½ lemon
1 tbs freshly ground coriander

Melt butter in a heavy saucepan and stir in sugar and lemon juice, cook and stir until sugar dissolves, then boil fast until a little of mixture will crack if dropped into hot water. Stir in coriander and pour mixture onto a buttered dish or shallow pan. Cut into squares while hot and leave to cool. Break into squares and store in an airtight container.

Coriander Fondant

⅔ cup sweetened condensed
milk
1½-2 tsp ground coriander

1 tsp vanilla essence
4¾ cups icing sugar

Combine sweetened condensed milk, coriander and vanilla in a basin and stir until well mixed. Gradually add icing sugar, stirring until mixture is thick and smooth. Use to stuff stoned dates, to stick walnut halves together, or form small balls and roll in grated coconut, chocolate, nuts or seeds.

Costmary

Costmary is of especiall use in the Spring of the yeare, among other such like herbes, to make Sage Ale, and thereupon I thinke it tooke the name of Alecoast.

John Parkinson

Costmary, *Chrysanthemum balsamita,* is a perennial with soft, aromatic, pale green leaves. Originally from Western Asia and naturalised in Southern Europe, it was introduced into Britain about the sixteenth century when it became very popular for flavouring drinks, hence its name of alecost. Costmary is grown from division of the creeping roots in spring or autumn and forms large clumps when grown in fertile soil and full sun. However, it is shallow rooted and needs water in dry seasons. During spring and summer the leaves are ready to use and can be added to drinks, salads, soups, stews and stuffings to taste. The flavour is somewhat minty but slightly more bitter and spicy and it has been used as a substitute for mace and nutmeg. Costmary leaves are either cut from their stems and minced, or finely chopped, or they can be infused whole and removed before a dish is served. If you like the flavour it is a herb to experiment with, noting quantities, and a good guide to using it is to adapt recipes using mint.

Costmary and Apple Dip

1 litre thick stewed apple   *½ cup mint jelly*
½ cup sour cream   *2 tbs minced costmary*

Blend thoroughly and serve with plain sweet biscuits.

Costmary with Chicken

Stuff a chicken with 1 small, peeled onion and 6 leaves costmary. Steam in a little water until meat is tender. Remove from pan, skin and bone, and arrange meat on a dish. Make a sauce by stirring 1 cup chicken stock into 1 tbs cornflour mixed with a little cold water and bring it to the boil. Cook, stirring, for 3 minutes until sauce is smooth and thick. Pour over meat and decorate with chopped parsley. Serve hot or cold.

Stuffed Courgettes with Costmary

4 medium sized courgettes   *1 tbs chopped parsley*
250 g minced veal   *2-3 tbs parmesan cheese*
50 g minced bacon or pork   *2 beaten eggs*
1 tbs butter   *pinch salt, pepper, nutmeg*
1 chopped costmary leaf

Cut courgettes in half lengthways and scoop out most of the flesh. Cook this with meat and herbs in butter, browning gently. Remove from the heat and add cheese, eggs and seasonings. Use this mixture to stuff the halved courgettes, lay them in a greased ovenproof dish, pour over a little white wine and bake until tender in a moderate oven.

Costmary with Eggs

Heat a small costmary leaf in butter melting for an omelette or scrambled eggs and remove it just before pouring in the eggs. This will give a pleasant minty tang to the dish.

Costmary Lemonade

Chop 2 lemons roughly into a basin and add 1 cup sugar and 4-6 chopped costmary leaves. Pour on 2 litres boiling water, stir well and allow to cool. Strain and serve iced.

Negus

6-8 lumps sugar
1 lemon
1 litre boiling water

3-6 costmary leaves
½ litre port or sherry
wine glass brandy (optional)

Rub sugar lumps over the lemon to extract the oil. Slice lemon and put it with the sugar into a jug and pour on the boiling water. Stir and add costmary and warmed port or sherry. Stand covered until it has cooled slightly. Strain into warm glasses and sip. Mrs Beeton writes that this quantity, without the brandy, is sufficient for a party of 9 or 10 children. Negus was drunk on *Twelfth Night*.

Cress

A Common Garden Plant raised for Sallets.

Sir John Hill

Cress, *Lepidium sativum,* land cress, *Barbarea verna,* watercress, *Nasturtium officinale* and Rocket, *Eruca sativa* are all members of the Cruciferae and taste 'hot'. They are mainly used raw, in salads, sandwiches and butters, but watercress is also cooked in soups. Cress, or garden cress, is an annual grown from seed and usually cut when it is 5-7 cm high. It may be grown in the garden, or in boxes all year round, and is an excellent source of vitamin C. It is often grown with mustard.

Land cress is a biennial, also grown from seed, and it will thrive in most ordinary garden situations as long as it is well watered in dry weather. It grows as a rosette of dark green, lobed leaves which may be picked round the plant like picking parsley. Land cress may be used winter and summer but once the plant begins to flower the leaves decline. It self-sows readily.

Watercress which is the most succulent of the cresses, only grows really well in water. It grows wild in streams but should not be gathered from streams which run through sheep pastures because it is host to the liver fluke. It should only be gathered wild if you are sure the water is unpolluted. Watercress is a creeping perennial, usually eaten in spring because once it begins to flower it tastes very hot.

Rocket or garden rocket (not to be confused with sweet

rocket, *Hesperis matronalis,* a night-scented, ornamental plant), is an annual grown from seed. Plants should grow quickly for best flavour, so rocket should be sown in spring and summer only in cold districts, but all year round in mild places. The leaves are bronzy green and look rather like land cress but grow more upright. They should be used before the plant flowers. It will self-sow. It is also known as regula or roquette.

Cress Butter

Chop 2 tbs garden cress or watercress finely and beat into 50 g softened butter with a little lemon juice to taste. Use on crackers or to make sandwiches.

Cress and Cottage Cheese

Chop any type of cress finely and fold into cottage or cream cheese to taste. Spread on savory biscuits or use in sandwiches.

Mustard and Cress Sandwiches

Butter thinly sliced bread and cover with a layer of finely chopped mixed mustard and cress. Close sandwich with another slice of buttered bread. Cut in triangles and serve.

Mustard and Cress Salad

1 cup each cress and young
*   mustard*
1 small lettuce
1 eating apple
juice ½ lemon

½ tsp salt
1 tbs cider vinegar
3 tbs oil
1 tbs finely chopped chives

Wash and dry greens and tear into bite-sized pieces. Core and dice apple and toss in lemon juice. Combine salt, vinegar and oil with chives, and shake well in a screw-top jar. Pour over salad, toss and serve.

Cress, Carrot and Celery Salad

Combine washed, torn land or garden cress, grated carrot and finely chopped celery. Toss in French dressing and serve.

Cress, Parsnip and Orange Salad

Wash and dry land or garden cress. Grate scrubbed, raw parsnip into a bowl and add an equal quantity of torn cress and a little grated orange rind. Toss in French dressing.

Cress and Orange Salad

Wash and dry land or garden cress, or watercress and arrange around a flat dish. Pile thin slices of peeled, de-seeded orange in the centre and serve with poultry.

Rocket Salad

Combine equal quantities of washed torn lettuce, rocket leaves and purslane, if available, and toss with French dressing.

Chicken and Watercress

chicken pieces	*1 tbs flour*
1 tbs each oil and butter	*1 cup chicken stock*
½ sliced onion	*salt and pepper*
1 bunch watercress	*2 tbs fresh or sour cream*

Brown chicken pieces well in heated oil and butter and remove from pan. Add sliced onion, and almost all the watercress, chopped (keep a little aside to garnish the finished dish) to the pan and fry gently until soft. Add flour and stir until frothy, then gradually stir in the stock. Season to taste, return chicken to the pan, cover and simmer gently for ½ hour. Remove chicken to a hot serving dish and keep warm. Puree the sauce in a blender or through a sieve or mouli, return to the pan and bring to the boil again. Remove from the heat, stir in cream, pour sauce over the chicken and garnish with remaining watercress. Fried sippets are nice with this dish.

143

Watercress Mayonnaise

Combine in a blender:
1 cup mayonnaise
3-4 tbs finely chopped
  watercress leaves

1 tbs finely chopped chives
1 tsp lemon juice

Blend well, taste and season with salt and pepper if necessary. Serve with green and egg salads or cold fish.

Watercress Omelette

4 tbs butter
1 cup finely chopped
  watercress leaves
1 tbs finely chopped chives

salt, pepper and nutmeg to
  taste
6-8 beaten eggs
salt and pepper

Melt 2 tbs butter in a frying pan and gently cook watercress and chives, stirring until limp and heated through. Season with salt, pepper and freshly grated nutmeg. Remove from heat and keep warm. Heat remaining 2 tbs butter in an omelette pan, add beaten eggs and cook omelette as usual. Spread with the warm watercress mixture, fold and serve.

Watercress Dip

bunch watercress leaves,
  stripped from stems
3-6 chopped radishes, or
  2-4 spring onions, chopped

1 small peeled, diced cucumber
¼-½ cup sour cream
strained juice 1 lemon
salt and pepper to taste

Combine all ingredients in a blender and blend until smooth. Store in the refrigerator and use as a dip.

Watercress Salad Dressing

Combine equal quantities of oil and lemon juice seasoned to taste with salt and a little pepper. Add finely chopped watercress and shake in a screw-top jar until well blended. Keep in refrigerator and use with salads or cold fish.

French Toast Sandwiches with Watercress

Make sandwiches of thin bread and butter spread with cream cheese and watercress leaves seasoned to taste. Dip them in beaten egg and fry gently in hot butter, browning both sides.

Watercress Sauce

125 g watercress
50 g butter
pepper and a pinch cayenne
1 tbs flour
¼ litre stock

salt to taste
lemon juice
50 g chopped, blanched
cucumber

Cook watercress in boiling water until just tender, drain and sieve. Stir in 25 g butter and blend well with pepper and a little cayenne to season. Melt remaining butter, stir in flour and stock and bring to the boil, stirring. Simmer 5 minutes, remove from the heat and gradually add watercress. Season with lemon juice and finely chopped cucumber. If used as a fish sauce, use fish stock and 1 tsp anchovy sauce to flavour the sauce, but if to accompany meat or chicken, use a meat or chicken stock.

Watercress Soup

500 g potatoes
1 large bunch watercress
2 tbs butter
5-6 cups water

¼ cup cream or top milk
2 egg yolks or 1 egg
salt and pepper to taste

Peel and dice potatoes. Cut off and reserve about 20 perfect watercress leaves, wash and cut up the rest and saute in hot butter in a saucepan until soft. Add water and potatoes, simmer about 20 minutes until soft, and puree through a sieve or mouli. Return to the pan, bring back to the boil, add remaining leaves and simmer for 2-3 minutes. Mix cream and egg together in a cup, add a little soup and mix well. Remove pan, stir in egg and cream mixture and serve.
  Watercress soups may be cooled and served chilled. Land cress may be used instead of watercress in soups. Freshly grated nutmeg and/or sliced tomato may be added as a garnish.

Watercress and Barley Soup

25 g butter
1 peeled sliced onion
1 cup cooked barley
1 large bunch watercress

1 litre chicken stock
pepper and salt
1-2 cloves crushed garlic
soya sauce to taste

Melt butter in a saucepan and gently cook onion until soft and transparent. Add barley, increase heat and saute to brown slightly, then add chopped watercress and saute. Pour in stock, stirring, and bring to the boil. Add salt, pepper, garlic and soya sauce to taste.

Potatoes and Watercress

Beat together and serve hot:
500 g cooked, mashed,
   hot potatoes
1 small bunch washed,
   chopped watercress

½ tsp savory
salt and pepper to taste
1 tbs butter

Cooked Watercress

Watercress leaves may be stripped from the stems, washed, shaken dry and cooked in a little butter over a low heat in the same way as cabbage or silver beet. Serve hot with a little salt and mashed potatoes.

or

½ cup sesame seed
2 bunches watercress

1 tsp soya sauce

Brown sesame seed gently in a hot pan and pound into a paste. Drop washed watercress into a pot of boiling water and cook 5 minutes. Drain, squeeze moisture out and chop. Add soya sauce and sesame paste, mix and serve.

Dandelion

You see here what virtues this common herb hath, and that is the reason the French and Dutch so often eat them in the spring; and now, if you look a little farther, you may see plainly, without a pair of spectacles, that foreign physicians are not so selfish as ours are, but more communicative of the virtues of plants to people.   Nicholas Culpeper

Dandelion, *Taraxacum officinalis*, is a common European weed which has become naturalised throughout most of the world. All parts of the plant have been used as food and/or medicine from ancient times, and the leaves, picked young and eaten raw in salads or sandwiches, are considered a tonic and purifier. Leaves and flowers may be gathered wild around the garden but best and most tender leaves come from a few plants cultivated in better soil. They can be prevented from spreading by removing seed heads, and grow without any trouble for years. The roots, scrubbed and roasted make a good coffee substitute and can also be used in dandelion beer. Because of their milky juice, dandelion leaves will discolour at the edges if they are cut with a knife, so raw dandelion leaves for use in salads should always be torn into bite-sized pieces like lettuce, not chopped. Dandelions may be blanched by covering the plants in the garden with a flowerpot to keep out the light, and this makes their flavour less bitter, but as a general rule young leaves are not too bitter and can be eaten without blanching.

Dandelion Beer

500 g dandelion leaves and
  tap roots
2 lemons, grated rind and
  juice

8 litres water
1 kg raw sugar
50 g cream of tartar
yeast

Wash dandelion leaves and roots and put with grated lemon rind into the water in a preserving pan. Bring to the boil and cook steadily for 15 minutes. Strain liquid over sugar and cream of tartar and stir well. When cooled, add strained lemon juice and yeast. Pour into clean 2-litre jars and fill nearly to the top. Put a little cotton wool in the neck of each jar to keep fruit flies out but to allow air to escape and leave 3 days. Then siphon into clean bottles and cap. Ready to drink in 1-2 weeks.

Dandelion Coffee

In summer dig, wash and dry roots well. Chop them small and roast them gently in a slow oven until crisp but not too brown, turning the pieces from time to time. When cold grind and store in an airtight container. The coffee may be made by simmering the powder or by pouring on boiling water, according to taste.

Dandelion Shrub

2 litres dandelion flowers
4 litres boiling water

juice 3 lemons
2 kg sugar

Put flowers in a large bucket, pour boiling water over them, cover and leave overnight. Strain and add lemon juice and sugar and heat gently until sugar is dissolved. Strain again into bottles and cork tightly. Leave a week before drinking and serve in glasses with ice.

Dandelion Wine

2 litres dandelion flowers

1½ kg sugar

148

4 litres boiling water   yeast and nutrient
4 oranges

Place flowers in a large bucket, pour boiling water over them, cover and allow to steep 2 days. Pare orange skin thinly and add to mixture in a saucepan. Bring it to the boil and simmer 10 minutes. Strain onto sugar and stir until dissolved. Add strained fruit juice, yeast and nutrient and pour into containers fitted with airlocks. Leave until fermentation ceases, then siphon off into clean bottles and cork. Leave at least 6 months before drinking.

Dandelion Salads

Combine equal quantities of cooked, peeled, sliced beetroot and washed, torn dandelion leaves. Season with salt and pepper and add wine vinegar to taste.

or

Tear 10 young dandelion leaves and the leaves of ½ lettuce into bite-sized pieces. Place in a salad bowl with a dessertspoon each of finely chopped chives, mint and sweet marjoram. Combine in a jar and shake well 1 clove crushed garlic, 4 tbs oil, 1 tbs vinegar, salt and pepper to taste. Pour dressing over the salad and toss well.

or

250 g washed dandelion leaves   2 sliced tomatoes
3-4 spring onions   French dressing

Tear dandelion leaves into bite-sized pieces and finely slice spring onions and tomatoes. Arrange all in a bowl and before serving add French dressing and toss well.

Hot Dandelion and Bacon

4 slices bacon   1½ cups dandelion leaves
¼ cup wine vinegar   salt to taste

Cook chopped bacon till crisp and add vinegar. When hot add chopped dandelion leaves and salt to taste. Cover and cook slowly until leaves are tender. Serve with mashed potato.

Dandelion Sandwiches

Dandelion leaves, finely chopped may be added to any sandwich to taste — particularly with Marmite or cottage cheese.

To Cook Dandelion Leaves

Wash leaves and cook 5 minutes in boiling water. Drain and discard water and cook 10 minutes in a pot of fresh, boiling water. Drain, chop finely and add a little butter and cream, salt and pepper to taste or a pinch of nutmeg.

Dandelion Bud Omelette

12 dandelion flowerbuds	*4 lightly beaten eggs*
4 tbs butter	*salt and pepper*

Cook buds gently in 2 tbs butter for 2-3 minutes. Drain. Make an omelette by heating 2 tbs butter in a pan and when hot, add lightly beaten eggs. Lift sides of omelette with a spatula to let the unset egg run underneath. Turn omelette, fill with buds, fold it over and season with salt and pepper.

Dandelion and Cheese Bake

2 litres dandelion leaves	*1-2 tbs Marmite*
2 cups water	*1 tsp salt*
2 tbs butter	*½ cup grated cheese*
1½ tbs flour	*½-1 cup buttered breadcrumbs*
2 cups hot milk	*pepper*

Wash dandelion leaves and cook in 1 cup water for 5 minutes. Drain and replace water with a fresh cup boiling water and continue to cook until leaves are tender. Melt butter in another saucepan, stir in flour and gradually make a white sauce by stirring in hot milk. Blend in Marmite and boil sauce about 5 minutes. Place drained dandelion leaves in an ovenproof dish and sprinkle with salt. Pour sauce over them and top with a mixture of grated cheese and buttered breadcrumbs. Season with pepper to taste and bake in the oven at 180 °C for about 20 minutes.

Dandelion and Barley Pudding

1 cup dandelion leaves
1 cup nettle tops
1 cup water

1 cup cooked barley
salt and pepper
1-2 tbs butter

Wash dandelion and nettles and cook 5 minutes in half the water. Drain and cook again in fresh water until tender. Drain and chop. Mix with barley and pour into a buttered pie dish. Season with salt and pepper to taste and dot with butter. Heat through before serving.

Sauteed Dandelion

1 kg dandelion leaves
oil
bunch spring onion or shallots

2-3 cloves garlic
salt and pepper
mushrooms to taste (optional)

Wash dandelion leaves and cut them in half. Heat oil and saute chopped spring onions or shallots (and mushrooms). Add crushed garlic and damp dandelion leaves and continue to saute for about 10 minutes. Season with salt and pepper to taste and serve on hot buttered toast.

Dandelion Soup

1 cup cooked dandelion leaves,
  pureed
1 tbs butter
1 tbs flour

1 cup milk
salt and pepper
1 hard-boiled egg

Make a sauce by melting butter in a pan and stirring in flour. Gradually blend in milk, continuing to stir, and bring to the boil. Cook several minutes, add pureed dandelion leaves and salt and pepper to taste. Sieve a hard-boiled egg into the soup and serve.

Dandelion Timbales

Combine and mix well:
2 beaten eggs
1¼ cups milk
2 tbs melted butter

pinch salt and pepper
1 tsp grated onion
1 cup cooked, minced
   dandelion leaves

Butter small ramekins and pour enough mixture in to half fill them. Set in a pan of hot water and bake at 180°C for 25-30 minutes. Serve on slices of fried bread and garnish with tomato.

Dill

*An umbelliferous Plant kept in our Gardens,
principally for the Use of the Kitchen ... The Seeds
of Dill are said to be a Specific against the
Hiccough, but I have known them tried without
Success.*
Sir John Hill

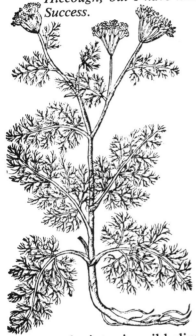

Dill, *Anethum graveolens*, is an annual grown from seed and will self-sow in favourable situations. It grows as a single stem and superficially resembles fennel but the two herbs taste quite different, and have quite different characteristics although they are both used with fish. Because it is tap-rooted, dill is best sown where it is to grow as it does not transplant easily. Both the bluish linear leaves and the flowering and seeding tops are used in cooking, and a succession of sowings will enable you to use it from early spring into autumn and winter in mild climates. However dill does need adequate moisture to produce good leaves and these may be picked until the flowers begin to form. The flowering sprays are used in dill pickles and the seeds may be used to flavour many foods too. Both seeds and leaves may be dried for winter use.

Dill is used with cucumbers, fish and potatoes and may be finely chopped as a garnish with many other dishes. The seeds may be used in breads, salads and pickles as well as to flavour fruit and vinegars. Dill makes food more digestible and has always been a remedy for babies suffering from wind. It is easy to grow and use.

Cottage Cheese with Dill

Combine 1 cup cottage or cream cheese with 2 tbs finely chopped dill leaves and mix well. Leave 30 minutes to allow flavours to blend. Salt may be added to taste.

Creamy Dill Dip

¼ cup sour cream or
*   250g carton plain yoghurt*
½ cup mayonnaise
1 tbs lemon juice

1 tbs milk
2 tbs finely chopped dill
salt, pepper and sugar to taste

Combine and whisk all ingredients together and keep in a covered container in the refrigerator. Use as a dip for biscuits, or as a sauce for fish, or with chunks of cucumber. Curry powder or chopped chervil, basil or tarragon may be used instead of dill.

Dill Cheese Dip or Spread

125 g cream cheese
2 tbs thin cream
2 tsp dill seed

2 tsp lemon juice
1 tbs grated onion
salt and pepper

Blend cream cheese and cream together, add the rest and mix well.

Dill and Cucumber Sandwiches

Lay thin slices of cucumber on buttered bread and sprinkle with pepper and finely chopped dill to taste. Cover with more buttered bread.

Dill and Fish Filling

Combine and heat in a small saucepan:
250 g cooked, flaked white fish   *squeeze lemon juice*
½ cup cream or sour cream   *1 tbs chopped dill*

Use hot to fill pancakes, or allow to cool and use to fill pastry cases for hot or cold savouries, or use as a sandwich filling.

Smoked Fish Pate

1-2 smoked fish, according to
  size
1 cup melted butter
½ cup cream cheese

salt and pepper
1 small clove crushed garlic
1 tbs finely chopped dill

Skin, bone and flake fish and beat in all remaining ingredients until well blended. Turn into a serving dish and chill at least 2 hours so pate sets and flavours blend. Garnish with sprigs of fresh dill and serve with biscuits. This recipe is suitable for 2 mackerel or 1 schnapper.

Onion and Dill Bread

1¼ cups milk
2 tbs sugar
2 tbs butter
1 tbs grated onion
2 tsp dill seed

1 tsp salt
3 cups flour
1 tbs dried yeast
1 beaten egg

Boil milk in a small saucepan. Remove from the stove and stir in sugar, butter, onion, dill seeds and salt. Leave to cool, place half the flour in a basin with yeast and beat in the cool milk mixture with a wooden spoon. Beat in egg and then gradually add remaining flour and beat really fast to blend evenly. Pour mixture into a greased loaf tin and allow to rise until double in size. Bake at 180 °C for about 30 minutes.

Potato Dill Sticks

100 g cooked, sieved potato
100 g butter
100 g flour

1 tsp salt and pepper to taste
milk
dill seeds

Combine potato, butter and flour, sprinkle with salt and pepper and work into a soft dough. Chill in a plastic bag in the refrigerator for 30 minutes. Roll out 1cm thick on a floured surface and brush with a little milk. Sprinkle with dill seeds and cut into strips about 2 x 100cm. Bake on a tray at 180 °C for 10-15 minutes.

Salmon Mousse with Dill

½ cup cold water
3 tsp gelatine
500 g tinned salmon
¼ cup mayonnaise
¼ cup sour cream

4 tsp fresh dill leaves
1 tbs lemon juice
sliced cucumber and olives to
    garnish

Pour water into the top of a double boiler and add gelatine. Allow to soften for 2 minutes then heat gently over hot water until gelatine dissolves. Set aside to cool. Empty salmon out of tins and remove bones and skin. Blend juice and salmon with mayonnaise and sour cream until smooth. Add finely chopped dill, lemon juice and gelatine and mix well. Pour into an oiled 2-cup mould and set in the refrigerator until firm. Unmould onto a cold serving plate, garnish with sliced cucumber and olives and serve with crackers.

Boiled Lamb with Dill Sauce

Simmer gently a loin lamb or hogget in about 5 cups of water with 1 bay leaf, 3-5 peppercorns, a sprig of dill and 1-2 tsp salt. Skim liquid when it first comes to the boil, then cover and cook until meat is tender. When nearly cooked make the sauce:

4 tbs butter
3 tbs flour
2½ cups stock from lamb
3 tbs chopped dill leaves

2 tbs vinegar
2 tsp sugar
1 beaten egg
salt and pepper to taste

Melt butter in a pan and stir in flour. Gradually add stock, stirring all the time, bring to the boil and simmer 3 minutes. Add 2 tbs dill leaves, vinegar and sugar. Remove from the heat, stir in beaten egg and season to taste. Drain the lamb, place on a hot serving dish, pour over sauce and garnish with remaining dill.

Fresh Cucumber and Dill Pickle

2 peeled, sliced cucumbers
2 peeled, sliced onions
⅔ cup tarragon vinegar
1 tsp salt
¼ tsp pepper

4 tbs sugar
1 tbs chopped dill leaves
2 tsp chopped parsley
1-2 grape leaves

Arrange cucumber and onions alternately in a bowl, add vinegar, seasonings and herbs, and mix through. Cover with grape leaves and put a plate on top to hold the cucumber in the liquid. Marinate 2-3 hours before using and keep leftover pickle in the refrigerator.

Dill and Garlic Pickle

Put small firm cucumbers in a basin, cover with cold water and leave overnight. Next day drain, dry and pack them into jars with 6 slivers garlic and 3 flowering heads of dill per jar. If cucumbers are large they may be cut lengthways but they should not be peeled. Make the pickling liquid by combining:

1 litre cider vinegar   *1 cup salt*
3 litres boiling water

Pour into a saucepan, stir until salt dissolves and boil 5 minutes. Pour this boiling liquid over the cucumbers in the jars, overflow and seal jars with Perfit seals. These dill pickles are ready to eat in 2-3 weeks. Once opened, the metal top should be replaced by a plastic lid that is not affected by the vinegar and salt.

Dill and Apple Sauce

500 g peeled, sliced apples   *1 tbs each sugar and butter*
2 tbs water   *1 tbs finely chopped dill*

Cook apples gently in the water until soft and dry. Add sugar, butter and dill leaves and mix well. Use as an omelette or pancake filling and serve as a dessert.

Dill and Cheese Tart

100 g melted butter   *⅓ cup finely chopped dill*
250 g biscuit crumbs   *1 tsp salt*
1 cup each cottage and   *1 tsp lemon rind*
   cream cheese   *freshly grated nutmeg*
2 beaten eggs

Combine melted butter and biscuit crumbs and when well mixed press into a shallow, buttered pie dish. Combine cottage and cream cheeses with beaten eggs, dill, salt and grated lemon rind. Pour into the biscuit shell, top with grated nutmeg and bake 30-40 minutes at 180 °C.

Swedish Apple Pudding

4 tbs butter
1½ cups fresh white
    breadcrumbs
750 g peeled, sliced cooking
    apples

¼-½ cup water
½ cup sugar
strip lemon peel
½ tsp dill seeds

Melt butter in a frying pan and brown breadcrumbs gently. Cook apples with water, sugar, lemon peel and dill seeds until soft in a covered saucepan. Remove lemon peel and beat apples until smooth. Place half the apple in the bottom of a buttered pie dish, top with half the breadcrumbs. Then add more apple and breadcrumbs. Bake about ½ hour at 180 °C. Serve cold with cream or custard.

Dill Sauce

Combine and use over cooked potatoes, carrots or beetroot:

4 tbs melted butter
1 tsp made mustard
a squeeze of lemon juice

1 tsp finely chopped fresh dill
leaves

Dill Sauce for Fish

Combine and blend until smooth and chill before serving:

½ cup mayonnaise
¼ cup sour cream
1 tbs lemon juice
1 tbs fresh milk

pinch each salt, pepper and
    sugar to taste
1-2 tbs finely chopped dill

Dill Seed Sauce for Fish

1½ cups bechamel sauce
1 tbs sherry

2 tsp dill seeds
salt and pepper

Heat sauce and stir in sherry and crushed dill seed. Cook, stirring a minute or two, taste and add salt and pepper if necessary. A sliced dill pickle may be added and the sauce cooked a little longer to heat it through.

Dill and Potato Soup

3 chopped bacon rashers
1 sliced onion
4 peeled, diced potatoes
1 cup water

2-3 cups milk
salt and pepper to taste
finely chopped dill leaves

Fry chopped bacon gently with onion until onion is soft. Add potatoes and water and cook until potatoes are tender. Mash, stir in milk, and continue cooking until soup is well blended and thick. Season to taste, sprinkle with dill and serve.

Pumpkin and Dill Soup

2½ cups cooked, mashed
  pumpkin
2½ cups chicken stock

2 tsp dill seeds
salt and pepper to taste

Combine all in a saucepan and bring to the boil, stirring. Add cream to each bowl when serving.

Cold Spinach and Dill Soup

250 g spinach leaves or
  turnip or beetroot tops
2 peeled, sliced cucumbers
2-3 cups stock

salt and pepper to taste
1 cup sour cream
finely chopped dill leaves

Cook chopped spinach leaves over a low heat in a pan with very little water until tender. Blend or sieve drained leaves and combine with thinly sliced cucumber and stock. Mix well, taste and season. Chill and serve in bowls topped with a whirl of sour cream and dill.

Tomato Soup with Dill

½ litre of fresh or canned
  tomato soup
1 small onion, grated

1 tbs fresh, chopped dill leaves
  or ¼ tsp dried dill
2-4 tbs cream if liked

Heat soup with onion and dill gently for 5 minutes to infuse the flavour. Stir in cream before serving.

Cold Cucumber and Dill Soup

4 small cucumbers
1 tsp salt
2 minced garlic cloves
1 tbs chopped dill leaves

juice ½ lemon
4 cups plain yoghurt
1 tbs chopped mint
1 tomato

Peel and slice cucumbers thinly and sprinkle with salt. Leave 30 minutes and drain. Combine with garlic, dill, lemon and yoghurt and whirl in a blender for 30 seconds. Chill and serve garnished with finely chopped mint and slices of tomato.

Green Beans with Dill

Cook sliced green beans as usual in a little boiling water. When tender, drain and add 1 tsp butter and 1 tsp finely chopped dill. Shake the saucepan with the lid on to blend thoroughly. Leave for flavour to infuse for 2 minutes, then taste and add salt and pepper as needed. Dill seeds may be added in place of dill leaves, but use less because flavour is stronger.

Hot Beetroot with Dill

1 onion, peeled and sliced
1 tbs butter
1 cup sour cream, seasoned
  with salt, pepper and sugar
  to taste

lemon juice if liked
500 g cooked, hot beetroot
1 handful chopped dill

Cook onion in butter until soft, add seasoned sour cream, lemon juice and most of finely chopped dill. Pour over hot beetroot, toss, and garnish with remaining dill.

Dill and Fennel Courgettes

Cook small courgettes whole in boiling water for 8-10 minutes and drain. Allow to cool, then cut into fingers and marinate in French dressing, flavoured with herbs, in the refrigerator for about 4 hours. Divide into 2 dishes and sprinkle one with fennel seeds and one with dill seeds. Garnish with sliced tomato sprinkled with a little sugar and finely chopped basil.

New Potatoes with Dill

Cook 500 g small new potatoes until tender in boiling water. Drain and add 25 g butter and 1-2 tsp finely chopped dill leaves. Shake well to mix the dill through, and serve.

Dill Potatoes

*1 kg potatoes, peeled and
   diced*
boiling water
2 tbs butter
2 sliced onions
1 crushed clove garlic

2 tbs flour
¼-½ cup cold water
3 tbs finely chopped dill
salt
4 tbs cream

Cook potatoes in boiling water until tender, and drain. Melt butter and saute onions and garlic until golden. Sprinkle in flour and stir in water to make a sauce. Add dill and simmer 5 minutes. Add potatoes and reheat, stirring in cream just before serving.

Cucumbers with Dill and Sour Cream

5 cucumbers
2 tsp salt
½ cup cider vinegar
2 tbs cold water

1 tsp sugar
3 tbs fresh dill leaves
pepper to taste
sour cream

Peel and slice cucumbers thinly and sprinkle with salt. Leave 30 minutes and drain. Combine vinegar, water, sugar and finely chopped dill leaves, add cucumber and mix well. Sprinkle with freshly ground black pepper and chill. Serve in individual dishes garnished with a dollop of sour cream.

Potato Salad with Dill

Boil potatoes as usual, drain and chop into bite-sized pieces. While still hot pour over French dressing and sprinkle with a little minced garlic and some dill seeds. Toss together and leave to cool.

161

Rice and Dill Salad

2 cups brown rice
water and salt
8 tbs safflower oil
2 tbs lemon juice

1 tbs grated onion
1 tbs dill seeds
½-1 cup chopped celery
sunflower or sesame seeds

Cook rice in boiling water with salt and when liquid is absorbed, rice should be tender. Combine all other ingredients and toss through the hot rice until well mixed. Chill and serve with lettuce and tomato.

Vegetable, Macaroni and Dill Salad

2 cups cooked, cold macaroni
1 cup cooked green peas
1 cup sliced celery
½ cup grated carrot
2 tbs chopped onion
1 tbs fresh, finely chopped dill
    leaves

½ cup mayonnaise
1 tbs vinegar
1 tsp sugar
pinch mustard powder
salt and pepper to taste

Combine macaroni and vegetables and mix well. Combine mayonnaise and all other ingredients and stir into macaroni mixture. Transfer to a serving dish and chill, before serving on a bed of lettuce garnished with tomato.

Dill and Tomato Omelette

6 eggs
2 spring onions
2 tbs finely chopped dill leaves
pepper to taste

2 tbs oil or butter
1 skinned, chopped tomato
½ cup alfalfa sprouts

Beat eggs, finely sliced spring onions, dill and pepper in a bowl with a wire whisk. Heat oil or butter in a frying pan with a lid and add egg mixture. Heat carefully until mixture begins to set, then add tomato. Cover with a lid until top of egg sets, then fold omelette over, slide onto a warmed plate and top with sprouts. Serve at once. Sprouts may be added with tomato.

Dill Water for Babies

Infuse ½ tsp dill seeds in a cup of boiling water. When lukewarm, strain and give 1 tsp after feeds to alleviate flatulence.

Elder

The vinegar in which the dried floures are steeped is wholsome for the stomacke: being used with meate it stirreth up an appetite.   John Gerard

The elder, *Sambucus nigra*, is a small deciduous tree native to Europe and the British Isles. It has become naturalised in other parts of the world, even in New Zealand where it is still appreciated for its lovely, useful flowers and berries. It is grown easily from cuttings and will flourish in any dampish, waste place, along hedges or the edges of woods. It is best pruned back in spring, which keeps the trees more compact. The elder has many uses in medicine, food and as a dye. It also has magical associations and traditionally before picking any part of it this charm should be said, 'Owd Girl, give me of thy wood, An' I will give thee some of mine When I grow into a tree.' Otherwise some misfortune may occur.

Both elder flowers and berries are used in cooking and a wide variety of dishes may be flavoured with them. If you have no source of wild plants it is well worth planting a hedge of elder to enjoy both flowers and fruit.

To Dry Elderberries

Collect berries when fully ripe on a dry day and strip them from their stems. Spread them on screens in the sun and bring them inside each night until no juice comes out of them when they are squeezed, or dry them in the oven at low heat. When dry like currants, store them in clean dry jars. Stew them gently with a little lemon juice and sugar before adding to cakes and pies.

To Dry Elderflowers

Pick whole heads of fully open elderflowers when they are dry of dew and spread them on fine mesh screens, snipping off their stalks. Dry in a hot cupboard and when they are brittle, cool completely and pack in screw-top glass jars.

Elderberry Chutney

*1½ litres elderberries, stripped
   from their stalks
¾ cup brown sugar
½ cup white sugar
1 tsp ground ginger*

*¼ tsp cayenne pepper
1 tsp mixed pickling spice tied
   in a bag
½ litre cider vinegar
1 cup chopped apple*

Put all ingredients except apple in a heavy pan, mix well, bring to the boil, stirring, and cook gently for an hour. Then stir in apple and cook till soft and thick. Remove spice bag. Pour chutney into jars and seal when cold. Serve with pork or poultry.

or

*½ kg peeled, sliced onions
½ litre malt vinegar
½ kg ripe elderberries
½ kg peeled, chopped apples*

*1 tsp each salt, ginger and
   pickling spice
100 g sultanas
450 g sugar*

Cook onion in a small quantity of vinegar until soft. Add rest of vinegar, fruit, and spices tied in a bag. Cook gently, stirring, until soft. Add sultanas and sugar, and boil till thick. Remove spice bag, bottle, and seal when cold.

Elderflower Champagne

4 litres water
2½ cups sugar
7 heads fresh elderflowers

2 lemons, chopped
2 tbs white vinegar

Boil water and pour over sugar in a large bowl or bucket. Stir well and allow to cool. Add elderflowers, sliced lemons and vinegar and stir again. Leave 24 hours, then strain, bottle and cap. Ready to drink in 1-2 weeks. Do not fill bottles too full for this can be very fizzy.

Elderflower Egg Nog

1 cup elderflowers
1 litre milk

2 eggs, separated
½ cup sugar

Simmer elderflowers in milk for 5-10 minutes. Beat egg yolks with sugar and strain hot milk onto them, stirring well. Allow to cool, fold in stiffly beaten egg whites and chill before serving. A pinch of cinnamon or nutmeg may be added before drinking.

Elderberry Juice

1 litre elderberries
2-4 tbs honey or 8 tbs sugar

juice 2 lemons
1-2 litres boiling water

Strip berries from their stems with a fork and measure into a basin. Add honey or sugar, lemon juice and boiling water to taste. Stir well and leave until cold. Strain into a jug pressing out the juice with a wooden spoon. Keep in the refrigerator and serve with ice.

Elderberry Rob

Rob comes from Arabic *rubb*, meaning the thickened juice of ripe fruits.

1 litre ripe elderberries
½ litre water
1 cup sugar

2½ cm stick cinnamon
12 cloves
1 tsp nutmeg

Crush berries against side of the pan with a wooden spoon, add water and simmer 10 minutes, stirring. Strain through a cloth or jelly bag and squeeze out all the juice. Measure and add enough water to make it up to 1 litre. Stir in sugar and spices and cook very gently for ½ hour. Strain into a jug and serve hot or cold.

or

2½ kg elderberries   500 g sugar

Strip elderberries from their stalks, put in a pan and press some juice out of them. Bring to the boil, stir in sugar and when it is dissolved, simmer gently until mixture resembles honey. Strain and bottle. Use by diluting 1-2 tbs rob in hot water and sip.

Elderberry Wine

1⅓ kg elderberries   4 litres boiling water
1½ kg sugar   wine yeast and nutrient

Strip berries from their stalks with a fork and weigh them into a plastic bucket, crushing them slightly. Pour on boiling water, stir well and leave to cool to lukewarm before adding wine yeast and nutrient. Stir daily for 3 days, keeping wine covered, then strain liquid onto sugar and stir to dissolve it. Ferment in dark glass containers to keep wine a good colour. If wine overflows in its first vigorous fermentation, top it up with some reserved liquid or a little water that has been boiled and allowed to cool. When fermentation ceases siphon into clean bottles and cork.

Elderflower Wine

2½ cups fresh elderflowers   juice 3 lemons
1½ kg sugar   4 litres boiling water
250 g raisins   wine yeast and nutrient

Trim flowers from their thicker stems and pack into cup measure lightly. Tip into a plastic bucket with sugar, raisins and lemon juice. Pour over boiling water and stir well. When mixture has cooled to lukewarm, add wine yeast and nutrient, cover and leave in a warm place for 5 days, stirring every day. Strain into a container with an airlock and leave to ferment. When fermentation ceases, siphon into clean bottles and cork.

Apple and Elderberry Jam

1½ kg elderberries
2 kg apples
½ cup water

¾ cup sugar to every 1 cup
fruit

Wash and remove stalks from elderberries and peel, core and slice apples. Put in a pan with water and boil gently until soft. Measure pulp and add sugar. Stir until dissolved and boil until the jam sets when tested on a saucer. Pour into hot jars and seal when cold.

Blackberry and Elderberry Jam

equal quantities of blackberries
and elderberries

375 g sugar to every 500 g fruit

Wash fruit and remove any stalks. Put in a preserving pan and mash slightly to cause juice to begin to flow. Bring to the boil slowly and boil gently about 20 minutes. Stir in sugar until dissolved and bring to the boil again. Boil until jam sets when tested on a saucer, 10-20 minutes.

Apple and Elderberry Jelly

2 kg elderberries
1 kg apples
½ litre water

1 cup sugar to each 1 cup of
strained juice
juice of a lemon

Cook chopped fruit in water until tender. Strain through a jelly bag overnight. Measure liquid back into pan. Reheat, stir in sugar and lemon juice and boil until it jells.

Gooseberry and Elderflower Jelly

large, green gooseberries
water

sugar
elderflowers

Top and tail gooseberries, place in a pan and cover with water. Simmer until fruit is tender and strain overnight through a jelly bag. Next day measure the juice, return to the pan and bring to the boil. Gradually stir in 500 g sugar to every ½ litre liquid and bring to the boil again. Add 3 heads of elderflowers, stripped from stalks and tied in a muslin bag, per ½ litre juice and infuse in the boiling syrup for about 5 minutes. Remove bag and test for setting after a further 5-10 minutes. When ready to jell, pour into hot jelly jars and seal when cold.

Rhubarb and Elderflower Jam

6 large heads elderflowers   6 cups sugar
1½ kg rhubarb   juice 1 lemon

Cut thick stems off elderflowers and tie them in a muslin bag and place in the bottom of a large glass, porcelain or enamel bowl. String rhubarb, cut in short pieces and add to the basin. Sprinkle with sugar, cover with a plate and press down with a weight. Leave 12 hours, stir well with a wooden spoon and leave a further 12 hours. Tip into a large pan and heat gently, stirring to dissolve sugar, but do not allow mixture to boil. Cool, return to the basin, cover again and leave 12 more hours. Remove bag of elderflowers and squeeze out all the juice. Put rhubarb and syrup into a preserving pan with strained lemon juice. Bring slowly to the boil, stirring, and boil rapidly for about 10 minutes, uncovered, when the jam should wrinkle if a little is tested on a cold saucer. Pour into warm jars and seal when cold.

Spiced Elderberry and Apple Tart

1 cup flour   400 g sliced apples
1½ tsp ground allspice   2-3 sprays ripe elderberries
100 g butter   rind and juice ½ lemon
1 tsp sugar   2 tbs each flour, sugar and
1 tsp baking powder   butter
1 beaten egg   1 tsp ground allspice

Make a short pastry by combining flour and allspice and rubbing in butter until mixture is crumb-like. Add sugar and baking powder and mix to a dough with beaten egg. Roll out on a floured surface and line a 25cm greased pie plate. Arrange sliced apples evenly in the pie dish, sprinkle elderberries, lemon rind and juice over them. Make a crumble by combining flour, sugar, butter and allspice and spread over top of fruit. Bake at 180 °C for about 30 minutes and serve hot or cold with cream.

Elderberry Sauce

1 litre elderberries
vinegar
6-8 shallots
3-6 cloves, pinch mace or
    nutmeg

½ tsp peppercorns
250 g sugar

Put elderberries in a casserole and cover with vinegar. Cover and cook in a cool oven, 100 °C, for about 3 hours. Strain liquid into a saucepan, add shallots and spices, stir in sugar and simmer gently over low heat until thick, about an hour. Strain and bottle.

or

½ litre elderberries
2 cooking apples
2 onions
½ litre malt vinegar
1 tsp salt

6 cloves
1 tsp cinnamon
1 tsp ground ginger
½ tsp ground mace
300 g brown sugar

Strip elderberries from their stems before measuring and place in a preserving pan with peeled, sliced apples and onions. Add vinegar, salt and spices, cover, bring to the boil and simmer an hour. Rub mixture through a sieve or mouli and return to the pan with sugar. Stir well, bring to the boil and cook uncovered until mixture is thick, about 20 minutes. Pour into warm, dry jars and seal when cold.

With apples:

2 peeled, cored, sliced apples
2 sprays elderberries

3 tbs water
1 tbs sugar

Cook apples and elderberries stripped from their stalks in water with sugar until soft and well blended. Serve hot or cold with pork, poultry or other meat.

Elderberry Pie

Combine elderberries, stripped from their stems and washed, with sugar to taste and a little lemon rind and juice. Line a pie plate with pastry, fill with elderberry mixture, cover with more pastry and bake at 220 °C for 10 minutes. Reduce heat to 180 °C and bake a further ½ hour. Serve with cream. A mixture of apple and elderberries may be used.

With blackberries:

2 cups elderberries	1 tbs flour
2 cups blackberries	1 tbs butter
1 cup sugar	enough short pastry to cover

Wash fruit and remove any stalks. Place in a deep pie dish and mix in sugar. Sprinkle with flour, dot with butter and cover with a thick, shortcrust pastry. Bake 180-200 °C for about 30 minutes. Serve hot or cold with cream or ice cream.

Apple pie may also be flavoured by adding elderberries to taste.

Prunes in Elderberry Wine

Soak 500 g prunes in 1 cup elderberry wine with a small piece of vanilla pod, for 12 hours. Transfer to a saucepan, bring to the boil and simmer 5-10 minutes. Remove from the heat, cool and chill. Serve with cream.

Elderflower and Gooseberry Ice Cream

1 ¼ cups water	500 g topped and tailed
2 cups sugar	gooseberries
juice ½ lemon	1 ¼ cups whipped cream
½ litre of elderflowers snipped off their stalks	

Place water and sugar in a saucepan and stir to dissolve sugar while bringing mixture to the boil. Boil 3 minutes, add gooseberries and strained lemon juice and boil 5 minutes. Remove from heat and add elderflowers tied in muslin. Stir well, cover and leave to get cold. Remove bag of elderflowers pressing all the liquid out, and sieve gooseberries or blend them with the liquid. Pour into trays and freeze until mushy. Remove from the freezer, beat until smooth, then fold in slightly whipped cream. Pour back into trays and refreeze until firm. Move from freezer to refrigerator 30 minutes before serving.

Elderflower Blancmange

1-2 sprays elderflowers or 2 tbs
    dried elderflowers
½ litre milk
1 tbs honey

1½ tbs cornflour
small pinch salt
2 tbs cream
freshly grated nutmeg

Put elderflowers in a saucepan with all but ½ cup milk, bring to the boil and allow to infuse, barely simmering for about 15 minutes. Strain, pressing all the milk out of the elderflowers and discard them. Stir honey into the hot milk. Combine cornflour and salt and stir in ½ cup cold milk to make a smooth paste. Gradually stir in hot milk and honey and return to the saucepan. Bring to the boil, stirring and cook 3 minutes. Remove from heat, stir in cream and pour into a wetted mould. Cool and chill. Before serving grate a little fresh nutmeg on top.

Elderflower Fritters

12 heads elderflowers
¼ cup plain flour
pinch salt
1 egg, separated

4 tbs milk
4 tbs water
oil for frying

Trim elderflowers leaving a short stalk to hold them by. Sift flour and salt together into a basin. Combine egg yolk, milk and water and whisk together with a fork. Stir it into the flour and beat until smooth with a wooden spoon. Whisk the egg white stiff and fold into the batter. Pour oil into a heavy pan about 1cm deep and when it is hot dip a spray of elderflowers into the batter and shake off excess before laying it flat side down into the hot oil. Trim off remaining stems while the fritter cooks and then turn it to brown the other side. Drain on brown paper, remove to a warm serving dish and sprinkle lightly with sugar. Serve with slices of lemon. 1 tsp chopped marigold petals and/or a pinch cinnamon or nutmeg may be added.

or

12 heads elderflowers
¼ cup sherry
2 tbs brandy
1 tsp cinnamon
6 tbs flour

pinch salt
2 eggs, separated
1¼ cups white wine
oil for frying

Snip each flowerhead into its four parts and lay in a flat dish in a mixture of sherry, brandy and cinnamon. Cover the dish with a cloth and leave the flowers to absorb the flavour for about an hour, stirring them from time to time.

Sift flour and salt into a basin. Make a well in the centre and beat in egg yolks with a wooden spoon, adding the wine little by little. Stand the batter until needed. Whisk the egg whites until stiff and fold them into the batter. Heat the oil in a heavy pan, dip drained flowerheads into batter, shake off excess and fry as above. When brown on both sides drain on brown paper and slide onto a warm dish. Serve with a sprinkle of sugar and orange or lemon slices.

Elderflower Water Ice

rind and juice 3 lemons or
  limes
1 cup sugar
3 cups water

heaped basin elderflowers
3 tsp gelatine softened in ¼
  cup cold water
2 stiffly beaten egg whites

Peel rind thinly into a saucepan with sugar and water and bring to the boil, stirring to dissolve sugar. Boil 5 minutes. Add elderflowers, softened gelatine and stir well to thoroughly dissolve gelatine. Cover and allow to cool off the stove. Before it begins to set, stir in juice, strain all into ice cream trays and freeze until mushy. Remove from freezer, break up water ice evenly and then fold in stiffly beaten egg whites and freeze. Half an hour before serving transfer from freezer to refrigerator.

Elderflower Semolina

1 large head elderflowers
½ litre milk
2 tbs semolina

2 tbs sugar
1 egg, separated

Strip flowers into milk in a saucepan, bring to boil and simmer 10 minutes. Sprinkle the semolina into the hot milk with the sugar and beaten egg yolk. Stir and cook gently 15-20 minutes until thick. Beat egg white stiff, fold into mixture, pour into a serving dish and eat hot or cold.

Fennel

Fennel is of great use to trim up and strowe upon fish, as also to boil or put among fish of divers sorts, cowcumbers pickled, or other fruits. The roots to be boiled in broths. The seed is much used to put in pippen pies and divers othersuch baked fruits, as also into bread to give it more relish.

John Parkinson

Fennel, *Foeniculum vulgare*, is a perennial, native to the Mediterranean, which has become naturalised in many countries. Fennel grows from seed and self-sows readily, being declared a noxious weed in some areas. However, in the garden it may be controlled by removing and using the seeds and it is a very decorative plant, growing up to 1½ metres high in flower. Both the feathery, bright green leaves and the brown, sweet-tasting seeds are edible, having a strong aniseed flavour. Florence fennel or finocchio, a variety cultivated as a vegetable for its white bulbous stalk base, may be used raw, or cooked in a variety of ways. Fennel may be collected from the wild but make sure the plants have not been sprayed and do not collect it from roadsides where it may be affected by petrol fumes. Its flavour may be more rank and less sweet when wild so it is generally better to transplant a seedling or two to better soil in the garden.

N.B. Do not confuse fennel with hemlock which often grows in similar situations. Hemlock has blotches on its stems, white flowers and leaves resembling chervil or plain parsley. Fennel has green stems, yellow flowers and feathery leaves and smells of aniseed. Hemlock is **poisonous** and no part of it should be eaten.

Florence fennel is grown from seed sown in autumn and will provide celery-like edible stalks without being prone to the diseases which often make celery difficult to grow. Although principally used with fish, fennel may be used with a variety of meats and vegetables, in soups, salads and sauces, biscuits and bread.

Fennel Omelette

Make an omelette in the usual way and either mix finely chopped fennel with the beaten egg or sprinkle it over the omelette before folding it. Use 3 tbs fennel to 4-6 eggs. Chopped chives may be added with the fennel.

Fennel with Scrambled Eggs

Mix 1 tbs finely chopped fennel leaves to every 2-3 eggs and scramble in the usual way.

Baked Chicken with Fennel

6 fresh or dried fennel stalks
2-3 bay leaves
150 g bacon or cooked ham
1½ kg roasting fowl
2 peeled cloves garlic
1 strip lemon rind
freshly ground black pepper
4 tbs butter

Place fennel stalks and bay leaves in the bottom of a casserole. Cut bacon or cooked ham into long strips and place in the cavity of the fowl with garlic and lemon rind. Sprinkle with pepper and dot with 2 tbs butter. Spread remaining butter over fowl and lay it on its side on top of the herbs. Cover and cook at 180 °C for 35-40 minutes. Remove from oven, turn and baste the fowl with butter before cooking a further ½ hour. Then remove lid, baste again and cook until brown.

Fish with Fennel

When grilling fish rub it with butter and sprinkle with pepper and salt. Lay the fish on a bed of fennel sprigs, cover with more fennel and cook 10-20 minutes until tender.

or

Place 2-3 leafy sprigs of fennel in the cavity of the cleaned fish. Place fish on a bed of fennel stalks, cover with melted butter and grill until tender, browning both sides.

To flambee, make a bed of dried fennel stalks in a baking dish and place cooked fish over it on the grilling grid. Warm a ladleful of brandy, light and pour it flaming into the dish. This sets the fennel alight and it burns giving off a strong scent which flavours the fish. Transfer fish to a hot serving dish and strain juices over it.

Baked Fish with Orange and Fennel

4 fish steaks
juice ½ lemon
½ tsp fennel seed
salt and pepper to taste

1 orange
1 onion
2 tbs butter

Butter a dish and arrange fish steaks in it. Sprinkle with lemon juice, fennel seed and salt and pepper to taste. Peel and slice orange and onion and divide rings among the fish. Dot with butter, cover and bake until fish is tender.

Fish Fillets, Shrimps and Fennel

250 g tin shrimps
25 g butter
4 large or 8 small fish fillets

salt and pepper to taste
2 tbs chopped fennel
2½ cups topmilk or cream

Put shrimps and butter in an ovenproof dish and heat gently until butter is melted. Remove shrimps and tilt dish until butter covers the sides and bottom of the dish. Sprinkle fish with salt and pepper, divide shrimps evenly among the fillets, sprinkle with 1 tbs finely chopped fennel and roll up the fillets. Place them in the dish, pour over the topmilk or cream, cover and cook at 180°C for 20-30 minutes. Serve garnished with remaining fennel.

Fish and Fennel Sauce

500 g filleted fish
1¼ cups milk
salt and pepper

2 tbs butter
1½ tbs flour
1 tbs finely chopped fennel

Place rinsed, drained fish in a saucepan with milk, and add salt and pepper to taste. Bring to the boil gently and simmer 10 minutes. Remove fish carefully, remove any skin or bones and arrange fish in a buttered ovenproof dish. Strain milk and reserve it. Melt butter in a small saucepan, gradually stir in flour, then strained milk. Continue stirring until sauce thickens smoothly and add fennel. Taste and add more salt and pepper if necessary. Pour sauce over fish and reheat gently in the oven or under a grill until evenly heated through.

Herring Salad

4 pickled herrings
1 eating apple
2 tsp lemon juice
1 small onion
1 cooked, peeled, sliced
  beetroot

250 g cooked, diced potatoes
½-¾ cup sour cream
1 tbs fennel leaves
salt and pepper to taste
sprigs of fennel to garnish

Cut each herring in half lengthways and cut each piece into four. Core and slice apple, put in a dish with herrings and toss lightly with lemon juice. Add peeled, sliced onion, beetroot, potatoes and sour cream, and mix altogether with finely chopped fennel leaves. Taste and add salt and pepper if necessary. Pour into a serving dish and garnish with sprigs of fennel.

Cottage Cheese, Cucumber and Fennel Spread

125 g cottage cheese
1 tbs cream or softened butter
2-3 tbs chopped, pickled
  cucumber

1-2 tsp finely chopped fennel
salt and pepper

Mash cottage cheese with cream or softened butter until smooth. Fold in other ingredients, mixing well and seasoning to taste. Serve on biscuits or bread.

Lamb and Rice with Fennel

1 cup rice	1 cup milk or cream or
2-3 tbs oil	yoghurt
750 g lamb, hogget or mutton	1 tbs chopped fennel
1 tsp cumin seeds	salt and pepper to taste
1 cup stock	

Wash and drain rice. Heat oil in a heavy saucepan and gently fry rice, stirring and turning. Add meat and cumin and saute until gently browned. Add stock, milk or cream or yoghurt. Cover, reduce heat and cook 10-15 minutes. Transfer to a casserole, add fennel, salt and pepper to taste, cover and cook in the oven at 180 °C for about 45 minutes, when liquid should be completely absorbed and the meat and rice tender. A pinch of nutmeg, cinnamon or cloves may be added to the casserole, and 1-2 tbs lemon juice.

Fennel Seeds with Liver or Kidneys

50 g butter	1-1½ cups stock
1 clove garlic	250g sliced mushrooms
1 finely chopped onion	1 tsp fennel seeds
250 g kidneys or liver	salt and pepper
1 tbs flour	

Heat butter in the pan and gently cook garlic and onion. Add sliced meat and cook, stirring and turning until done. Stir in flour and allow to brown before adding stock, mushrooms and fennel seeds. Cook until gravy thickens, season to taste and serve with hot buttered toast.

Boiled Sausage with Fennel

1 kg sausage meat	1 finely chopped onion
4 cups breadcrumbs	salt and pepper to taste
2 tbs fennel seeds	2 beaten eggs

Combine all ingredients and mix well — a little chopped parsley can also be added. Flour a clean cloth and form the mixture into a sausage shape on it. Wrap it up in the cloth and tie the ends and middle with white string. Lower sausage into a large saucepan of boiling water and boil gently for 2½ hours. Lift out, untie the cloth and roll the sausage in a small quantity of breadcrumbs. Leave to cool and serve cold with salad or on bread.

Fish and Fennel Filling

Heat gently together in a small pan:
250 g cooked, flaked fish, or   *2 tsp finely chopped fennel*
   smoked fish
½ cup cream with a squeeze
   of lemon juice

Mix well and season with salt and pepper to taste. Use hot on toast or to fill savoury pancakes, or cold as a spread.

Fish and Fennel Pate

400-500 g tinned fish, e.g. tuna   *lemon juice to taste*
1 finely chopped onion
¼-⅓ cup finely chopped
   fennel leaves

Mince or blend first three ingredients and stir in enough lemon juice to give the desired consistency. Press into a bowl and chill. Garnish with fennel and serve with crackers.

Fennel Biscuits

150 g butter   *2½ cups flour*
150 g sugar   *2 tsp baking powder*
1 beaten egg   *2 tsp fennel seeds*

Cream butter and sugar until smooth and stir in beaten egg. Sift flour and baking powder together and stir into mixture with fennel seeds. Knead well and press into a well-buttered, flat baking tin. Bake at 180 °C for about 30 minutes or until brown. Remove from oven and cool slightly before cutting into fingers. If mixture is too soft add a little more flour.

Fennel Seed Bread

1 tbs dried yeast
4-6 cups flour
1 tbs sugar
1-1½ cups warm water

½ tsp salt
1-1½ tbs fennel seeds
4 tbs oil or melted butter

Combine yeast and 1 cup flour and sugar and add warm water to make a batter. Leave 5 minutes to allow yeast to begin to work and then stir in more flour, salt and fennel seeds. Gradually add oil or butter and sufficient flour to knead dough comfortably on a floured surface. Put bread in an oiled basin, cover and leave to double in size. Knock back dough and form into rolls or a loaf or divide into three and make into long sausage-shaped rolls for plaiting. Place on a greased tray. Cover and allow to rise for 30-45 minutes and then bake at 220 °C for 10 minutes for rolls, lower the temperature to 200 °C and continue to bake loaf or plait for a further 20-25 minutes.

Fennel and Apple Pudding

6 apples
1 cup brown sugar
2 tbs flour

1 tsp finely chopped fennel
leaves or 1 tsp fennel seeds
2 tbs butter

Peel and slice apples finely and mix them with combined flour, sugar and fennel. Tip into an ovenproof dish and dot with butter. Cook in a moderate oven 30-40 minutes.

Apple Tart with Fennel Seeds

When making apple pies or tarts combine 2 tsp fennel seeds with ½ cup sugar to every 500 g apples and layer the fennel sugar with sliced apple in the dish. Bake in the usual way.

Beetroot Salad with Fennel

500 g cooked, peeled, diced
    beetroot
½ cup wine vinegar

1 tsp salt
2 tbs oil
50 g grated horseradish

½ cup water   2-3 tsp fennel
50 g sugar

Arrange beetroot in a serving dish. Combine vinegar, water, sugar, salt, oil and grated horseradish in a screw-top jar and shake to combine thoroughly and dissolve sugar. Pour this over beetroot and garnish with finely chopped fennel.

Parsnip Salad

Cut parsnips into bite-sized pieces and cook gently in very little water until tender. Season to taste with salt and pepper, dress with mayonnaise and finely chopped fennel.

Fennel Butter Sauce

Combine ½ cup of melted butter and 2 tbs chopped fennel leaves. Add a pinch of salt and keep warm for 5 minutes to extract flavour before serving as a sauce with fish.

Fennel Sauce for Grilled or Steamed Fish

1 cup white sauce   1 hard-boiled egg (optional)
2 tbs chopped fennel leaves   juice of a lemon

Combine white sauce and fennel and heat, stirring, for 2 minutes. Add chopped hard-boiled egg if desired, warm through and finally add lemon juice. Serve hot.

Uncooked Fennel Sauce

1 cup thick cream   3-4 tbs finely chopped fennel
2 tbs lemon juice   salt and pepper

Whip cream lightly and stir in strained lemon juice and fennel. Taste and season with salt and pepper. Serve with chilled salmon or other cold fish, or with hot pork chops.

Fennel and Gooseberry Sauce for Grilled Fish

250 g gooseberries
2 tbs water
1 tbs sugar
50 g butter
1 tbs flour

1 cup hot water
2-3 tsp finely chopped fennel
salt, pepper and nutmeg to
    taste

Top and tail gooseberries and put in a saucepan with 2 tbs water.
Simmer gently until gooseberries are soft and rub them through a
sieve. Stir sugar into this hot puree and set mixture aside. Melt 1 tbs
of butter, stir in flour, adding hot water until mixture thickens
smoothly. Remove from heat and stir in remaining butter, chopped
into small pieces. Stir in gooseberry puree and return to heat. Add
fennel and mix well. Taste and season with salt and pepper and a
little nutmeg. Keep warm and serve with grilled fish.

Chilled Borsch

500 g beetroot
5 cups beef or chicken stock
1 tsp sugar
juice ½ lemon
salt and pepper

½ tsp crushed fennel seed
2 sliced, hard-boiled eggs
½ cucumber sliced finely
2 spring onions, chopped
½-¾ cup sour cream

Peel and chop beetroot small and cook in stock until tender. Add
sugar, lemon juice, seasoning and crushed fennel seeds, stir well
and allow to cool. Chill soup and when quite cold, add chunky,
sliced hard-boiled egg, cucumber and spring onions. Mix well and
serve in individual small bowls topped with a little sour cream.

Polish Borsch

Slice finely and cook gently in butter until soft:
1 medium-sized onion
2 leeks
½ cabbage

2½ cups raw beetroot
a stalk celery
1 parsnip

When soft add:
500 g brisket of beef
a piece of lean bacon

a bouquet garni
a sprig marjoram and fennel

Bring to boil, skim and simmer gently until meat is nearly cooked. About 15 minutes before serving, add 8 small sausages and cook them in the soup. Lift all the meat out of the soup, cut it into bite-sized pieces and keep hot in a serving dish. Add 1 tbs each chopped fennel leaves and parsley and 1 cup sour cream to the soup, and serve in bowls with the meat garnish separate. The sour cream may be served separately too. If soup is not a good red colour, grate a raw beetroot, cook it gently in a cupful of stock, simmering for 2-3 minutes and strain liquid into soup.

Broad Beans with Fennel Sauce

500 g shelled broad beans	*1 cup broad beans stock or*
1 cup water	*milk*
2 tbs butter	*salt and pepper*
1½ tbs flour	*2-4 tbs finely chopped fennel*

Cook beans in boiling water until tender. Drain, keeping the liquid, and keep hot in a serving dish. Melt butter in a small saucepan, stir in flour and gradually add broad beans stock, making quantity up to 1 cup with milk. Cook and stir until sauce is smooth and thick, and season to taste with salt, pepper and finely chopped fennel. Pour over beans and serve.

Green Beans and Fennel

Cook green beans in usual way and when ready drain and add a little butter. Toss with finely chopped fennel leaves and add salt to taste. Serve hot or cold.

Cabbage and Fennel

1 cabbage	*1 tsp mixed mustard*
salt and water	*1 tbs chopped parsley*
6 tbs oil	*1 tsp fennel seeds*
3 tbs cider vinegar	*pepper to taste*

Slice washed cabbage finely, cook in a little boiling, salted water until just tender. Mix together all other ingredients in a screw-top jar and shake well. Drain cabbage, turn into a serving dish, add dressing, toss and serve.

Beetroot with Fennel Sauce

25 g butter
1 finely chopped onion
500 g cooked, diced beetroot

salt, pepper, sugar to taste
1 cup sour cream
2-4 tbs finely chopped fennel

Melt butter in a saucepan and gently cook onion until soft. Add beetroot and season to taste with salt, sugar and pepper. Stir in sour cream and heat gently until it boils. Mix in fennel and serve with hot bacon or veal.

Cooked Cucumber with Fennel

1 large green cucumber
salt
2 tbs melted butter
several spring onions

1 tbs chopped fennel leaves
freshly ground pepper
4 tbs cream

Peel and slice cucumber lengthways and place in a colander. Sprinkle with salt and leave to drain for 20-30 minutes. Melt butter in a pan and gently cook cucumber and sliced spring onions until tender. Add fennel and season with pepper to taste about 5 minutes before cooking is finished. Finally add cream and reheat but do not boil. Serve as a vegetable.

Fennel Potatoes

500 g peeled, sliced potatoes
water
2 tbs each oil and butter

1 tsp fennel seed
salt and pepper
parsley

Cook potatoes in a little boiling water until barely tender. Drain thoroughly. Heat oil in a frying pan, add butter and when this melts add potato slices, crushed fennel seeds and season to taste. Saute until slices are well browned and serve garnished with finely chopped parsley.

Fennel Seed and Potato Bake

Butter an ovenproof dish and fill with layers of peeled, sliced raw potato sprinkled with ½-1 tsp fennel seeds to each layer and salt and freshly ground pepper to taste. Add ½ cup creamy milk and dot top with butter. Bake in a moderate oven till potato is cooked.

Sweet Florence Fennel

Fennel with Bacon and Vegetables

Trim and wash fennel bulbs and cook 5 minutes in boiling water.
Cool under running water and drain and dry in a cloth. Quarter
them and arrange in a casserole with pieces of bacon, onion and
carrots. Moisten with a little meat stock and cook, covered, in a
slow oven until tender.

Creamed Fennel

1 litre water	fennel bulbs
1 tbs lemon juice	butter
1 tbs butter	cream
1 tsp salt	finely chopped fennel leaves
6 peppercorns	pinch nutmeg and paprika

Combine water, lemon juice, butter, salt and peppercorns and
bring to boil in a large saucepan. Add washed, trimmed fennel
bulbs cut into thick slices. Cover and simmer slowly until tender.
Drain and serve with a little hot melted butter and cream, garnished
with finely chopped fennel leaves and a pinch of nutmeg and
paprika.

Fennel a la Nicoise

2-3 fennel bulbs	4-5 tomatoes
boiling water	½ cup white wine
2 onions	sprig fresh thyme
2 cloves garlic	salt and pepper to taste
4 tbs oil	

Cook fennel in boiling water for 10 minutes, drain and cut in
quarters. Saute peeled, sliced onions and garlic in oil until soft.
Add fennel, tomatoes, wine, thyme and seasonings and simmer
covered until cooked.

Pickled Fennel a la Grecque

Trim, wash and quarter 4-5 fennel bulbs and cook them for 10 minutes in a court bouillon of:

1 litre water
100 ml olive oil
1 tsp coriander seeds
1 tsp salt
½ tsp peppercorns

bouquet garni of bay leaf,
1 sprig each thyme, fennel
and celery
juice 2 lemons, strained

Cool in the liquid in a covered crock and serve as hors d'oeuvre.

Fennel and Lemon Salad

1 bulb Florence fennel
1 thin-skinned lemon
2 tsp parsley
1 tbs lemon juice

2 tbs oil
2 tbs cream
2 tsp sugar
salt and pepper to taste

Quarter fennel and blanch in boiling water for a minute. Drain, dip into cold water to cool, drain and dry it. Slice fennel finely. Pare ½ lemon rind thinly and blanch in boiling water. Drain and cut it finely onto a plate. Peel the lemon, removing all the pith, and chop it into small pieces removing any pips. Combine fennel, diced lemon, and finely chopped parsley and lemon rind. Combine salad dressing ingredients in a screw-top jar and shake to blend well. Pour over the salad and toss.

Cream of Finocchio Soup

1 bulb finocchio or 4-6 stalks
fennel
1 small, chopped onion
25 g butter
2 cups chicken stock

1 tbs butter
1 tbs flour
1 tsp salt
2 cups milk

Slice finocchio finely, combine with onion and cook in hot butter in a saucepan, covered, until soft. Add chicken stock and cook 5-10 minutes more. Blend soup or put through a mouli, and set to one side. Melt 1 tbs butter in a small pan, stir in flour and salt, and gradually add milk, stirring to form a smooth sauce. Combine with blended finocchio soup and reheat, but do not boil. Serve garnished with finely chopped fennel leaves.

Baked Fennel

2 Florence fennel bulbs *2 tbs milk*
1 tbs butter, melted *2 tbs grated cheese*

Cook fennel in boiling water for 20 minutes. Drain, cut into quarters and arrange in a baking dish on top of melted butter. Add milk, sprinkle with cheese and dot with more butter if liked. Bake 10-20 minutes at 200 °C.

Florence Fennel in White Sauce

Simmer trimmed, quartered fennel in boiling water until tender. Drain and arrange in an ovenproof dish and cover with white sauce seasoned with a little nutmeg, and a cup of cooked ham (optional). Heat in oven until brown.

This recipe can be varied by adding cheese to white sauce, and either dish can be topped with breadcrumbs.

Garlic

The offensiveness of the breath of him that hath eaten garlic will lead you by the nose to the knowledge thereof ... Therefore let it be taken inwardly with great moderation.

Nicholas Culpeper

Garlic, *Allium sativum*, has been used for so long for food and medicine that no one knows its country of origin. Several varieties are available, differing in size and the colour of the skins, some being white and others pink or purplish. There is also a giant or elephant garlic which is more closely related to the leek, with very large cloves but a milder flavour. Garlic is grown from the cloves, each bulb being made up of 8-16 small pieces each in its own skin, held together by the papery outside skin of the bulb. They are called clove from 'cleave', meaning to divide or break apart. Only perfect garlic should be used. It should be firm, not soft or shrunken from the skin, and it should not have any discolourations, for imperfect garlic tastes rank and even a small piece of it can ruin a dish. To prepare garlic, hold it on a board with the concave side down and press it firmly with the handle of the knife. The skin will separate from the flesh and can then be slipped off before the garlic is chopped or crushed. A garlic press is useful for extracting the juice, and gives a very finely broken clove, while crushing garlic with salt helps prevent the aftertaste of garlic. Garlic vinegar is also a way of using the

188

flavour without lasting effect. If flavour is wanted without texture, garlic cloves speared on toothpicks may be included during cooking, then easily removed before serving.

To store garlic, plait the dry stalks together and hang in a warm, airy place. If the bulbs have no tops keep them in a net or string bag where they are airy and dry. Damp causes garlic to soften and taste bad.

Garlic and Asparagus Spread

Mash together cooked asparagus with crushed garlic to taste and use as a spread on sandwiches or toast.

Garlic Bread

1 French loaf
50-75 g butter

1-2 crushed cloves garlic
parsley or thyme (optional)

Slice bread diagonally without cutting right through. Cream butter with crushed garlic until well blended. Spread on slices, wrap loaf in foil and heat at 180 °C for 10-15 minutes and serve hot. Finely chopped parsley or thyme may be added to garlic butter, and/or a little lemon juice.

Garlic and Parsley Butter

Combine with a fork and blend thoroughly:
100 g butter
8 crushed cloves garlic
½ tsp salt

1 tsp prepared mustard
2 tbs finely chopped parsley

Garlic butter is delicious spread on outside of toasted sandwiches.

Garlic for Breakfast

Rub a piece of fresh or fried bread all over with a piece of peeled garlic, sprinkle with salt and a few drops of olive oil.

Garlic Fingers

Cut rolls in half lengthways and spread with garlic butter. Sprinkle with poppy seeds and grill until browned. Serve hot.

Honeyed Garlic

Peel cloves of garlic and cook gently in salted water until tender. Drain and dry them and place in a saucepan with 3 tbs melted butter and ¼ cup honey. Cook gently, turning often until garlic cloves are glazed. Serve on toothpicks.

Hummus

2 cups cooked, drained chick
   peas
⅔ cup tahina
¾ cup lemon juice

2-6 minced cloves garlic
1 tsp salt
1 tsp ground cumin
parsley to garnish

Whirl all ingredients, except parsley, in a blender until smooth. Serve as a salad or dip, garnished with finely chopped parsley. If too thick as a dip it may be thinned with more lemon juice.

Toulouse Garlic Dip

Pound together in a mortar:
2-3 cloves peeled garlic   75 g skinned walnuts

Add a pinch of salt and, drop by drop, 3-5 tbs olive oil, mixing to make a thick sauce. Serve as a dip with celery or fresh bread, or as a sauce with cold meats.

Turkish Eggplant Pate

2 eggplants
4 tbs olive oil
juice of a lemon

1 crushed clove garlic
salt and pepper
finely sliced onion rings

Score eggplant skins with a knife to stop them bursting and bake whole in a moderate oven, 180 °C, until soft, about an hour. Cut them in half when they are cool and scoop out pulp. Mash this in a bowl until it is smooth, gradually beat in oil, then add lemon juice, garlic and pepper and salt to taste. Tip into a serving dish, garnish with onion rings and serve with biscuits.

Piperade

¼ cup olive oil
2 cups peeled, sliced onions
3 cups green peppers,
   de-seeded and sliced in rings
3 cloves garlic
2 cups tomato slices, drained

1 slice white bread, cubed
¼ cup milk
6 beaten eggs
¼ cup finely chopped parsley
2 tsp salt
½ tsp pepper

Heat olive oil and gently cook onions, peppers and garlic for 5 minutes. Add drained tomatoes and stir fry 10 minutes. Soak bread cubes in milk and add beaten eggs to this with seasonings and half the parsley. Mix well and stir into the mixture in the pan. Cook gently, all together, over a low heat, until egg is set, stirring occasionally. Sprinkle with parsley and serve.

Garlic and Potato Eggs

500 g potatoes, grated
1 tbs each oil and butter
6 slivered cloves garlic
1-2 tbs finely chopped parsley

salt and pepper
knob butter
3 beaten eggs

Put grated potatoes into a heavy pan with hot oil and butter and fry till cooked and brown on both sides. Add garlic and continue cooking, then add parsley, salt and pepper to taste. Mix well, and move potato mixture into centre of pan. Add a knob of butter and when hot pour in beaten eggs. Cook gently until set, spreading potato mixture evenly over them. Turn with a fish slice and allow other side to brown. Serve with a green salad. If hard to turn, place under a hot grill to brown top.

To Flavour Grilled Meat with Garlic

1. Rub a little crushed garlic over the meat before grilling.
2. Marinate the meat in a mixture of oil, lemon juice or wine, and crushed garlic for 1-2 hours before cooking.
3. Spread the meat or fish with butter and a few thin slivers of peeled garlic. Grill and discard the garlic before serving.

For Roasts:

1. Crush garlic and rub it on the outside of the joint.
2. Make small slits in the meat and insert slivers of garlic.
3. Rub the outside with a cut, not crushed, clove of garlic.
4. Use 2-3 peeled cloves of garlic instead of stuffing.

Leftover Meat Fritters

Mince any leftover cooked meat and mix with 1 crushed clove garlic, chopped parsley, and salt and pepper to taste. A few breadcrumbs or a little mashed potato may be mixed in. Bind with 1 beaten egg and shape into fritters. Roll in flour and fry in hot oil and/or butter. Drain on brown paper.

Garlic Stuffed Steak

750 g steak
1 cup soft breadcrumbs
2 chopped bacon slices
2 cloves garlic, slivered
2 tsp each chopped onion,
celery and parsley

1 tbs melted butter
seasoned flour
oil
1 cup wine or stock

Cut steak into several pieces. Combine all other ingredients except flour, oil and wine or stock and mix well. Spread this stuffing on the steak and roll each piece up, fastening it with a toothpick. Roll the pieces in seasoned flour. Fry in hot oil to brown on all sides and then place in a casserole with wine or stock. Cover and cook at 180°C for 1½-2 hours, until steak is really tender.

Garlic and Apple Chutney

12 large, green apples	1 tbs salt
8 large onions	1 tsp cayenne pepper
25 g garlic	1 tbs whole cloves
4 cups brown sugar	malt vinegar to cover

Peel and core apples and chop them with peeled onions and garlic. Put them into a preserving pan with all other ingredients — cloves tied in muslin — and cover with malt vinegar. Stir well, bring to boil and simmer slowly for about 2 hours, until chutney is thick. Remove cloves, bottle and seal when cold.

Garlic Pickle

Peel garlic cloves and sprinkle with salt. Stand 2 days and drain. Place in jars and cover with liquid made in the proportions of:

1 litre white vinegar	25 g chillis
50 g mustard seed	25 g ground turmeric
25 g bruised root ginger	75 g sea salt

Bring this to the boil, simmer 10 minutes, strain over garlic and seal. Stand 3 days before using.

Apple and Garlic Sauce

1½ kg apples	4 tbs peppercorns
½ kg garlic	4 tbs chillis
4 tbs whole ginger	4 litres vinegar
4 tsp cloves	1 kg treacle

Chop unpeeled apples and garlic. Bruise ginger and tie it with spices in a muslin bag. Put all ingredients in a pan except treacle, bring to the boil and simmer about 2 hours. Remove spice bag, sieve pulp and return to the pan with treacle. Boil 5 minutes and bottle, overflow and seal.

Garlic Rice

After cooking brown rice stir about 1 finely chopped tsp garlic into it for every 1 cup raw rice. Add finely chopped parsley or marjoram, toss well and serve.

Sausage Casserole with Garlic

500 g sausages
seasoned flour
25 g butter
2 peeled, sliced apples
4 peeled, sliced shallots or
  1 onion

2-3 cloves garlic
1 tbs finely chopped sage
salt and pepper
1 cup cider or stock
parsley to garnish

Roll sausages in seasoned flour and fry until brown in hot butter. Transfer to a casserole and layer with apple, onion and slivered garlic sprinkled with a little sage and seasoned with salt and pepper. Add cider or stock, cover and cook at 180 °C about 45 minutes. Garnish with finely chopped parsley.

Garlic Sauces

Stir 1 tbs garlic vinegar into a cup of melted butter.

or

Blanch 2 cloves peeled garlic in 2 waters and then pound them in a mortar with a tsp of butter or oil. Rub this mixture through a sieve and simmer it in butter.

Serve sauce in a separate dish on the table.

Steak sauce

Chop finely a few slices of onion and 2 cloves of peeled garlic. Place in a mortar and pound with a little olive oil until smooth. Add a pinch of mustard, pepper and salt and a little finely crumbled dried basil and rosemary. Put in a bottle and thin to a ketchup mixture by adding a little dry red wine.

Creamed sauce

12 cloves garlic
1 litre milk
4 egg yolks

½ cup cream
salt and pepper to taste

Chop garlic and combine with milk in a saucepan. Bring to the boil slowly. Beat egg yolks, warm cream and add to egg yolks and stir this mixture slowly into the milk, stirring to avoid lumps. Stir well, taste and season as necessary, then rub through a sieve, reheat and serve without boiling. This may also be used as a spread, chilled, on toast.

Pesto with Butter

2 cloves garlic
6 sprigs basil and parsley

50 g butter
2 tbs parmesan cheese

Pound peeled garlic in a mortar and add minced herbs and continue to pound until blended. Add softened butter and cheese and beat until well combined. Use as a spread on cooked meat or fish, and grill briefly before serving.

Skordalia

2 cooked potatoes
salt and pepper
3 cloves garlic

1 ¼ cups olive oil
4 tbs wine vinegar

Mash peeled potatoes very finely, and pound peeled garlic in a mortar before combining the two. Gradually add oil and vinegar alternately and season to taste. The sauce should be thick and smooth and is served with fish or cold vegetable salads.

Garlic Soup

4 large cloves garlic
2 tbs butter
6 cups chicken stock

toast, grated cheese and
parsley to garnish

Peel and slice garlic finely and cook gently in melted butter in a saucepan until soft but not brown. Add stock and simmer, covered, for 20 minutes. Strain into bowls and serve with a small slice of toast sprinkled with grated cheese and chopped parsley floating on top.

or

50 g butter or lard
24 cloves garlic
1 ½-2 litres stock

salt, pepper and nutmeg
3 egg yolks
3 tbs olive oil

Heat butter and cook crushed garlic gently in it without browning. Add stock and seasonings and cook ¼ hour, sieve and reheat the soup. Beat egg yolks with oil, stir in a little soup, mix well and return mixture to the soup pot. Heat gently but do not boil. Serve poured over toast in individual bowls.

L'Aigo Boulido

1 litre water
salt and pepper
8 cloves crushed garlic
2 cloves garlic

4 slices bread
1 bay leaf
sprig each sage, thyme and bay
1 beaten egg

Bring water to boil, add salt and pepper and crushed garlic and simmer 5 minutes. Rub 2 cloves of garlic over the bread and place a slice in each bowl. Add sage, thyme and bay to soup, remove from heat and stand, covered, for 5 minutes. Strain. Pour beaten egg into the hot soup holding egg high so that it runs in a thin stream into the soup and curdles. Serve poured over the bread in the bowls.

Garlic Butter for Vegetables

6 cloves garlic
25 g butter

1 tbs parsley

Boil peeled garlic in a small pan of salted water for ¼ hour. Strain, discard liquid and pound garlic with butter. Add finely chopped parsley, and serve stirred into hot beans, lentils or mushrooms, or add to soup to taste.

Lettuce Salad with Garlic

Rub a small chunk of bread with peeled garlic and place in bottom of a salad bowl. Add torn lettuce, and oil and vinegar dressing, and toss salad before serving.

Courgette Salad

750 g courgettes
½ cup olive oil
¼ cup lemon juice

3 crushed cloves garlic
½ tsp salt
1 tbs minced oregano

Wash courgettes and slice thinly. Arrange in a shallow dish and pour over a dressing of remaining ingredients. Toss well and chill, covered, about 2 hours for flavours to infuse. Season with pepper, and garnish with olives.

Globe Artichokes and Garlic

Cook artichokes in water flavoured with 1 tbs olive oil, 1 crushed clove garlic and juice of a lemon, for 30-45 minutes. Drain and serve hot with butter.

Green Beans and Garlic

After cooking fresh green beans in a little boiling water until tender, drain them and add ½-1 clove crushed garlic and 1 tbs butter or oil and salt to taste. Cover and shake the saucepan to mix the flavours.

Garlic and Nasturtium Dressing

¼ cup wine vinegar
1 tbs lemon juice
½ tsp mustard powder
salt and pepper
1 clove garlic, crushed

1 tbs grated onion
1 tsp chopped, pickled
    nasturtium seeds
¾ cup olive oil

Combine vinegar and lemon juice, add other ingredients except oil and mix well. Then blend in oil a few drops at a time to make a creamy dressing. Store in a screw-top jar and shake to blend thoroughly before using.

Garlic Potatoes in Foil

8 medium-sized potatoes
75 g melted butter
2-3 cloves garlic, crushed

salt and pepper
finely chopped parsley

Peel potatoes and cut each into thick slices not quite through to the base and stand on pieces of foil. Combine melted butter, crushed garlic, salt and pepper and pour a little over each potato, allowing to run between slices. Seal foil around potatoes and bake at 210 °C for 40 minutes or until done. Unwrap and serve garnished with finely chopped parsley.

197

Garlic and Potato Puree

10 cloves garlic
½ cup ground almonds
½ cup water
3 medium-sized, cooked
   potatoes

juice of 1½ lemons
½ cup olive oil
1 egg yolk
salt and black pepper

Press garlic into a large bowl and pound to a creamy consistency. Add ground almonds and water, a little at a time, and mix till smooth. Add mashed potato and blend well, then gradually blend in lemon juice, oil and beaten egg yolk. Beat until whole mixture is smooth. Season to taste with salt and freshly ground black pepper. Serve with fish, eggplant or salads. This may be kept in a sealed container in the refrigerator for up to a month.

Stewed Vegetables with Garlic

3 tbs oil
2 peeled, sliced onions
3 peeled, sliced cloves garlic
4-6 skinned, sliced tomatoes

1-2 green or red capsicums
2 sliced courgettes
eggplant (if available)
salt, pepper and parsley

Heat oil and gently fry onion and garlic until soft. Add tomatoes, stir well, then add remaining vegetables cut in slices. Cover and cook gently until tender. Taste and season, and garnish with chopped parsley.

Spicy Tomatoes

1 tbs oil
½ tsp black mustard seeds or
   cumin seeds
4 cloves garlic
2½ cm root ginger, grated

2 chillis, ground
1 onion, chopped
1 tbs vinegar (optional)
1 kg tomatoes, sliced

Heat oil in a pan and add seeds. When they begin to pop, add garlic, ginger, chillis and onion and cook gently until onion is tender. Add tomatoes and simmer until thick, about 20 minutes. Vinegar may be added to give a sharper flavour.

Silverbeet and Garlic

silverbeet
salt and pepper
1 tbs butter

1 crushed clove garlic
4 tbs top milk

Wash silverbeet and drain, cut finely and cook gently with a little salt and pepper in butter. When silverbeet is tender, drain and keep hot. Combine garlic and milk in a saucepan and heat without boiling. Add silverbeet, warm through and serve.

Horseradish

The root is long and thicke, white of colour, in taste sharpe, and very much biting the tongue like mustard.

John Gerard

Horseradish, *Cochlearia armoracia*, which is native to eastern Europe, is cultivated and used more in north-eastern Europe and England than in other countries. It is a very persistent perennial with large dock-like leaves, and although it dies back in winter every little piece of root will grow. Horseradish grown in well-manured and light, well-drained soil in a sunny situation, will develop roots that are large and tender for using. The roots should be washed, sliced, and minced or blended without scraping, because the pungency is close to the skin. Preparing horseradish can be a painful experience because the volatile oils react on the eyes in the same way as onions. Therefore, it is best to mince the roots outside rather than in an enclosed space, with a hand covering the top of the mincer (and even dark glasses on to protect the eyes). A blender is a more comfortable way of preparing it. Horseradish loses its pungency when exposed to the air, so must be immediately covered with lemon juice or vinegar and may then be stored in the refrigerator for future use. To make sauce: Remove 1 or more tablespoons of horseradish from the storage jar and squeeze out vinegar or lemon juice. Mix it with 1 tablespoon of cream or top milk or to taste. Once the horseradish has been mixed with cream it must not be replaced in the storage jar or the stock may turn sour, so only remove as much as you are going to use at any one time. Horseradish also loses its pungency if heated, so it is generally served cold. It is most commonly served as a sauce with beef, but it also tastes good with all types of fish, with chicken, and in salads, and is combined with apple and cream and vinegar in various garnishes.

Cheese and Horseradish Spread

250 g cottage or cream cheese
2 tsp horseradish sauce
pinch salt

1 tbs chopped parsley or
    chervil
50 g softened butter

Combine all ingredients and blend well.

Open Sandwich of Horseradish

rye bread, thinly sliced and
    buttered
2 rashers bacon per slice

1 strip liver pate per slice
2-3 slices tomato per slice
grated horseradish

Arrange rye bread on plates, allowing 2 slices at least per person. Cut rind from bacon and fry until cooked. Cool and lay 2 rashers on each slice of bread. Lay a strip liver pate on one slice bacon, and slices of tomato on the other and sprinkle grated horseradish on top.

Apple and Horseradish Fresh Chutney

2 apples
3 tbs lemon juice
½ tsp mustard powder

1 tsp water
1 tsp sugar
2 tbs grated horseradish

Grate peeled, cored apples and mix with lemon juice. Combine mustard powder with water to make a smooth paste and stir into apples. Add sugar and grated horseradish and blend well. Serve with hot or cold fish, meat or poultry. This should keep 2-3 weeks in the refrigerator.

Horseradish and Apple Sauce for Smoked Fish

½ cup horseradish sauce
2 peeled, grated apples

lemon juice
pinch sugar

Combine all and mix well. Serve with hot, poached, smoked fish and use any leftover fish and sauce for sandwich filling.

Sardine Jelly

3 tbs gelatine
¾ litre tomato juice
1 tbs grated horseradish
2 tbs lemon juice
1 tbs grated onion or chopped
  chives

250 g tinned sardines
100 g cottage cheese
¼ cup chopped celery

Soften gelatine in a little tomato juice. Add rest of juice and heat gently until gelatine dissolves. Add grated horseradish (according to taste), lemon juice, onion or chives and mix well. Pour a thin layer of this liquid into a wet mould and allow to set firmly. Arrange half the drained sardines on the set jelly, pour half the remaining jelly over them and allow to set. Mash the remaining drained sardines with the cottage cheese and celery, and combine with the remaining jelly. Pour this over the rest and chill until firm. Serve unmoulded on a bed of lettuce, and decorate with slices of hard-boiled egg. Other fish may be used in the same way.

Pickled Beetroot with Horseradish

Bring to the boil:
1 cup vinegar
2 sliced onions
2 tsp grated raw horseradish

4 tbs sugar
1 bay leaf
6 peppercorns

Pour over 8 small, cooked, sliced beetroot and marinate for a day before using as a salad or pickle.

Meat Loaf with Horseradish and Sage

1 tbs butter
2 tbs finely chopped onion
125 g pork sausage meat

1 tsp salt
freshly milled black pepper
1 tsp finely chopped sage

500 g mince
2 tsp horseradish sauce
½ tsp Worcestershire sauce

1 beaten egg
50 g breadcrumbs
3 slices cheese

Melt butter in a frying pan and cook onion until golden. Put in a basin with meat, sauces, salt, pepper and sage, and blend. Mix in beaten egg and roll meat in breadcrumbs. Grease a loaf tin, arrange slices of cheese along the bottom, and pile meat mixture on top. Bake at 180 °C for about an hour, and serve hot or cold.

Devilled Mutton

1 peeled, sliced onion
1 peeled, sliced clove garlic
25 g butter
2 tsp Worcestershire sauce
1 tbs grated horseradish

½ tsp mustard powder
2-3 tbs tomato sauce
3 tbs apple or plum chutney
½ cup water
cooked, diced mutton

Cook onion and garlic gently in hot butter until tender. Stir in remaining ingredients except mutton and mix well. Put mutton into a casserole and pour over the sauce. Place in the oven at 180 °C and bake about 30 minutes. Serve with rice or mashed potatoes.

Horseradish and Beetroot Relish

250 g cooked, sliced beetroot
100 g grated horseradish
salt to taste

½ cup white vinegar
1 tbs sugar

Combine all ingredients and stand for an hour before serving. This can be kept in the refrigerator about 2 weeks in a covered jar.

Corned Beef and Potato Pie

hot mashed potato
1¼ cups white sauce
1 tbs grated horseradish
1 tbs chopped parsley

250 g cold, minced corned
beef
50 g grated cheese
salt, pepper and parsley

Arrange mashed potato to line a pie dish. Combine white sauce, horseradish, parsley and corned beef and heat gently. When hot, tip into the lined dish and sprinkle with cheese. Season to taste and heat in oven until cheese bubbles. Garnish with more chopped parsley and serve hot.

Horseradish Sauces

Bread:

2 tbs breadcrumbs	pinch salt
4 tbs grated horseradish	2 tbs cream
1 tsp sugar	2 tbs cider vinegar

Combine all ingredients and beat together until well blended. Serve with hot beef, or cheese or meat fondue.

Cold:

Mix together, until well blended, 4 tbs grated horseradish, 2 tsp mustard powder, 1 tsp wine vinegar, and a pinch pepper or paprika. Add 4 tbs cream, sour cream, or yoghurt, to taste.

Hot:

25 g butter	½ cup grated horseradish
2-3 tbs flour	½ tsp salt
1 tsp mustard powder	½ tsp sugar
1 cup stock or milk	3 tbs vinegar

Melt butter in a small saucepan, and stir in flour and mustard powder. Gradually stir in milk or stock and heat, stirring, until sauce is thick and creamy. Boil 5 minutes. Add remaining ingredients and stir well. Reheat but do not boil.

Whipped Cream:

2 mashed, hard-boiled eggs	pinch salt
1 tsp mustard powder	½ cup whipped cream
1 tbs grated horseradish	

Mash eggs, mustard and horseradish together with salt, and fold into cream until well blended. Chill before serving.

Hyssop

Garden Hyssope is so well knowne to all that have beene in a Garden ... the whole plant is of a strong sweet sent.   John Parkinson

Hyssop, *Hyssopus offici-nalis*, is a perennial, native to southern Europe. It grows as a small, nearly evergreen, shrubby bush and has generally blue, but sometimes white or pink flowers. Hyssop may be grown from seed, cutting or division, and prefers a position in full sun and a light, calcareous soil. It does not do well in heavy soils or damp situations. Formerly hyssop was used as a medicinal herb and for strewing. It was grown for making edges in knot gardens for it is readily clipped to make a neat bush, and its essential oil is used in perfume. In cooking hyssop has a somewhat hot and spicy flavour — a little like thyme and savory but also with overtones of mint and rue — so it must be used carefully. It can be added, finely chopped to soups, stews, stuffings and meat dishes, savory egg and cheese dishes, as well as to salads and pickles. Made into a syrup it is used to flavour fruit dishes and custards, and tea may be made with leaves or flowers.

Hyssop Honey

Gently warm honey with a bunch of bruised flowering tops of hyssop. This is best done in a double boiler, using new season's 'runny' honey before it sets. When flavour is sufficiently strong, strain out hyssop and bottle honey.

Fish Pate with Hyssop

250 g tuna or salmon, tinned
1 hard-boiled egg
2 tbs drained cottage cheese

1 tsp finely chopped hyssop
salt and pepper to taste

Mash fish and its liquid with all other ingredients and blend till smooth. Serve chilled with crackers.

Ham, Cheese and Hyssop Spread

250 g minced, cooked ham
¾ cup cream cheese
½ cup soft butter

2 tsp finely chopped hyssop
salt and pepper

Combine all ingredients, blend well, add seasoning to taste. Place in a serving dish and chill before serving with crackers.

Baked Fish with Hyssop

4 flounder fillets
salt and pepper
2 shallots
2 tsp finely chopped hyssop

½ cup top milk or cream
¼ cup grated cheese
½ cup fresh breadcrumbs

Sprinkle fish with salt and pepper to taste and roll it up. Place in a buttered ovenproof dish and pour over a mixture of finely chopped shallots and hyssop and top milk. Mix cheese and breadcrumbs, and sprinkle on top. Bake at 180 °C for 20-30 minutes. The cheese may be omitted.

Chicken with Hyssop

Stuff a roasting chicken with any favourite stuffing substituting 2 tsp finely chopped hyssop for any other herb usually used in the recipe. While chicken is roasting baste it with its own fat or 2 tbs melted butter and a little lemon juice. Sprinkle it with 1 tsp finely chopped hyssop.

An unstuffed chicken may be cooked with a sprig of hyssop in the cavity and the flavour is improved by adding a knob of butter and thinly peeled lemon rind to this.

Meat Balls with Hyssop

250 g minced meat
1 minced onion
1½ tbs finely chopped parsley
1½ tbs finely chopped hyssop

salt and pepper
1 beaten egg
seasoned flour
oil for frying

Combine minced meat and onion, mix in herbs and season to taste. Stir in beaten egg and mix well. Form into small balls, roll in seasoned flour, fry quickly in very hot oil, turning to brown them on all sides. Reduce the heat, and cook a little longer if they are not cooked in the middle. Drain on brown paper before serving.

Hyssop Sauce for Poultry or Game

Combine and cook gently together until fruit is tender and sauce thick:

¾ cup sugar
½ cup water
250 g cranberries

2 tbs seedless raisins
1 tsp finely chopped hyssop

Hyssop Custard

4 eggs
1½ cups milk

6 tbs hyssop syrup
added sugar to taste

Separate eggs and combine egg yolks with ½ cup cold milk, beating lightly with a fork. Heat remaining milk, pour into egg mixture stirring all the time. Return to the rinsed pan, add syrup and reheat, stirring, until mixture coats the back of the spoon. Remove from the heat and pour into a basin. Beat egg whites stiff and fold in 1-2 tbs sugar, and fold into custard. Leave to cool before serving with fresh fruit.

Marinated Peaches

1 tbs liquid honey
1 cup orange juice
2 tsp finely chopped hyssop
6 ripe peaches

1 cup whipped cream
hyssop flowers to garnish
slivered almonds (optional)

Combine honey and orange juice and mix well. Add hyssop. Halve and stone peaches and pour liquid over them. Place in a shallow dish, cover and marinate overnight. Next day put 2 halves in each serving dish, decorate with a little whipped cream and hyssop flowers, and slivered almonds. The syrup may be strained around the peaches.

Hyssop Syrup for Fruit

20-30 sprigs flowering hyssop
1½ cups water

¾-1 cup sugar

Simmer hyssop in water in a covered saucepan for 10 minutes. Strain and press liquid out of the hyssop with a wooden spoon. Return liquid to the pan with sugar, stir to dissolve it and boil hard for 5 minutes. Cool, strain through a fine strainer into a jar and, when cool, store in the refrigerator. Use as a syrup to flavour fresh sliced fruit or fruit salad, or as a syrup in which to cook peaches, apricots or plums, or use in compotes, pies, flans or tarts.

Fruit pies, e.g. apricot or peach, may be cooked with hyssop, adding ½ tsp finely chopped hyssop to every 500 g fruit.

Cauliflower and Hyssop Salad

2 cups thinly sliced, raw
    cauliflower
1 diced red apple
2-4 tsp finely chopped hyssop

1½ cups plain yoghurt
1 tsp salt
1 tbs lemon juice

Mix cauliflower and apple together in a salad bowl. Combine other ingredients in a basin, mix well, pour over cauliflower. Toss and chill before serving. Decorate with hyssop flowers.

Cottage Cheese and Carrot Salad

1 cup cottage cheese or
   yoghurt
2 tsp chopped hyssop
2 large carrots
1 grated onion, or 2-3 chopped
   spring onions

1 chopped green pepper
salt and pepper
1 lettuce

Combine cottage cheese and hyssop and stir in grated carrots and onion or chopped spring onions, and green pepper. Season with salt and pepper and mix well. Pour onto a bed of washed, dried lettuce and serve.

Potato and Apple Salad

500 g cooked, diced potatoes
1 sliced apple
1 tbs lemon juice
2 tsp finely chopped hyssop

½ cup chopped walnuts
5 tbs mayonnaise
salt and pepper
1 tbs chopped parsley

Combine ingredients, mix well and serve with green salad.

Savoury Pancakes with Hyssop

1 cup flour
pinch salt
1 egg

1¼ cups milk
1 tsp finely chopped hyssop
butter, fat or oil for frying

Sift flour and salt into a bowl. Make a well in the middle and stir in egg and about half the milk. Beat to a smooth batter and then add remaining milk and hyssop. Stand 10 minutes before heating a little butter in a pan and pouring some batter in to cook. When the lower side is brown and the top bubbling, turn each pancake over to brown the other side. Fill each pancake with a mixture of cheese, mushrooms, previously cooked in butter or milk, cooked, finely chopped ham, chicken or fish combined in a little hot white sauce or any other combination, but include 1 tsp finely chopped hyssop with whatever filling you choose. Makes 8.

Yorkshire Pudding with Hyssop

4 tbs flour
pinch salt
1 ¼ cups milk

2 eggs
1 tbs water
1-2 tsp finely chopped hyssop

An hour before you wish to cook the pudding, mix flour and salt in a basin. Stir in a little milk to make a smooth paste and drop in eggs. Beat well and then stir in rest of milk. Cover the bowl with a cloth and leave an hour. Heat some dripping from the meat, or some oil, in a large shallow ovenproof dish or several small dishes. Whisk 1 tbs water and hyssop into the batter, and when fat or oil is smoking hot, pour batter into the dish and cook 15 minutes in the middle of the oven at 180 °C. Move to the top shelf and brown the top for 5 minutes more. Serve with roast beef.

Potato Soup with Hyssop

25 g butter
1 peeled, sliced onion
500 g peeled, sliced potatoes
3-4 cups stock

a little flour
cold milk to thicken soup if
   necessary
1 tbs finely chopped hyssop

Melt butter in a saucepan, add onion and potato and cook gently until onion is tender. Add stock, stir well and bring to the boil. Cook until the potatoes are tender. Mouli vegetables and, if the soup is not thick enough, combine a little flour with cold milk and gradually stir into the soup to thicken it. Season to taste and stir in hyssop just before serving.

To Dry Hyssop Flowers

Gather flowers on a dry day when they are fully out and spread them on paper, cardboard box lids or screens and dry in the hot water cupboard or any warm place out of direct sunlight. Store in screw-top jars when quite dry.

Glazed Carrots with Hyssop

2 carrots
1 tbs water
1 tbs butter

1 tsp honey or sugar
2 tsp finely chopped hyssop
salt and pepper

Slice carrots into thin strips and place in a saucepan with all other ingredients. Bring to the boil, cover and simmer about 10 minutes over a gentle heat until moisture is absorbed and the carrots tender. Be careful that it does not burn. Serve hot.

Mushrooms with Hyssop

250 g mushrooms
25 g butter
1 tsp finely chopped hyssop

salt and pepper to taste
1 tbs lemon juice

Cook mushrooms in butter with finely chopped hyssop sprinkled over them in a covered pan. Season to taste and add lemon juice.

Lemon Balm

For the herbe without all question is an excellednt helpe to comfort the heart, as the very smell may induce any so to believe.   John Parkinson

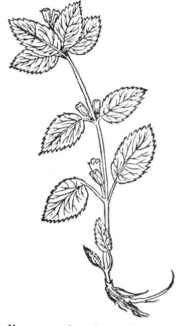

Lemon balm, *Melissa officinalis*, is native to Europe, and is a sweet smelling perennial which grows and looks rather like mint. However it may readily be distinguished from mint by the lemon fragrance of its leaves. It is easily grown from seed, cuttings or root division, and will grow in sun or semi-shade but it does need water in dry weather. In flower it will grow about 75cm tall, but it dies back to a low clump in winter. Lemon balm may be dried for winter use in places where it dies right back — simply pick leafy stalks on a dry day, tie them in small bundles and hang in a warm, airy place until crisp. Then strip the leaves off into a dark glass airtight container. The leaves may be used for tea, etc, in winter.

Lemon balm may be used to give a lemon flavour to drinks, punches and teas, to fruit and other salads, and to fish dishes. The fresh young leaves may be finely chopped, or left in whole sprigs. It is not wise to cook balm for long as the essential oils evaporate and leave a bitter taste — it is better to use it as a garnish or cook it only for a short time. Like sweet cicely, lemon balm may be used to sweeten tart fruit. Add it to a light syrup, poach the fruit gently and less sugar will be needed. Lemon balm is a great asset to people who like the

212

flavour of lemon but find lemons hard to grow, so it is particularly useful in colder climates. As a tea it has the reputation of relieving depression and making the heart 'merrie'.

N.B. The flavour of balm when added to green salads can be quite over-powering so add it with a light hand and taste before adding more.

Apple Balm Crumble Cakes

6-8 cooking apples
sprig of balm to sweeten
water
sugar
250 g short crust pastry
½ cup each wholemeal and
    plain flour

pinch sea salt
75 g butter
2 tbs chopped lemon balm
3 tbs raw sugar

Cook finely sliced apples with a sprig of balm and a little water until soft. Remove balm and sweeten with sugar to taste. Roll out pastry, line 30 small tart tins and fill with stewed apple. Sift flour and salt, rub in butter until mixture is like breadcrumbs. Add balm and sugar and sprinkle over apple. Cook at 180 °C for 20 minutes. Serve hot or cold with cream, ice cream or yoghurt.

Matrimonial Cake

1 cup wholemeal flour
1 tsp baking powder
½ cup wheatgerm
½ cup rolled oats
1 cup brown sugar
1 tbs finely chopped balm
175 g melted butter

Topping:
1 cup minced dates
1 cup minced raisins
grated rind of 1 lemon
2 tbs flour
½ cup brown sugar
½ cup water

Combine base ingredients in a bowl and mix to a paste with melted butter. Press into a greased Swiss roll tin. Combine all topping ingredients in a saucepan and simmer, stirring, for 5 minutes. Spread this topping over base mixture and bake about 40 minutes at 180 °C. Poppy seeds or other seeds may be sprinkled on the topping before baking.

Finely chopped balm may be added to taste to any plain cake mixture when lemon is not available.

Iced Orange with Balm

½ litre boiling water
1 bunch balm
100 g sugar
½ litre orange juice

1 cup lemon juice
1 litre ginger ale
ice cubes
balm leaves to garnish

Pour boiling water over balm and sugar in a jug. Stir well and allow to cool. Strain and combine with fruit juices and chill overnight. Strain and add ginger ale just before serving in glasses half full of ice cubes and float a balm leaf in each glass.

Balm Liqueur

1 handful of finely chopped
    balm leaves
½ litre brandy

1 cup sugar
1 cup water

Infuse balm in brandy for 24 hours, standing bottle in a warm place. Strain out balm and add a syrup made by boiling sugar in water for 10 minutes and allowing to cool. Filter mixture into bottles and seal.

Balm Wine

a big bunch of balm
4 litres boiling water

1½ kg sugar
wine yeast

Pour boiling water over balm in a plastic bucket and crush leaves well. Stir in sugar so that it dissolves. Cover and allow to cool, strain out balm and add wine yeast. Pour into a bottle or bottles fitted with an airlock and allow to ferment until very few bubbles rise to the surface. Siphon into clean bottles, cap and stand 6 months before drinking.

Balm Butter

Cream together:
100 g softened butter
1 tbs finely chopped fresh
    balm leaves

a squeeze of lemon juice
freshly ground white pepper

Serve on grilled fish or veal steak, or use to spread on chicken, fish or veal before grilling, or to butter bread for chicken or fish sandwiches.

Fish with Balm Sauce

Make a court bouillon by combining:

½ litre water   ½ bay leaf
1 small sliced carrot   1 tsp salt
1 small sliced onion   2 peppercorns
1 sprig parsley   1 tbs white vinegar
1 sprig lemon thyme or balm

Bring to the boil, add 4 fish fillets and poach gently until tender, about 10-15 minutes. Remove fish to a serving dish and keep hot. Strain liquid.

Melt 25 g butter in a small pan, remove from heat and stir in a scant 25 g plain flour. Gradually blend in ¼ litre milk and reheat, stirring until boiling. Cook gently for 1-2 minutes, add salt and pepper and 1 tbs finely chopped fresh balm leaves, and serve.

The milk may be replaced with fish stock or half of it replaced by onion stock made by cooking 1-2 onions in ½ cup water for 10 minutes, according to taste.

Balm-Flavoured Yoghurt

To every cup plain yoghurt add 1-2 tbs clear honey and 1 tbs finely chopped balm. Mix well and stand 15 minutes before using with fresh fruit or fruit salad or muesli.

Balm may also be used in place of other herbs in chicken liver or fish pates.

Balm Stuffing

¾ cup fresh breadcrumbs   salt and pepper
2 tbs butter   1 beaten egg
1 tbs finely chopped balm

Mix all ingredients, binding with beaten egg. This may be used to stuff fish, lamb, poultry or veal.

Balm and Rice Stuffing

2 tbs butter or oil
1 finely chopped onion
2 finely chopped sticks celery
⅓ cup rice

½ cup chicken stock
2 tbs finely chopped balm
salt and pepper to taste
1 tsp grated lemon rind

Heat butter in a small pan and gently fry onion and celery. Add rice and stir well, frying for about 5 minutes. Add stock, cover and simmer until rice absorbs liquid, about 10 minutes. Remove from heat and add balm, salt, pepper and lemon rind, stirring well to blend seasonings evenly. Allow to cool before using to stuff chicken.

Baked Apples with Balm

Stuff peeled, cored apples with a mixture of 2 tsp ground almonds, 1 tsp brown sugar and 1 tsp finely chopped balm. Top with a small knob of butter and bake at 180 °C until done.

Balm Custard

Make a custard by beating together 2 tbs sugar and 2 eggs. Add ½ litre milk and beat well, and 1 tsp vanilla essence. Pour into a dish and sprinkle 1 tbs finely chopped balm leaves on top. Place dish in a shallow pan of water and bake at 150 °C until set. Serve cold with fruit and cream.

Fruit Salad with Balm

Add 1 tbs finely chopped lemon balm to any fruit salad mixture and chill slightly before serving.

Orange Compote and Balm

4 sweet oranges
1 cup sugar
1 cup water

1 tablespoon finely chopped
balm

Peel oranges and slice them in rounds. Combine sugar and water in a saucepan and bring to the boil, stirring until sugar is dissolved. Simmer syrup for 10 minutes. Chop balm finely and sprinkle over sliced oranges in an ovenproof dish. Pour hot syrup over, cover dish and allow to cool. Then chill compote before serving with whipped cream or ice cream.

Stewed Pears and Balm

Stew pears in the usual way adding a sprig of balm to syrup. Remove when fruit is cold and sprinkle finely chopped balm on top just before serving. When bottling pears, a small sprig of balm can be added to each jar.

Rhubarb and Balm

1 kg rhubarb   *175-250 g sugar*
6-12 sprigs balm   *knob butter*

Trim off rhubarb leaves and cut stems into 5cm lengths, stringing off the pink skin. Layer in a casserole with sprigs of washed balm, sprinkle with sugar and dot a little butter on top. Cover and cook at 180°C until fruit is tender. Remove balm and serve warm with cream or custard.

Apple and Balm Salad

Combine thinly sliced apple and finely chopped balm to taste and toss in a little French dressing with a handful of sultanas and chopped walnuts. Serve on a bed of lettuce torn into bite-sized pieces.

Beetroot and Balm Salad

Mix together:
250 g cooked, sliced beetroot   *½ cup yoghurt or sour cream*
250 g stoned cherries

Chill and serve garnished with finely chopped lemon balm.

Orange Salad with Balm

4-6 oranges
2 green peppers

4 tbs French dressing
1 tbs finely chopped balm

Peel and slice oranges in rounds, removing pith and pips. Arrange in a shallow dish with thin slices of green pepper. Pour over a mixture of French dressing and finely chopped balm and allow salad to marinate for 1-3 hours before serving with roast poultry.

Potato and Leek Soup with Balm

25 g butter
2-3 peeled, sliced potatoes
1 washed, sliced leek
3 pieces celery

2 cups water or stock
1 cup milk
pepper and salt
1 tbs lemon balm

Melt butter in a saucepan and gently fry sliced vegetables with the lid on until soft, about 10 minutes. Add water and continue to cook until tender. Remove from heat and pass through a mouli. Gradually stir in milk and reheat, but do not boil. Taste, season and add balm, stir well and serve.

Lemon Grass

Lemon grass, *Cymbopogon citratus*, is a tropical grass native to South East Asia. It is a perennial and grows up to a metre high in our climate if in a favourable position. It is generally propagated from division of the stolons which should be carefully separated as they break easily from the wirey roots. Lemon grass needs a hot, sunny, sheltered spot, enjoying humidity and lots of water in summer. The leaves are tough, strong and slightly 'cutty', brownish green in colour. They sheath the base of the stems, and both the leaves and stolons are used in cooking. However the plant is tough so it is generally used as an infusion or marinade and removed before the dish is served. Lemon grass is used in Ceylonese, Indonesian, Malaysian, Thai and Vietnamese recipes and it can be used in place of lemon or other lemon-flavoured herbs with fish, rice, jellies and drinks. Commercially it is grown for lemon oil, and sometimes dried lemon grass may be bought for flavouring or tea. It is rich in vitamin A and may be used in moderation as a medicinal tea too.

Stolons should be lightly crushed before using to bring out the flavour. For easy removal, chopped lemon grass may be tied in muslin and cooked in any dish that is difficult to strain.

Stewed Fish

oil for frying
1 small, chopped onion
2 chopped cloves garlic
3 chopped red chillis
2½ cm bulbous lemon grass
   stem, pounded
1 tsp grated lime peel

pinch salt
1 kg filleted fish pieces
3 tbs soya sauce
1 tbs lemon juice
1 cup water
2 bay leaves

Heat oil and gently fry onion, garlic, chillis, lemon grass, lime peel and salt. When onions soften, add fish and fry for 5 more minutes at medium heat. Add soya sauce and lemon juice and fry 2 minutes, then add water and bay leaves, reduce heat and allow mixture to simmer until everything is tender and sauce is thick. Remove piece of lemon grass and serve with rice.

Lemon Grass Cordial

6 green lemon grass leaves
2 litres boiling water
½-⅔ cup sugar

2 litres cold water,
approximately

Chop lemon grass roughly and infuse in a bucket with boiling water for 5-8 minutes. Strain liquid over sugar and stir to dissolve it. Allow to cool and dilute with cold water to taste. Keep in the refrigerator and use as a cordial.

Fish with Lemon Grass

Fish may be marinated in a mixture with lemon grass before cooking, or a small quantity of lemon grass may be tied in a bunch and added to liquid for poaching fish and removed before fish is served.

Stir Fry Beef with Lemon Grass

1 kg lean beef steak
¾ tsp salt
pepper to taste
2 cloves crushed garlic
1 tsp crushed ginger root
1 tbs flour or cornflour
3 tbs chopped lemon grass
2 tbs each sherry and soya
    sauce

1 tbs sugar
½ cup water
oil for frying
1 sliced onion
125 g sliced mushrooms
sliced spring onions for garnish

Slice beef in long, thin strips and roll in a mixture of salt, pepper, garlic, ginger and flour. Set aside. Combine lemon grass, sherry, soya sauce, sugar and water in a saucepan. Bring to the boil and simmer 15 minutes. Strain and reserve the liquid. Heat a little oil in a wok and quickly fry meat mixture in two lots for about 4 minutes each, stirring continuously and browning gently on both sides. Remove from the wok, add a little more oil, and stir fry onion and mushrooms 1 minute. Replace meat and lemon grass liquid, bring

to the boil and heat through. Serve garnished with sliced spring
onions.

Shrimp and Lemon Grass Soup

2 litres chicken stock
3 dried red peppers
1-2 tbs chopped lemon grass
500 g prepared shrimps

⅓ cup lemon juice
bunch coarsely chopped spring
  onions
finely chopped coriander

Put chicken stock in a large saucepan and heat with red peppers
and lemon grass, tied in a piece of muslin. Bring to the boil, cover
and simmer 20 minutes. Add shrimps and simmer 6-10 minutes.
Add lemon juice and chopped spring onions and cook gently.
Remove muslin bag, garnish with coriander and serve.

Lemon Grass Jelly

Make lemon grass tea and set it with gelatine softened in a little
cold water. Use 3 tsp gelatine to every 2 cups strained tea, stir well
until gelatine dissolves and when cool place in the refrigerator.
Serve with fruit, ice cream or cream.

Cold Beef with Lemon Grass Dressing

1 kg sliced, cold, cooked beef
2 stalks lemon grass
lime or lemon rind
3-4 cloves garlic
1 chilli

soya sauce
lemon juice
honey
coriander or parsley to garnish

Arrange thin slices of cold beef on a serving dish. Crush lemon
grass stolons and pare thin strips of lime or lemon rind, crush garlic
and chilli and combine with enough soya sauce, lemon juice and
honey to make a sauce. Pour this over the beef and leave to
marinate for an hour. Remove lemon grass and rind, garnish with
finely chopped coriander or parsley and serve.

Rice with Lemon Grass

1½ cups long grain rice
2 tbs oil or butter
1 sliced onion
3 cloves
10 peppercorns

6 cardamon pods, bruised
1½ tsp ground turmeric
1½ tsp salt
3 lemon grass leaves
2½ cups coconut milk

Wash and drain rice. Heat oil and fry onion until golden. Add spices and rice and fry 2-3 minutes. Add lemon grass and coconut milk, bring to the boil and lower heat, cover and simmer 20-25 minutes without lifting the lid, until liquid is absorbed. When rice is cooked the spices will have come to the top. Remove them, fluff up rice with a fork and serve.

Lemon Verbena

Lemon Verbena, *Lippia citriodora*, is a perennial shrub, native to South America, and was brought to Europe by the Spanish in the seventeenth century. It has a slender trunk and branches and will grow from 2-4 metres high in a warm, sheltered situation. The pale green leaves, which are lanceolate, veined and slightly rough or sticky, are 5-10 cm long and often grow in threes. When brushed or crushed they release a beautiful lemon fragrance. The tiny, light purple flowers grow in spikes at the end of the branches and smell sweet, especially in the evening. The shrub is deciduous, and in winter looks quite dead but, if pruned back in early spring, will shoot away vigorously and provide plenty of leaves for cooking and scent. It is usually propagated by cuttings taken in winter or early spring.

Lemon verbena leaves may be finely chopped into stuffings for fish, poultry or veal. They may also be used in place of lemon rind in cakes and puddings, and to make tea and jelly like lemon grass. They retain their lemon fragrance when dried and are useful in pot pourri and other scented mixtures.

Lemon Verbena Butter

Chop finely or mince 2-4 lemon verbena leaves and blend with 50 g butter, or to taste. Use as a lemon spread on toast, with fish or grilled meat, or with potatoes.

Lemon Verbena Cake

4 chopped lemon verbena leaves	¾ cup sugar
4 tbs boiling water	1 cup flour
2 eggs, separated	1 tsp baking powder

Infuse lemon verbena leaves in boiling water and allow to cool a little. Beat egg whites stiff and fold in half the sugar. Strain hot water onto egg yolks, beating until smooth and thick, and continue to beat in rest of sugar. Then add egg whites and fold in sifted flour and baking powder. Turn into an ungreased tin and bake at 180 °C for 35 minutes.

Lemon Verbena with Fish

Lemon verbena may be used to flavour fish pies in the same way as lemon thyme, or it may be used in poaching liquid or as a stuffing in baked fish. It may be substituted for lemon thyme in any stuffing recipe, but should be minced finely to remove its chewy texture.

Lemon Verbena Rice Pudding

2 tbs rice	½ litre milk
2 tbs sugar	3-4 lemon verbena leaves

Combine rice, sugar and milk in a buttered ovenproof dish and stir well. Add lemon verbena leaves and place in centre of oven. Cook at 160 °C for about 2 hours until rice absorbs milk. Stir now and then, and remove leaves before serving.

  Lemon verbena may be used to flavour any milk pudding by infusing the leaves to taste in hot milk and straining them out before continuing with the recipe. It may also be used in the liquid for poaching fruit and be finely crumbled or minced into sponge pudding mixtures.

Angel's Food

2 cups milk	3 tbs sugar
2-6 lemon verbena leaves	3 tsp gelatine
2 eggs, separated	¼ cup cold water

Heat milk with lemon verbena leaves and sugar and pour onto lightly beaten egg yolks. Stir well, return to the heat and bring just to the boil. Remove from heat and strain out lemon verbena onto gelatine, softened in cold water. Stir to dissolve, and allow to cool. Then fold in stiffly beaten egg whites and pour into a serving dish. Put aside to set, and serve with fruit and/or cream.

Lemon Verbena Custard

4-8 lemon verbena leaves	125 g sugar
1 litre milk	6 eggs

Put leaves and milk in a saucepan and heat gently. Leave 30 minutes to infuse, strain and cool. Place milk in a double boiler with sugar and lightly beaten eggs, and cook over gently boiling water, stirring until custard thickens. Serve hot, warm or cold, with fruit or puddings.

Lemon Verbena Stuffing for Chicken

Combine:
1 tbs lemon verbena   *2 tsp finely chopped parsley*
180 g stale white breadcrumbs *salt and pepper*
80 g bacon or ham chopped

Bind with 2 beaten eggs and a little melted butter if needed.

Lemon Verbena Sauces

Leaves may be infused in hot milk, stock or water, and strained out before thickening is added to give a lemon flavour with puddings, fish or meat.

Claret Cup with Verbena

8 lemon verbena leaves   *½ tsp freshly grated nutmeg*
1 tbs sugar   *1 bottle lemon fizz or soda*
2 tbs boiling water   *water*
finely peeled lemon rind   *sprigs borage, or borage*
1 glass sherry   *flowers*
1 bottle claret

Combine leaves, sugar and boiling water, crush and stir well. Then pour into a jug and add lemon rind, sherry, claret and nutmeg. Infuse ½-1 hour and strain. Add fizz and sprigs of flowering borage or single borage flowers to garnish.

Lemon Verbena Wine

This is not for drinking but for flavouring jellies, fruit salads, etc. Infuse 2 tbs chopped lemon verbena leaves in 1½ cups dry white wine. Leave 3-4 days, strain and bottle.

Lovage

The seed therof warmeth the stomacke, helpeth
digestion, wherefore the people ... in times past
did use it in their meates, as wee doe pepper ...
John Gerard

Lovage, *Levisticum offici-nale*, is a tall growing, umbelliferous perennial, native to southern Europe. It grows from seed or root division and 1-2 plants are ample for the average garden. Lovage dies back in winter but comes up quickly from the roots in spring, and in a damp place with adequate sunshine will grow 2 metres high in flower. The leaves and stems may be used in salads, stews, sauces and especially in soups, so much so that the Dutch call it the Maggi plant. The seeds may also be used like celery seeds and sprinkled on bread and biscuits before baking. They taste good on cheese straws. Lovage has a strong flavour and should be used carefully until you discover how much suits your taste. It adds a good flavour to stock when steaming poultry. For flavouring soups and stews it is better to add a leafy sprig or two and remove it before serving. Because lovage dies back in winter it is useful to freeze young leaves and stems whole, or blended, in ice-cubes. The stems may also be candied like angelica.

Lovage Sandwiches

Spread buttered bread with cottage cheese and finely chopped lovage. Cover, cut in triangles and serve.

or

Mix finely chopped lovage with grated apple, a little lemon juice and honey, salt and pepper. Lay between lettuce leaves on buttered bread.

Tomato and Lovage Cocktail

1 litre tomato juice	*2 sprigs lovage*
1 peeled, sliced onion	*1 sprig basil*
pinch salt	

Combine in a saucepan, bring to the boil and simmer 10 minutes. Strain, cool, and serve chilled, garnished with a lemon wedge.

Lovage with Fish

Combine:

250 g drained, tinned tuna	*2 tbs finely chopped lovage*
½ cup cottage or cream cheese	*2 tbs finely chopped parsley*

Mix well and serve on lettuce leaves as a salad, a sandwich filling, or an appetiser with biscuits.

To Freeze Lovage

Blend 1 cup chopped, young lovage leaves and stems with ½ cup water in a blender and freeze in ice-cube trays.

or

Freeze water in half-filled ice-cube trays and tip blocks out. Place a small sprig of lovage in each compartment and replace ice block. Top up tray with water and freeze until solid. When quite frozen tip blocks into a plastic bag, label and store in the freezer. 1 cube may be used to flavour ½-1 litre of stock, soup or stew.

Lovage Omelette

For each person use:
1 tbs butter
1 chopped slice bacon
½ chopped onion
1 tomato, chopped and
   skinned
1 sliced, cooked potato
   (optional)

1 tbs cooked peas (optional)
2 tsp chopped lovage
salt and pepper
2 eggs

Melt butter and cook bacon and onion until tender. Add tomato, vegetables and lovage, and cook 5 minutes. Season to taste, and add lightly beaten eggs. Stir and lift gently until egg mixture is set, slide onto a hot plate and serve.

Meat Balls with Lovage

500 g minced steak or veal
1 finely chopped onion
1 tbs finely chopped lovage
grated rind and juice ½ lemon

1 beaten egg
salt and pepper to taste
flour
oil for frying

Combine meat, onion, lovage, lemon rind and juice and mix well. Stir in beaten egg and seasoning and with floured hands shape mixture into small balls. Dip in more flour to coat evenly and fry in hot oil until well cooked, turning to brown all sides. Serve with lovage sauce and mashed potato.

Lovage Sauce

2 tbs butter
2 tbs flour
1 cup milk, or ½ cup milk
   and ½ cup chicken stock

1 tbs finely chopped lovage
salt and pepper to taste

Melt butter, stir in flour and cook about one minute. Remove from the heat and stir in milk, blending well. Return to the stove, bring to the boil and stir until mixture thickens. Stir in lovage and season to taste.

Lovage Piccalilli

2 kg chopped green tomatoes
½ kg chopped ripe tomatoes
4 peeled, chopped onions
3 each chopped, de-seeded
    red and green peppers
2 large cucumbers, peeled and
    chopped

1 cup finely chopped lovage
⅔ cup salt
6 cups cider vinegar
4½ cups brown sugar
1 tsp mustard powder
1 tsp pepper

Place chopped vegetables in a bowl and sprinkle with salt. Leave overnight and drain. Combine all ingredients in a large pan, bring to the boil and simmer for 1-1½ hours stirring now and then. Bottle, and seal when cold.

Lovage and Cheese Pudding

1½ cups fresh white
    breadcrumbs
2 cups milk
2 tbs butter

1½ cups grated cheese
3 beaten eggs
salt and pepper to taste
1 tbs finely chopped lovage

Put breadcrumbs in a bowl, pour milk, heated with butter, over them and leave about 10 minutes. Add cheese, beaten eggs, salt, pepper and lovage and mix gently. Pour into a buttered ovenproof dish, bake at 200 °C for about ½ hour, until pudding is golden brown and well risen, and serve.

Lentil Soup with Lovage

3 tbs oil
1 sliced onion
1 sliced carrot
2 sprigs lovage
3 cups lentils

4 cups water
2 cups skinned, chopped
    tomatoes
salt and pepper to taste
250 g frankfurters (optional)

Heat oil in a large saucepan and fry onion and carrot gently for 10 minutes. Add chopped lovage and lentils, and saute. Gradually stir in water and tomatoes. Cover and simmer 30 minutes until lentils are tender. If a cream soup is wanted, mouli the soup, otherwise season, add frankfurters cut into rounds, reheat and serve.

Lovage Soup

1 tbs butter
2 tbs wholemeal flour
½ litre chicken stock

1 tbs finely chopped lovage
1 tbs lemon juice
salt and pepper to taste

Make a sauce by melting butter, stirring in flour and gradually adding stock, stirring all the time. Bring to the boil and cook 3 minutes. Add lovage and lemon juice, season and simmer 15 minutes. Garnish with a little finely chopped lovage.

Lovage and Potato Soup

500 g peeled, diced potatoes
25 g butter
1 litre water

2-3 tbs finely chopped lovage
salt and pepper to taste
1 cup milk

Cook sliced potatoes in butter very gently, without letting them brown, for 15 minutes. Add water and lovage, bring to the boil and simmer until potatoes are cooked. Blend or mouli the soup, return to the pot, season and add milk. Reheat but do not boil. A little finely chopped lovage and/or chives may be added as garnish.

Chilled Tomato and Lovage Soup

4 cups beef stock
3 cups tomato pulp
1½ cups finely chopped celery
1 clove minced garlic
1 tbs minced lovage
2 tbs minced parsley

¼ tsp thyme
¼ tsp ground celery seed
½ tsp pepper
salt and sugar to taste
sour cream
chopped chives or lovage

Combine all except the last 3 ingredients in a large saucepan. Bring to the boil and simmer about 30-45 minutes, until celery is quite soft. Puree in a blender or through a mouli, taste and season with salt and sugar. Chill. Serve topped with a little sour cream and sprinkled with finely chopped chives and/or lovage to taste.

Green Salad with Lovage

Toss together 1 washed, dried lettuce torn in bite-sized pieces, sliced cucumber and tomatoes to taste, a little cress or watercress and 1 tbs finely chopped lovage. Pour French dressing over and toss well just before serving.

Marigold

The yellow leaves of the floures are dried and kept throughout Dutchland, against the winter to put into broths ...　　　　　　John Gerard

Marigold, *Calendula officinalis*, or pot marigold, should not be confused with French or Mexican marigolds which are a species of *Tagetes*. The *Calendula* marigold is a short-lived perennial usually grown as an annual from seed, and it forms a neat plant with slightly sticky, long, narrow, green leaves and daisy-type yellow or orange flowers made up of several layers of rays around a central brown disk. The rays of the petals, fresh or dried, have been used to colour and flavour food for hundreds of years, and the marigold is also used medicinally as an ointment to heal surface wounds. In our climate there are always a few flowers to be seen on the marigolds, even in winter. They prefer a reasonable soil and a sunny situation and, if cut back to prevent them becoming straggly, the plants will go on for several years. They also self-sow readily so there are always young seedlings to plant out to replace old plants. I do not think the petals have much flavour but they make an attractive edible garnish for a variety of dishes.

To Extract Orange Colouring from Calendula

Simmer 1 cup calendula ray in 2 cups milk or water and, when the rays begin to soften, remove from the heat and blend till smooth. Strain and use as a food colouring for sweet or savory dishes.

Drying Marigold Flowers

Pick whole flowers with some stem and hang in small bunches in a warm, airy place. When rays seem almost dry, strip them from the central discs and finish drying by spreading them out thinly on brown paper. When quite dry, store in dark glass containers.

or

Rays may be stripped at once from fresh flowers and dried as above.

Calendula Spread

Combine:

5 tbs mayonnaise
1 tbs finely chopped onion
6 tbs finely chopped celery
½ tsp curry powder
¼ tsp mixed mustard

pinch salt
2 hard-boiled eggs, mashed
4 tbs finely chopped calendula
  petals

Mix well, sprinkle with a little paprika and keep in refrigerator.
   This may be thinned by adding ¼ cup yoghurt and 1 tbs lemon juice, and served as a dip.

Cottage Cheese and Calendula Dip

250 g cottage cheese
250 g sour cream
1 tsp sherry

1 tsp each minced summer
  savory and chives
1 tbs minced calendula rays

Blend cottage cheese, cream and sherry until smooth, then blend in herbs. Season to taste, cover and chill at least an hour before serving with biscuits or chips.

Marigold Biscuits

125 g butter
125 g sugar
2 beaten eggs
½ tsp vanilla essence

2 cups flour
2 tsp baking powder
petals from 2-3 marigold
flowers

Cream butter and sugar until soft and blended. Add beaten eggs and vanilla essence and beat until smooth. Add sifted flour and baking powder and marigold petals and beat well to distribute them evenly. Drop spoonfuls on a greased tray and bake at 180 °C for about 10 minutes. Cool on a rack.

Calendula Cakes

100 g butter
½ cup sugar
2 eggs
2 cups flour

2 tsp baking powder
pinch salt
½ cup fresh calendula petals
6-8 tbs milk or calendula water

Cream butter and sugar, add eggs and beat well. Sift together flour, baking powder and salt, and add alternately with washed, chopped calendula petals and milk or calendula water to the creamed mixture. Fill paper patty pans or greased patty tins three-quarters full with mixture and bake at 180 °C for about 15 minutes, until cakes are well risen and golden brown. Place on a rack to cool and ice with icing made by combining icing sugar and calendula water while still warm.

Calendula Scrambled Eggs

4 eggs
4 tbs milk
salt, pepper and nutmeg to
taste

1 tbs butter
finely chopped rays of
2 marigolds

Beat together eggs and milk, season with salt, pepper and nutmeg. Melt butter in a pan, pour in egg mixture and sprinkle with calendula. Stir carefully until set. Serve with hot buttered toast.

233

Marigold Sandwiches

Arrange on slices of buttered, wholemeal bread, slices of cheese and/or liverwurst, marigold rays and mayonnaise. Sesame seeds may be added.

Mutton and Marigold Broth

2-3 kg neck of mutton
4 litres water
125 g barley or rice
bundle of sweet herbs
1 onion

1-2 turnips
1 tbs each chopped chives,
*   parsley, calendula rays*
salt and pepper to taste

Put meat cut in several pieces in a large saucepan with water and rice or barley. Bring to the boil and skim. Add bunch of sweet herbs — marjoram, basil, summer savory — and whole, peeled onion. Cover and simmer 1-2 hours. About 15 minutes before serving, add chopped turnips, chives, parsley and calendula rays. Season to taste. The broth can be thickened by adding oatmeal, or served over bread or toast in the soup plates.

Beef Stew with Calendula

Any beef stew or casserole may have the rays of 1-3 marigolds added 10-15 minutes before the end of cooking, depending on the size of the stew.

Bread and Butter Pudding with Calendula

Layer slices of buttered bread in a buttered, flattish, ovenproof dish, sprinkling 1½ tbs finely chopped marigold rays among the layers. Make a custard by combining:

2 beaten eggs
1-2 cups milk
4 tbs sugar

½ tsp vanilla essence or finely
*   grated lemon rind*

Pour this over buttered bread, and sprinkle top with a little more sugar. Sultanas may be added to the layers. Bake at 180 °C for about 40 minutes until custard is set and bread is crisp and sugary on top.

Marigold Custard

1 cup bruised calendula rays
½ cup sugar
½ litre boiling milk
3 egg yolks

pinch each salt, allspice and
nutmeg
rays to garnish

Combine calendula rays and sugar in a basin and pour boiling milk over them. Stir well, infuse 10 minutes and strain. Beat egg yolks slightly in a basin and gradually add milk, stirring all the time. Pour into a saucepan, season with salt and spices, and cook stirring until mixture thickens and coats the back of the spoon. Remove from the heat and pour into a jug or serving dish. Serve with whipped cream garnished with fresh rays.

Yellow Plum and Marigold Jelly

Put yellow plums or greengages in a large saucepan and cover with cold water. Bring to the boil and simmer until fruit is soft. Tip into a jelly bag and leave to drip overnight into a basin. Next day measure the liquid and add ¾ cup sugar to every cup liquid, and juice of 1-2 lemons. Bring to the boil, stirring until sugar dissolves, and boil until jelly will set when tested. Remove from the heat and leave 10 minutes. Stir in marigold petals to taste — this will allow them to be evenly distributed rather than all rising to the top. Pour into warmed jars and cover when cold.

Marigold Wine

1½ litres marigold rays
250 g raisins
4 litres water
1¼ kg sugar

375 g honey
2 oranges
yeast and nutrient

Gather marigold flowers daily until the rays when stripped will fill a 1½-litre container. Hang whole flowers by their stalks so that petals do not spoil while you are collecting them. Add raisins to them in a large container and pour over water, sugar and honey mixture which has been boiled and skimmed. Cover and stand 24 hours, stir, and cover and stand another 24 hours. Add the strained juice of 2 oranges and thin strips of orange peel and warm liquid gently. Add yeast and nutrient to the strained liquid, pour into containers fitted with airlocks and ferment as usual.

Marjoram

*Sweet Marjerome is a low and shrubby plant, of a
whitish colour and marvellous sweet smell ...*
John Gerard

Marjoram, *Origanum
majorana*, also known as
sweet or knotted marjoram,
is a tender perennial, related
to oregano and a member
of the large *Origanum*
family. In cold and wet climates marjoram cannot
survive the winter and must
be grown fresh from seed
each spring. It may be also
grown from cuttings and
can be overwintered in pots
inside. In the garden it
needs a good, light soil and
a sunny situation, and in
such a place will grow fast,
giving lots of tender, soft,
green leaves for use in cooking. Marjoram is one of the
'sweet herbs'. Its flavour is similar to thyme but more delicate
and sweeter, so it is usually added either to dishes that do not
need to be cooked for long, or at the last minute as a garnish.
Used both fresh and dried, marjoram blends well with egg
and cheese dishes, chicken and meat, and with different vegetables such as beans and tomatoes. It may be used in place of
thyme or oregano but the flavour will then, of course, be
different.

To Dry Marjoram

Pick sprigs of marjoram just as they are coming into flower and
hang them in small bunches in brown paperbags in a warm, airy

place. When leaves are crisp, rub them off into a dark glass, screw-top jar and use in place of fresh marjoram but in half the quantity.

Potted Meat with Marjoram

750 g cooked ham/chicken/
    turkey
1 tbs finely chopped marjoram

1 tbs brandy
salt and pepper to taste
6 tbs butter

Mince meat and blend with marjoram and brandy. Season to taste. Melt 3 tbs butter in a pan, add meat mixture and cook gently for 5 minutes. Pack into a bowl and leave to get cold. Melt remaining butter and pour over to seal the dish. Store in refrigerator and remove butter before serving with crackers.

Marjoram Spread

1 tsp grated onion
½ cup milk
1 beaten egg
1 tsp chopped marjoram
    and/or chives

pinch curry powder
1-2 tsp butter

Simmer onion in milk for 5 minutes. Stir in beaten egg, herbs, curry and butter, and cook until thick. Cool and use as a spread on biscuits. Nice topped with mint jelly.

Marjoram Scones

2 cups flour
2 tsp baking powder
pinch salt
50 g butter

2-4 tbs finely chopped
    marjoram
cold water to mix

Sift together flour, baking powder and salt. Cut in butter and rub into flour until mixture is like breadcrumbs. Add marjoram and enough water to make a stiff dough. Stir lightly, and pat dough out gently on a floured surface. Cut into squares and bake at 200-220 °C until golden brown and light, about 10 minutes.

Savoury Pikelets with Marjoram Filling

1 cup flour	1 beaten egg
1 tsp baking powder	¾ cup milk
1 tbs sugar	

Sift together flour, baking powder and sugar and make a well in the middle. Beat egg and milk together, and stir into dry ingredients to make a smooth mixture. Heat a lightly oiled heavy pan and cook pikelets in the usual way. When cooked, fold each pikelet into a cornet shape and slip ends under the edge of a plate to hold the shape. When cool fill with marjoram filling:

2 mashed, hard-boiled eggs	1 tsp finely chopped marjoram
2 tsp softened butter	1 finely chopped shallot
salt and pepper	

Mash all ingredients together to blend well, and fill pikelets.

Vegetable Quiche with Marjoram

50 g butter	3 beaten eggs
1 cup flour	½ cup top milk or cream
pinch salt	1 tbs finely chopped marjoram
water to mix	salt and pepper
1 peeled, sliced onion	
2-3 cups cooked vegetables —	
peas, carrot, cauliflower	

Make a pastry by rubbing butter into combined flour and salt until it resembles breadcrumbs. Mix in enough water to make a dough. Knead lightly, roll out and line a greased pie plate. Fill with mixed vegetables. Combine beaten eggs, cream and marjoram, and pour over vegetables. Sprinkle with salt and pepper to taste. Bake at 190 °C for about 30 minutes, until pastry is crisp and filling set. Serve warm or cold.

Marjoram Omelette

Make omelette of 4 eggs and combine 1 tbs finely chopped marjoram with beaten eggs before cooking as usual. This omelette may be filled with cheese.

Scrambled Eggs with Marjoram

To every 4-5 eggs add 1 tbs finely chopped marjoram and cook as usual. About 25 g cheese may also be added.

Fish with Marjoram and Mushroom Sauce

750 g fish fillets, poached
  gently in salted water
  and served hot
50 g butter
1 finely chopped onion
150-200 g sliced mushrooms

1 cup cream
2 tbs lemon juice
3 tsp vinegar
salt and pepper
1 tbs chopped marjoram
¼ tsp paprika

While fish is cooking make sauce by melting butter in a pan and gently cooking sliced onion without browning it. Add mushrooms and gradually stir in cream, lemon juice and vinegar. Season with salt and pepper and marjoram and simmer gently about 15 minutes. The sauce may be thinned with a little milk if too thick. When cooked pour sauce over hot fish and sprinkle with paprika.

Whitebait with Marjoram

1-2 cups whitebait
50 g butter
3 tbs chopped shallots
1 cup white wine
1 tbs lemon juice

1 tbs chopped marjoram
salt and pepper
1 tbs flour
1 cup cream
freshly grated nutmeg

Wash and drain whitebait and set on one side. Melt butter and gently cook shallots without browning. Add wine, lemon juice and marjoram and season to taste. Simmer slowly until sauce is slightly reduced. Combine flour with cream, stirring to a smooth consistency. Gradually add to sauce stirring until thick. Remove from the heat and add whitebait. Pour into buttered ramekins, sprinkle with a little grated nutmeg and heat through in the oven at 180 °C for 5-10 minutes. Serve hot. Oysters, scallops, or other fish may be served in the same sauce.

Chicken and Marjoram in Aspic

Steam a small chicken on a rack in a large pot with about 1 ½ litres boiling water and a bouquet garni. Remove chicken when tender and cool before skinning it and cutting meat into bite-sized pieces. Soften 4 tbs gelatine in a little cold water and then stir in hot stock to dissolve it. Strain and make up to 2 litres, if necessary, with boiling water. Arrange chicken pieces in a rinsed mould or basin with 2-3 tsp finely chopped marjoram layered among the chicken or 2-3 whole sprigs of marjoram, and pour in hot gelatine mixture. Allow to cool before setting firmly in the refrigerator. Serve unmoulded with salad.

Chicken and Marjoram Roll

2 cups flour	250 g cooked chicken
100 g butter	½ cup cooked peas
cold water to mix	½ cup cooked rice
25 g each butter and flour	1 peeled, minced onion or
2 chicken bouillon cubes	3 shallots
1 cup boiling water	2-3 tsp finely chopped
pinch each salt, pepper, mace	marjoram

Make a pastry by sifting flour into a basin, rubbing in butter to make a fine crumb-like mix and blending to a dough with cold water. Roll out on a floured surface and make an oblong about 30 x 25cm. Melt 25 g butter in a saucepan and stir in flour. Remove from heat. Dissolve chicken stock cubes in boiling water and gradually stir this into the butter-flour roux to make a smooth sauce. Bring to the boil, season with salt, pepper and mace and cook 5 minutes. Remove from heat. Mince cooked chicken and stir into sauce with remaining ingredients and allow to cool before spreading over half the rolled-out pastry. Damp edges and fold pastry into a roll. Prick or slash top to allow steam to escape. Place in a large meat dish in a hot oven, 200-220 °C, and cook about 20 minutes until pastry is crisp and golden.

Liver with Marjoram

50 g butter	salt and pepper to taste
1 peeled, sliced onion	2 tbs flour

500 g liver   ½ cup stock or water
2-3 tsp finely chopped
   marjoram

Heat butter in a frying pan and gently cook onion. Thinly slice
liver, move onions to the side of the pan and cook liver about 5
minutes, turning to brown both sides and adding marjoram.
Sprinkle with salt and pepper and remove to a warm serving dish.
Stir flour into remaining fat and gradually add stock or water, stirring to a thick gravy. Cook gently 3 minutes and serve poured over
the liver.

Moussaka with Marjoram

3 eggplants   500 g skinned, chopped
salt   tomatoes
oil for frying   2-4 tbs finely chopped
2 finely sliced onions   marjoram
750 g minced meat   25 g each butter and flour
pepper   1 cup hot milk
1 tsp ground allspice   1 egg yolk

Slice eggplants, sprinkle with salt and leave 30 minutes to drain.
Dry them, fry in hot oil and drain on brown paper. Fry onions in
oil until soft. Add meat and cook, turning until brown. Season with
salt, pepper and allspice and add tomatoes and marjoram. Stir
well, add a little water if mixture is too dry, and cook 15 minutes.
Make a sauce by heating butter, stirring in flour, and gradually
adding hot milk, stirring to make a smooth sauce. Blend in beaten
egg yolk, season with salt and pepper to taste and cook 3 minutes
but do not boil. In a large, buttered ovenproof dish arrange
alternate layers of eggplants and meat mixture, and cover with
sauce. Place dish in the oven and bake at 180°C for about 45
minutes.

Eggplant with Marjoram

Peel and slice eggplant and dip in beaten egg. Drain, roll in
seasoned flour and fry in oil until brown on both sides. Lift into a
casserole, sprinkling finely chopped marjoram between layers of
eggplant. Moisten with a little tomato puree and top with grated
cheese. Bake in a moderate oven, 180°C, for 20-25 minutes.

Pork Baked with Marjoram

750 g lean pork, cut in pieces
2 tb seasoned flour
oil for frying
1 sliced clove garlic
1 sliced onion

1 tbs finely chopped marjoram
1 bay leaf
salt and pepper
1 cup cider or water

Roll pork pieces in seasoned flour and fry in hot oil until browned on all sides. Remove meat to a casserole and add garlic and onion to oil and cook gently 2-3 minutes. Combine all ingredients in the casserole, seasoning to taste, cover and cook at 180 °C for about one hour.

Rolled Schnitzel with Marjoram

4 large slices veal, halved
salt and pepper
8 thin slices cheese
8 small sprigs marjoram

1 tbs oil or butter
1 tsp cornflour
1-2 tbs water

Flatten meat slices and cut them in half. Sprinkle with salt and pepper and place a slice of cheese on each piece. Chop marjoram leaves onto cheese and roll up each piece and fasten with a toothpick. Heat oil in a frying pan and brown the rolls. Reduce heat, cover and cook about 30 minutes turning meat occasionally. When tender remove to a hot serving dish. Mix cornflour with 1 tbs cold water to a smooth paste. Add to liquid in frying pan and stir until it thickens. Taste and season as necessary. Pour over meat and serve.

Shepherd's Pie

oil for frying
2 rashers bacon
1 onion, peeled and sliced
1 clove crushed garlic
500 g minced leftover meat

1-1½ cups leftover gravy
1 tbs finely chopped marjoram
salt and pepper
500 g mashed potato
butter

Heat oil in a pan and gently fry bacon cut into small pieces, sliced onion and garlic until soft. Add meat, brown and then stir in gravy and marjoram. Mix well and turn into a greased ovenproof dish. Season with salt and pepper and top with mashed potato. Dot with a little butter and bake at 180 °C for 45 minutes.

Steak and Marjoram Stew

1 kg steak	*1 cup tomato puree*
salt and pepper	*1 glass red wine*
2 tbs oil	*1 tbs finely chopped*
1 kg small, whole onions	*marjoram*
2 sliced cloves garlic	

Trim and cut steak into bite-sized pieces and season with salt and pepper. Fry in hot oil with peeled onions and slivers of garlic until meat is brown. Add tomato puree and wine, cover and simmer gently about 2 hours until meat is tender and sauce is thick. Add marjoram about 15 minutes before end of cooking.

Liver and Kidney Stuffing with Marjoram

50 g butter	*2 tbs chopped fresh marjoram*
1 finely chopped onion	*2 tbs chopped parsley*
minced pig's liver and kidneys	*salt and pepper*
250 g fresh white breadcrumbs	*1 beaten egg*

Melt butter and gently cook onion till soft. Add minced meat and saute at a greater heat for several minutes. Turn out into a bowl and cool. When cold add fresh breadcrumbs and herbs. Season and bind with beaten egg. Use as stuffing for pork.

Poultry Stuffing with Marjoram

Mix together:

100 g breadcrumbs	*2 tsp marjoram*
grated rind of 1 lemon	*salt and pepper to taste*
1 tsp thyme	

Rub in 50 g butter and bind with 2 beaten eggs.

Onion Soup with Marjoram

2-3 onions
50 g butter
4 cups chicken stock
salt and pepper

2-3 tsp finely chopped
marjoram
grated cheese

Slice onions finely and cook gently in butter for about 10 minutes until soft but not brown. Add stock, cover and simmer 20-30 minutes. Season to taste and serve with finely chopped marjoram sprinkled on each bowl of soup with a little grated cheese melting on top.

Spaghetti Sauce with Marjoram

2 tbs oil
2 sliced onions
1 clove sliced garlic
500 g skinned, chopped
   tomatoes

salt and pepper
1 tbs finely chopped
   marjoram

Heat oil and fry onions gently but do not allow to brown. Stick a toothpick in each piece of garlic and fry with onion for 5 minutes. Discard garlic and add tomatoes. Stir well and cook rapidly so liquid evaporates and sauce thickens, but be careful it does not burn. Season to taste and add marjoram. Remove from the heat but keep hot and serve with boiled, drained spaghetti and grated cheese.

This sauce may also be used as a pizza filling, topped with cheese, bacon or anchovies.

Potato Pie with Marjoram

500 g peeled, sliced potatoes
1 peeled, sliced onion or
   4 shallots
100 g butter

2 tbs finely chopped marjoram
salt and pepper to taste
a little milk

244

Arrange potatoes and sliced onion in layers in a well-buttered ovenproof dish, dotting each layer with pieces of butter and sprinkling with marjoram, salt and pepper. Add a little milk and cook slowly at 160-180 °C for about one hour.

Vegetable Stew with Marjoram

3 stalks celery, chopped
2 cloves garlic
1 peeled, sliced onion
2 cups sliced mushrooms
2 tbs oil or butter
3 carrots, peeled and sliced
500 g small, new potatoes

4 skinned, chopped tomatoes
1 cup water
1 tsp marjoram
1 tsp salt
1 sliced green pepper
2 tbs chopped parsley

Cook celery, garlic, onion and mushrooms in oil, stirring gently until onion is tender. Add all remaining ingredients except parsley and green pepper, cover and cook gently for about 30 minutes until tender. If stew is too thin, thicken by blending 1 tbs flour with a little cold water until smooth, stirring into stew and cooking a further 5 minutes. Garnish with chopped parsley and green pepper.

Marjoram Jelly

apples
water

sugar
marjoram

Chop up apples and cover with water. Bring to boil and simmer until fruit is soft. Strain liquid through a jelly bag overnight. Next day measure liquid, return to pan and heat. Add a bunch of marjoram sprigs and 1 cup sugar to every cup of liquid. Stir well to dissolve sugar and boil rapidly until jelly will set when tested on a saucer. Remove sprigs of marjoram and stir in finely chopped marjoram instead. Pour into warm jars, and seal when cold.

Marjoram Wine

Crush 25 g fresh marjoram and infuse in a bottle of wine for 7 days. Strain through a fine cloth and drink in small glassfuls after meals.

Meatballs with Marjoram and Nutmeg

500 g minced beef	½-1 tsp grated nutmeg
1 tbs minced, mixed basil and savory	½-1 tsp grated lemon rind
1-3 tsp minced marjoram	1-2 beaten eggs
2 tsp finely chopped parsley	flour
	oil and butter

Combine beef, herbs, nutmeg and lemon rind, and mix well. Bind with beaten egg and roll into small balls. Roll them in flour and fry in mixed oil and butter until brown on all sides and cooked. Vary seasoning to taste.

Mint

There are many different types of mint which are perennial creeping plants. Those used most in cooking are spearmint, *Mentha spicata*, and the similarly flavoured winter mint and rust-free mint; apple mint, *M. suaveolens*, and peppermint, *M. x piperita*, though other varieties may be used to taste. Mints are propagated by root division because they tend to hybridise from seed. They need a rich, moist soil with water in dry seasons and, because they are shallow-rooted, they should be well dressed with compost every year, or lifted, divided and reset in fresh soil, or they may be infected by mint rust.

Mints are usually picked in sprigs and the leaves stripped and finely chopped or minced before adding to vegetables and sauces, salads and jellies. They are used whole in sprigs in different drinks and are a favourite herb in Middle Eastern cooking.

Pineapple with Mint

Add finely chopped mint — about 12 leaves to an average-sized tin of pineapple. Mix well, cover and chill before serving.

Minted Cream Cheese

250 g cream cheese   2 tbs finely chopped mint
salt and pepper   1-2 tbs cream

Mash cream cheese with a little salt and pepper. Blend in mint and add enough cream to make into a smooth spread. Store in a dish for at least 30 minutes in the refrigerator to allow flavours to blend. Serve on biscuits.

Mint Sandwich Spread

1 cup chopped dates   1 tbs water
rind and juice 1 Lisbon lemon   1 tbs finely chopped mint

Combine in a saucepan and heat gently, stirring until well blended. The lemon rind may be finely grated or peeled into large strips, with no pith, and removed at end of cooking. The spread is ready when well mixed and the dates are soft. Store, covered, in a jar in the refrigerator and use on sandwiches or biscuits.

or

Combine equal quantity of minced raisins and finely chopped mint and add a little hot water to improve consistency.

or

1 cup tender cooked peas   squeeze lemon juice to taste
1 tbs finely chopped mint   dab butter
pinch sugar

Mash peas and blend in other ingredients to taste. ½ cup cottage cheese may be added to taste.

Lime and Mint Jelly Spread

1 packet lime jelly   ½ cup finely chopped mint
1 cup boiling water
½ cup vinegar
2 cups mixed grated carrots,
   apple, chopped celery and
   chives

Pour jelly crystals into a bowl and add boiling water. Stir to
dissolve and add vinegar. Allow to cool a little, then stir in vegetables and herbs to make a thick jelly. Set in the refrigerator and
use as a spread on crackers.

Mint Cake

50 g butter	½ cup chopped mint
2 cups flour	½ cup currants
½ cup sugar	1 beaten egg
½ tsp salt	¼-½ cup water

Cut butter into flour until mixture is like breadcrumbs. Add sugar,
salt, mint and currants and mix to a dough with beaten egg and
water. Knead lightly and press into a buttered flat tin. Prick the top
with a fork and bake 20 minutes at 190-200 °C. Cool, glaze with
lemon icing and serve cut in fingers.

Cheese Pieta with Mint

250 g cheddar cheese	4 cups self-raising flour
6 beaten eggs	1 tbs chopped mint
1 cup milk	pinch salt and pepper

Chop cheese into 1cm squares and put in a bowl with eggs and
milk. Gradually stir in flour, mint and seasoning and mix well.
Pour into a buttered deep tin and bake at 180 °C for about 40
minutes. Cut into squares and serve.

Orange and Mint Loaf

2 cups flour	1-2 tbs finely chopped mint or
2 tsp baking powder	eau de cologne mint
½ tsp salt	1 beaten egg
25 g butter	½ cup orange juice and milk
2 tbs sugar	mixed
1 tsp grated orange rind	

Sift together flour, baking powder and salt and rub in butter. Add
sugar, orange rind and mint and mix well. Make a well in the centre
and stir in beaten egg and orange and milk, adding more milk if
necessary to make the right consistency. Pour into a greased loaf
tin and bake at 180 °C for 30-45 minutes. Cool on a wire rack and
leave a day before cutting.

Lime-Mint Avocado Pie

500 g plain biscuits
200-250 g melted butter
½ cup lime juice
¼ cup mint leaves
2-3 avocados

250 g cream cheese
1 tbs grated lime rind
1 tin sweetened condensed
    milk
whipped cream

Crush biscuits with a rolling pin and stir in melted butter to make a soft dough mixture. Line a large or 2 small pie dishes with biscuit crumb crust and set in the refrigerator overnight. Heat lime juice, add mint leaves and simmer 3 minutes. Strain after it has cooled. Peel and de-seed avocados and put in a blender with softened cream cheese, lime rind and cooled juice. Blend to a puree, add condensed milk and blend smooth. Pour into biscuit pie shells and allow to set at room temperature for one hour before refrigerating until quite firm and chilled. Spread with a little sweetened whipped cream before serving in thin slices. Crystallised mint leaves may be used to decorate the pie.

Mint Pasties

Roll out flakey pastry and cut into rounds the size of a saucer.

50 g finely chopped peel
50 g currants
50 g sugar

2 tbs finely chopped mint
25 g melted butter

Stir well to combine all ingredients in a bowl and place a large spoonful of mixture on each thin round of pastry. Damp edges of pastry, fold each circle in half and press edges together. Bake 20 minutes at 200 °C.

Mint Ale

¼ cup each applemint and
    spearmint
1½ cups boiling water

1 tbs sugar
juice ½ orange and ½ lemon
small bottle ginger ale

Pour boiling water over mints in a bowl, stir in sugar until dissolved, cover and cool. When cold, strain and add strained fruit juice. Combine with chilled ginger ale and serve. Ice may be added.

Citrus and Mint Cup

Combine and cool, and drink over ice:

1 cup grapefruit juice	sprigs of crushed mint
2 cups orange juice	2 cups water
½ cup lemon juice	sugar or honey to taste

Mint and Grape Juice Punch

1 litre fresh mint sprigs	juice of 1-2 lemons
1 litre boiling water	castor sugar to taste
2 cups chilled grape juice	1 litre ginger ale

Put mint sprigs in a jug, crush with a wooden spoon and pour over boiling water. Allow to infuse 10 minutes before straining. Cool and chill. Add chilled grape juice, lemon juice and castor sugar to taste. Finally add chilled ginger ale and serve with ice in each glass.

Mint and Honey Syrup

6 tbs chopped mint	1 cup honey
1 cup water	½ cup lemon juice

Boil mint gently in water for 10 minutes. Strain over honey and lemon juice and stir until dissolved. Bottle and keep in the refrigerator. Use like cordial, diluting to taste with water or lemonade.

Mint Julep

large bunch fresh spearmint or eau de cologne mint	3 bottles dry ginger ale ice blocks
1 cup sugar	slices of lemon
1 tin pineapple juice	fresh mint to garnish
juice 4 lemons	

Put washed mint in a bowl and bruise with a wooden spoon. Add sugar and fruit juices and stand 2-4 hours. Strain liquid into a bucket and add remaining ingredients. Serve as a punch.

Mint Lemonade

Peel rind of 3 lemons thinly into a jug or basin. Add pulp but not pith, 5 tbs sugar and a handful of finely chopped mint leaves. Crush all together with a wooden spoon. Add 1 litre of water and stand an hour. Strain, chill and serve garnished with fresh mint sprigs.

Orange Mint Punch

Simmer for 10 minutes:

1 cup eau de cologne or orange mint

½ cup sugar
1 cup water

Add 1 litre pineapple juice and ½ cup lime juice and chill. Add 2 litres ginger ale and garnish with orange mint.

Raspberry and Mint Cooler

2 cups sugar
3 cups boiling water
1 handful mint

2 cups lime juice
1 cup raspberries
mint sprigs to garnish

Dissolve sugar in boiling water and pour over mint. Allow to cool. Strain out mint, add lime juice and raspberries and infuse 3 hours in the refrigerator. Serve in glasses partly filled with ice and garnish with mint sprigs.

Orange may be substituted for lime juice, and strawberries for raspberries.

Mint Syrup

2½ cup water
2 cups sugar

2 cups mint
½-1 cup lemon juice

Put water and sugar in a saucepan and bring to the boil stirring. Boil gently 5 minutes. Either infuse chopped mint in hot syrup, covered, until cold and then strain, or allow syrup to cool slightly and blend it with mint. When syrup is cold, strain blended mint out through muslin and add lemon juice to taste. Bottle and keep in the refrigerator. Use diluted like cordial in cool drinks, use as a flavour in other drinks or in fruit salad or fruit cocktails. If using in milk mixtures do not add any lemon juice to syrup for this will cause milk to curdle.

Mint Tea Punch

Make a strong mint or peppermint tea and steep 15 minutes. Strain and to 3 cups of tea add juice 3 lemons, 2 oranges and ¾ cup sugar. Stir well to dissolve sugar, cool, ice and serve with sprigs of mint in each glass.

Mint and Yoghurt Drink

1 cup cold water	*pinch salt*
1 cup yoghurt	*10 mint leaves*

Beat cold water and yoghurt together until well mixed and add salt and finely chopped mint. Pour into a jug, cover and chill in the refrigerator.

Baked Eggs

For 6 eggs:

1 tbs finely chopped mixed parsley and mint	*pepper and salt*
100 g finely chopped, cooked ham or bacon	*butter*

Butter small individual ovenproof dishes and sprinkle with herbs and bacon. Break an egg into each dish, season with salt and pepper and add a little butter. Cook at 180°C until set, about 8 minutes. Serve on buttered toast.

Scrambled Eggs and Mint

Add 1 tbs finely chopped mint or 1 tbs each mint and parsley to every 4 eggs when beating and scramble as usual.

Cold Mint and Egg Pie

250 g short pastry
100 g cottage or cream cheese
4 eggs

1 tbs finely chopped mint
1 tsp salt

Line a pie plate with half the pastry, rolled out thinly. Beat cottage cheese until smooth and spread over pastry. Make little hollows and break an egg gently into each depression. Sprinkle with salt and mint and cover with the rest of the thinly rolled pastry. Prick the top but be careful not to prick the eggs and bake at 190 °C for about 20 minutes until pastry is cooked and nicely brown. Serve cold with salad. A layer of cold cucumber may be arranged on cottage cheese.

Duck Roasted with Mint Butter

25 g softened butter
1 tbs chopped mint
salt
2 kg duck
2 chopped, small carrots
2 chopped sticks celery
2 chopped leeks
1 slice chopped bacon

1 sprig thyme
1 bay leaf
2 tbs wine or Madeira
½ cup stock or water
2 tbs lemon juice
pepper
2 tbs finely chopped mint

Combine butter and mint. Rub salt and then mint butter over the duck. Place sliced vegetables, bacon, thyme, bay and wine in the bottom of a roasting pan, lay the duck, breast up on this, cover and cook about 1½ hours. When duck is tender, remove to an open pan and return to the oven to brown. Boil pan vegetables and juices with stock or water for 5 minutes and strain into a basin. Cool quickly which will allow fat to rise to the surface. Skim off fat and reheat sauce in pan. Add lemon juice, pepper and mint. Serve sauce separately.

Mint Crust for Hogget

For a 2 kg leg of lamb, hogget or mutton use:
6 cloves crushed garlic
6 tbs fresh white breadcrumbs
6 tbs finely chopped mint

100 g butter
juice of a lemon
salt and pepper to taste

Pound all ingredients together to make a paste and spread firmly over the outside of meat. Stand an hour to allow flavours to develop and roast at 190 °C for 1½-2 hours, according to taste. Baste during cooking so top crust is well browned.

Lamb Stuffed with Mint

large bunch of long-stemmed
  fresh mint
leg of lamb or hogget, boned

25 g butter
salt and pepper to taste

Wash mint, shake dry and push, stalks first, into the hole where bone was removed. When stalks appear on the other side, pull them through to leave the leafy tops of the mint in the widest part of the meat. Cut off any long stalks, spread butter over meat and season with salt and pepper. Roast in a pan at 190 °C for about 1½ hours until meat is tender, basting occasionally.

Mint and Almond Stuffing for Chicken

100 g day-old breadcrumbs
1 beaten egg
pepper and salt to taste
1 grated apple
1 tbs lemon juice

2 tbs grated onion
1 tbs finely chopped mint
1 tbs sugar
2 tbs blanched almond slivers,
  toasted

Put breadcrumbs in a bowl and mix in egg. Season with salt and pepper. Toss grated apple in lemon juice and add, with grated onion, to breadcrumbs. Chop mint finely, add sugar to absorb its flavour and mix in with almonds so all is evenly distributed. Use to stuff a 1½ kg chicken.

Mint Stuffing for Fish or Mutton

100 g butter
4 tbs grated onion
½ cup finely chopped mint
3 cups soft breadcrumbs

3 tbs chopped parsley
1 tsp salt
1 tsp sugar

Heat butter in a pan and fry onion until golden. Add remaining ingredients and mix well.

Lamajoon

Dough:
1 tsp sugar
1 tbs D.Y.C. yeast
¼ cup warm water
250 ml scalded, cooled milk
2 tbs oil
250 g flour
½ tsp salt
4 tbs mint, finely chopped

Filling:
500 g minced lamb or hogget
2 tbs oil
2 cloves minced garlic
1 finely sliced onion
1 green pepper, de-seeded and
  chopped
3 tbs tomato paste
6 tbs mint, finely chopped
3 tbs parsley, finely chopped
1 tsp salt
¼ tsp each pepper and cumin

Dissolve sugar and yeast in warm water and milk, adding oil and flour gradually as yeast begins to froth. Sprinkle in salt and mint and stir well. Knead to form a soft dough and set aside in a covered basin to rise.

Fry meat, onion, garlic and green pepper gently in oil, and when lightly browned add tomato paste, herbs and seasonings and continue cooking at a low temperature for 10-15 minutes. Allow to cool.

When dough has risen, knock it back and roll out on a floured surface. Cut into eight 15cm rounds, divide filling into 8 portions and place each in the centre of a round of dough, like small pizzas. Bake at 200 °C for 15 minutes.

Mint and Mutton Patties

500 g cooked potato
500 g cooked, minced mutton
1 tsp salt
pepper to taste

1 tbs finely chopped mint
1 beaten egg
½ cup breadcrumbs
oil for frying

Combine mashed potato and minced mutton and mix in salt, pepper, mint and beaten egg, blending well together. Wet your hands and form mixture into 12 round patties, roll in breadcrumbs and rest them in the refrigerator for 20-30 minutes. Heat oil in a frying pan and cook patties about 10 minutes each side, until golden brown and heated through.

Turkish Meatballs

500 g minced meat
1 grated onion
1 tbs rice
1 tbs finely chopped parsley
1 tbs finely chopped mint

salt and pepper to taste
3 beaten eggs
just over ½ cup water
2 tbs milk
4 tbs oil or butter

Combine meat, onion, rice, herbs and seasoning and bind with 2 beaten eggs. Roll into 12 balls and cook in a shallow covered pan with water on a low heat for about 30-40 minutes until water has evaporated. Allow meat balls to cool enough to handle, then dip them in a mixture of 1 beaten egg and milk, and fry in oil.

Mint and Apple Chutney

2 kg peeled, cored and
  chopped cooking apples
450 g skinned, chopped, ripe
  tomatoes
600 ml vinegar
450 g brown sugar

2 tsp ground ginger
1 tsp salt
pinch cayenne pepper
450 g sultanas or raisins
50 g chopped mint

Cook apples and tomatoes in half the vinegar, stirring, until thick and pulpy. Add remaining ingredients except mint, stir well and cook 15-20 minutes more. When mixture is thick enough, add finely chopped mint and cook a further 5 minutes. Pour into sterilized jars and seal when cold.

Crystallised Mint Leaves

Gather perfectly shaped, young mint leaves and strip them from their stalks. Coat both sides with lightly beaten egg white, using a small paint-box brush. Sprinkle both sides with castor sugar and arrange leaves on a wire-rack covered with waxed paper. Dry in a very slow oven, below 110 °C, with oven door open. When dry wait until leaves are quite cold, then store in an airtight container with waxed paper between each layer.

Fresh Mint Chutney for Curry, Kebabs or Lamb

Combine ½ litre plain yoghurt, 1 small, finely chopped onion or 2 cloves chopped garlic, 1½ tsp ground cumin or caraway and 3 tbs chopped mint. Serve chilled.

Fresh Mint or Coriander Chutney

1 cup finely chopped mint or coriander leaves	*1 tsp salt*
	2 tsp sugar
8 finely chopped shallots or small onions	*1 tsp garam masala*
	4 tbs lemon juice
1 crushed clove garlic	*2 tbs water*

Combine all ingredients in a blender till smooth. Cover and chill before serving.

or

25 g fresh tamarind	*1 tsp salt*
4 tbs water	*1½ tsp sugar*
2 tbs each fresh mint and coriander leaves	

Soak tamarind in water for 30 minutes then squeeze out pulp. Mince mint and coriander leaves through a mouli parsmint, add tamarind pulp, season and serve with curry.

Mint and Crab Apple Jelly

Place crab apples in a large saucepan and cover with water. Cook gently until fruit is soft and liquid a good colour. Strain overnight through a jelly bag. Next day measure liquid and bring to the boil with a large bunch of mint. Stir in 1 cup sugar for every cup of liquid and boil until jelly sets when tested on a saucer. Remove mint and add a little finely chopped fresh mint before pouring into jars. Cover when cold.

Mint and Gooseberry Jelly

1 kg gooseberries	*1 cup water*

Cook fruit in water until soft. Tip into a jelly bag and strain overnight. Measure liquid and add ¾ cup sugar, 2 tsp white wine vinegar and 2 tbs freshly chopped mint to each cup of liquid. Stir well and boil until it jells.

Mint and Apple Jam

1 kg apples
¾ litre water
¾ kg sugar

1 bunch mint
½ cup chopped mint leaves

Peel, core and slice apples and cook in a pan with water until tender. Stir in sugar until dissolved, add a bunch of mint and boil fast until jam will set on a saucer. Remove mint sprigs, add ½ cup finely chopped mint leaves, cook 5 minutes, bottle, and seal when cold.

Bulk Mint Sauce

Pick mint leaves from their stalks and place in wide-mouthed screw-top jars, packing them fairly tightly. Fill jars with vinegar, turning to remove air bubbles, screw on plastic lids and store in a cool, dark place. To make, simply pour off the quantity needed, add hot water and sweeten to taste. Lemon juice or more vinegar may also be added.

Orange and Eau de Cologne Mint Jelly

Pour 1 cup boiling water over 1 sprig of eau de cologne mint leaves and leave to cool, covered. Dissolve 1 packet of orange jelly in 1½ cups boiling water and stir well. Add strained mint-flavoured water, pour into a mould and leave to set.

Blackcurrant and Mint Crumble

For every 500 g blackcurrants use 2 tbs finely chopped mint and 2-4 tbs sugar. Cover with any crumble mixture or make a pie or sponge by using pastry or a sponge topping instead of the crumble. Bake 30 minutes at 180 °C for crumble, at 200 °C for a pie, and about one hour at 180 °C for a sponge.

Minted Apple Compote

1 cup water	¼ cup chopped mint
½ cup sugar	2 large apples

Heat water, stir in sugar and bring to the boil. Add mint, boil 3 minutes and add peeled, quartered apples. Turn the heat low and gently poach apples in syrup so that they remain whole. When tender remove apples with a slotted spoon and strain the syrup over.

Minted Fruit

2 tbs sugar	2 tbs water
¼ cup finely chopped mint	3 cups mixed fresh fruit
½ cup mint-flavoured jelly	

Sprinkle sugar over mint and leave in a small bowl for one hour. Melt jelly with water over a low heat and chill. Chill chopped mixed fresh fruit and arrange in a serving dish. Spoon over the mint jelly and mint and sugar mixture and combine lightly. Serve cold with cream.

Minted Grapefruit and Strawberry Cocktail

Halve grapefruit and remove pulp by working with a teaspoon from centre of fruit outwards, lifting out each segment. Cut out dividing pith and put skins in cold water to keep them firm. Combine grapefruit pulp with strawberries, about ½ cup to each grapefruit, add sugar to taste and chill well. Just before serving, drain and dry grapefruit skins, line them with fresh mint leaves and fill with chilled fruit.

Mint Sorbet

½ cup boiling water	½ cup sugar
2 tbs chopped mint	⅓ cup water
1 cup water	¼ tsp cream of tartar
½ cup lemon juice	2 egg whites
1 egg white	

Pour boiling water over mint in a basin, cover and allow to cool. Strain and combine with 1 cup water, lemon juice and 1 egg white, whisk lightly, pour into a tray and freeze until partly set.

Put sugar, ⅓ cup water and cream of tartar in a saucepan and stir over heat until sugar dissolves. Bring to the boil and boil rapidly for 5 minutes, then remove from heat. Beat egg whites to soft peak stage and then pour hot syrup into egg whites in a very thin, slow steam, beating steadily all the time. Remove partly frozen mint mixture and fold in the meringue. Whisk lightly and pour into a deep tray or cake tin. Return to freezer until set, stirring to blend mixture evenly. Eau de cologne mint and orange juice may be used in the same way.

Mint Water Ice

3 tsp powdered gelatine
½ litre water
½-¾ cup sugar

2 tbs finely chopped mint
2 egg whites

Soften gelatine in ¼ cup water for about 5 minutes. Heat rest of water and sugar, stirring, and boil 5 minutes. Stir in softened gelatine and mint and leave to infuse one hour. Strain into an ice cream tray and freeze until partly set. Remove from freezer into a cold basin and beat until mixture is opaque. Beat egg whites until quite stiff and fold into cold mixture. Pour back into tray and freeze at least 2 hours.

Beetroot and Mint Salad

4 cooked, peeled, sliced
   beetroot

3-4 tbs French dressing
2 tbs finely chopped mint

Combine and toss well together to blend. Serve on a bed of washed, dried lettuce or chicory, or with cress or watercress.

Heat Wave Cucumber and Mint

Peel and slice cucumber and serve in individual bowls of salted ice water, garnished with sprigs of mint.

Courgette and Mint Salad with Honey Dressing

Combine in a bowl:

2 cups thinly, sliced courgettes   ½ cup chopped celery
1 cup grated carrot   2 tbs finely chopped mint

Combine 2 tbs clear honey, 4 tbs lemon juice, 5 tbs safflower oil and a pinch of salt and pepper in a jar and shake well. Pour dressing over salad and toss well.

Cucumber and Mint Salad

Combine and chill before serving:

1 cup yoghurt   ¼ tsp each salt and pepper
1 cup chunked cucumber   1 tbs chopped walnuts
1 small, finely sliced onion or   1 tbs finely chopped mint
  chopped spring onions

Lettuce Salad with Mint

Wash and dry a lettuce and tear into pieces. Add minced onion or chopped chives and 6 finely chopped sprigs of mint. Toss with French dressing and garnish with sliced tomato or hard-boiled egg.

Orange and Onion Salad

3 oranges, peeled and sliced   ¼ cup oil
  in rounds   1 tbs wine vinegar
1 peeled, sliced onion   salt, pepper to taste
2 tsp each finely chopped mint
  and parsley

Place orange and onion slices on a serving dish. Combine all other ingredients in a screw-top jar and shake well. Pour over salad.

Mint and Pea Salad

Mix together well:

2 tbs wine vinegar   6 tbs oil

262

½ tsp salt, pepper to taste   2 tbs finely chopped mint
1 tsp sugar

Add 375 g cold, cooked green peas and toss. Serve on lettuce.

Potato, Mint and Caraway Salad

500 g hot, cooked, diced   1 tsp caraway seed
  potatoes   1 tsp salt
2 tbs minced onion   2 tbs finely chopped mint
1 cup yoghurt

Combine and toss together well. Cool and chill.

New Potato and Mint Salad

500 g small new potatoes   3 tsp sugar
boiling water   ½ cup boiling water
4 sprigs mint   3 tbs vinegar

Wash new potatoes and cook gently in boiling water until tender
but still firm. Drain, skin if necessary and season with a little salt.
Chop mint finely and combine with sugar and boiling water. When
sugar has dissolved add vinegar and infuse one hour. Turn potatoes
into a serving dish and pour mint sauce over them. Chill and serve
as a salad or as a snack with a toothpick in each potato.

Minted Rice and Carrot Salad

500 g young carrots   salt and pepper to taste
2 tbs butter or oil   2 tbs finely chopped mint
2 tbs brown rice   1 tbs lemon juice

Scrub or scrape carrots, cut off ends and slice lengthways. Heat
butter or oil in a heavy pan, add carrots and cook gently about 3
minutes. Stir in rice, add enough water just to cover, season to
taste, cover and cook over a low heat until water is absorbed and
carrots and rice tender. Remove from heat, stir in mint and lemon
juice and allow to cool before serving.

Tabbouleh

125 g cracked wheat
1 cup finely chopped parsley
4 shallots
250 g tomatoes
⅓ cup finely chopped mint

⅓ cup lemon juice
⅓ cup oil
pinch chilli powder
salt to taste

Put cracked wheat in a bowl and cover with boiling water. Stand 15 minutes. Drain wheat and rinse under cold running water. Dry on absorbent paper. Put wheat in blender with other ingredients and blend well. Keep refrigerated.

Tomato and Mint Salad

Combine all ingredients and serve chilled:
3 sliced tomatoes
3 tbs finely chopped mint
2 tbs lemon juice

1 tbs sugar
salt and pepper to taste

Turkish Cabbage Salad

½ cabbage
sprig mint
2 tbs oil
juice of 2 lemons

1 tsp finely chopped mint
salt and pepper
2-5 cloves garlic, according to taste

Wash and separate leaves of cabbage and cook in boiling water with a sprig of mint for 2 minutes — cabbage must still be crisp. Drain cabbage, remove hard stalks and slice into strips. Combine oil, lemon juice, mint and seasoning and mix well. Add crushed garlic and pour over cabbage in a bowl, toss well and serve.

French Dressing with Mint

Combine in a screw-top jar:
1¼ cups oil
⅓ cup lemon juice

pinch pepper
3 tbs sugar

⅓ cup vinegar (cider or white)   *¼ cup finely chopped mint*
1 tsp salt

Store in refrigerator and shake well before using.

Cucumber Sauce with Mint and Dill

1 kg cucumbers   *½ cup sugar*
2 tbs salt   *1 tsp dill seed*
2 peeled, chopped apples   *1 tbs chopped mint*
1 peeled, sliced onion   *1 cup white vinegar*

Peel and quarter cucumbers and scoop out seeds with a teaspoon. Grate cucumber flesh into a bowl, sprinkle with salt, cover and stand overnight. Next day drain off liquid, rinse in cold water and drain again. Put all ingredients in a saucepan and simmer gently until thick, stirring from time to time. Put through a mouli or sieve until quite smooth. Reheat to boiling, pour into hot, dry jars and seal when cold.

Mint Butter

Combine and mix until well blended:
100 g butter   *1-2 tsp lemon juice*
2 tbs finely chopped mint   *salt and pepper to taste*

Roll into balls and serve with hot, grilled lamb chops, new potatoes, green peas or any other dish, or spread on any lamb or hogget before grilling.

Jellied Mint Sauce

1 tbs gelatine   *½ cup wine or cider vinegar*
¼ cup cold water   *1 tbs lemon juice*
½ cup boiling water   *½ cup finely chopped mint*
50 g sugar

Soften gelatine in cold water and add boiling water to dissolve it. Stir in and dissolve sugar and add remaining ingredients. Leave to cool, then stir to distribute mint evenly. Set in a shallow dish or small individual moulds, and serve cut in cubes with any lamb or mutton dish.

Apple Sauce and Mint

Add finely chopped apple mint to apple sauce about 5 minutes before end of cooking.

Lemon and Mint Sauce for Meat

Melt 25 g butter and stir in 25 g flour and cook slowly until sauce is brown. Remove from the heat and add 1½ cups stock, 1 tbs red currant jelly and juice of ½ lemon and ½ orange. Blend until smooth and cook stirring over a low heat until boiling. Just before serving add 1 tbs finely chopped mint. Serve with lamb or hogget.

Mint Sauce

Pound 2 tbs chopped fresh mint with 1 tbs castor sugar until smooth. Add 1-2 tbs boiling water and stir to melt sugar. Add vinegar or lemon juice to taste.

Mint Sauce for Serving with Fish

25 g butter
1 tbs anchovy sauce or to taste
½ cup dry sherry

2 tsp each chopped parsley and mint
2 tbs lemon juice

Melt butter in a saucepan, add anchovy sauce and cook very gently for 5 minutes. Add sherry, cook another minute before adding mint and parsley and cooking a further 5 minutes. Finally remove from heat, add lemon juice and pour over fried fish in a serving dish.

Mint and Cardamon Sauce for Fruit

Combine and simmer for 2 minutes:
½ cup water
½ cup honey

¼ tsp ground cardamon
6 finely chopped mint leaves

Cool and add:
½ cup port

⅛ cup Benedictine

Pour over fresh fruit and chill slightly before serving.

Mint and Fruit Sauce for Pork or Sausages

750 g peeled, sliced apples
250 g peeled, sliced quinces
3 tbs water
juice of 1 lemon

2 tbs sugar
50 g butter
1-2 tbs finely chopped mint

Cook fruit gently in water until tender — quinces should be sliced more finely than apples. Add lemon juice, sugar and butter, stir well and fold in finely chopped mint.

Mint and Plum Sauce for Lamb

500 g stoned plums
1 cup white wine vinegar

100 g sugar
1-2 tbs fresh mint

Stew plums in vinegar and sugar until soft. Stir in finely chopped mint and serve hot with lamb.

Chicken Soup with Mint

1 litre chicken stock
2 tbs rice

salt and pepper
finely chopped mint

Heat chicken stock and cook washed rice until tender. Taste, season and sprinkle with finely chopped mint.

Choko Soup with Mint

3 chokos
2 onions
4 sticks celery
¾-1 litre chicken stock
1 bay leaf

25 g butter
2 tbs flour
1 cup milk
½ cup finely chopped mint
salt and pepper

Peel and slice chokos and onions, slice celery and cook gently in chicken stock until tender with bay leaf to flavour. Remove bay and mouli or blend the vegetables. In another saucepan melt butter and stir in flour, gradually adding milk to make a sauce. Stir in vegetable mixture, cook until it thickens. Just before serving add mint, taste and add salt and pepper. A little cream may also be added and soup served hot or iced.

267

Chilled Mint and Cucumber Soup

1 large cucumber, grated
1¾ cups cream
½ cup yoghurt
1 clove garlic, crushed

2 tbs tarragon vinegar
2 tbs chopped mint
salt and pepper
sprigs of mint to garnish

Grate cucumber coarsely into a bowl and add remaining ingredients except garnish. Mix well, season to taste. Chill an hour and serve garnished with a sprig of mint for each bowl.

Minted Summer Soup

1 large cucumber, peeled and
   chopped
250 g natural yoghurt

5-6 sprigs mint, chopped
salt and pepper to taste

Blend all ingredients together, chill and serve garnished with mint.

Mint and Pea Soup

250 g cooked green peas
½ cup cooking water
½ litre chicken stock
2-3 sprigs finely chopped mint

1 tbs butter
1 tbs flour
½-1 cup milk
salt, pepper and sugar

Mouli green peas with ½ cup of cooking liquid. Pour into a saucepan with chicken stock and bring to the boil. Add mint and simmer gently 5 minutes. Melt butter in a small pan, stir in flour and gradually add milk to make a smooth sauce. Stir in a little soup to blend, gradually return all to the same pan and heat gently. Season and serve.

Prune Soup with Mint

250 g prunes
1 chopped onion
2 tbs long grain brown rice
2 tbs chopped parsley
2 tbs chopped mint

½ cup lentils
5 cups chicken soup
5 cups water
1 tsp salt
½ tsp pepper

Soak prunes overnight, drain, remove stones and chop. Combine all ingredients in a large saucepan and bring to the boil. Cover, reduce heat and simmer about 2 hours.

Courgettes with Mint

25 g butter
500 g sliced courgettes

salt and pepper
1-2 tbs finely chopped mint

Melt butter in a saucepan and gently cook courgettes, covered, until just tender. Turn while cooking and season with salt and pepper. Pour into a serving dish and sprinkle with mint.

Mint with Green Peas, Carrots or Potatoes

Cook fresh or frozen peas with 1 tsp sugar and 1 sprig mint. When tender, remove mint sprig and drain. Add a little piece of butter and finely chopped mint to taste and a little salt. Shake saucepan so butter melts and mixes with peas. The mint will mix through with the butter.

Carrots or potatoes may be garnished with mint in the same way.

Minted Pilaf

6 tbs butter
1 finely chopped onion
2 cloves garlic, crushed
1 tsp each ground cloves,
    cardamon and cinnamon
1½ cups rice
1 large tomato, peeled and
    sliced
¾ cup peas

3 finely chopped carrots
1 cup raisins or sultanas
2 tbs lemon juice
3 cups water
1 tsp salt
1 cup cashew nuts
¾ cup each finely chopped
    fresh mint and coriander
    leaves

Saute onion and garlic in heated butter until soft. Add spices and rice and saute several minutes. Add all other ingredients except mint and coriander, stir well, bring to the boil and reduce the heat. Cook covered until liquid is absorbed. Add mint and coriander leaves, stir well, cover and stand 5 minutes before serving.

Courgettes with Dill and Mint

500 g small courgettes
½ cup oil
1 finely chopped onion
250 g skinned tomatoes
1 tsp sugar

½ cup water
2 tsp finely chopped dill
1 tsp finely chopped mint
salt and pepper to taste

Cut ends of courgettes and halve lengthways unless they are very small. Heat oil and fry onion gently for about 5 minutes before adding tomatoes and sugar and cooking a further 10 minutes. Stir in water and bring to the boil. Add courgettes, herbs and season to taste. Cover and simmer gently until courgettes are tender.

Peppermint Marshmallows

2 tbs peppermint
1 cup boiling water
2 cups sugar

1 tbs gelatine
2 tbs lemon juice
1 cup coconut

Infuse peppermint in ½ cup boiling water and allow to cool. Strain and combine with sugar in a bowl and beat at high speed. Dissolve gelatine in remaining ½ cup boiling water and pour gradually into the mixture, continuing to beat until thick and smooth — this may take 15 minutes or more. Add lemon juice, beat briefly and pour into a lightly-oiled flat tin and set in the refrigerator. When set, cut into cubes and roll in coconut.

Peppermint Drops

½ cup crushed peppermint
   leaves
1½ cups water

2 cups white sugar
¼ tsp cream of tartar

Boil peppermint in water for 15 minutes. Strain onto sugar in another pan and boil until mixture reaches the soft ball stage, i.e. when a little of mixture is dropped into a basin of cold water it forms a small ball. Remove from heat, add cream of tartar and beat standing saucepan in a bowl of cold water until mixture is creamy. Drop teaspoonfuls onto waxed paper and allow to set.

Peppermint Biscuits

½ cup honey
125 g melted butter
2 eggs
2 tsp vanilla

1 cup wholemeal flour
1-1½ cups coconut
1 cup sultanas
1 tsp dried peppermint

Stir honey into melted butter and blend well. Allow to cool, then beat in eggs and vanilla. Stir in flour, coconut, sultanas and crumbled peppermint and mix well. Turn into a greased 20 x 30cm tin and bake at 180 °C for 20-30 minutes. Cut into fingers while hot, but leave to cool in the tin.

Peppermint Geranium Chocolate Cake

1½ cups flour
1½ tsp baking powder
1½ tbs cocoa
1 cup sugar

3 beaten eggs
6 tbs milk
1 tsp vanilla essence
125 g melted butter

Sift together flour, baking powder and cocoa into a basin. Stir in sugar, then combined egg, milk and vanilla essence. Gradually beat in melted butter until mixture is blended. Pour into a greased 21cm cake tin lined with peppermint geranium leaves. Bake at 160 °C for 30-40 minutes.

Nasturtium

*The Spaniards and others use the leaves hereof
instead of ordinary Cresses, because the taste is
somewhat sharpe agreeing thereunto ...*

John Parkinson

Nasturtium, *Tropaeolum majus*, is native to Peru, and was introduced to Europe by the Spanish in the seventeenth century when it was known as 'yellow lark's heels'. There are many varieties, some spreading, some dwarf, some compact, but all have shield-shaped, single, green leaves growing on long hollow stems and bright flowers with long spurs at the back. The flowers, which may be many shades of yellow or orange and even tawny red, look and taste good. Nasturtiums are easy to grow, but if the soil is too rich and moist they often have more leaves than flowers. They are grown from seed and, once the soil is warm, will germinate quickly if soaked overnight before planting where the plants are to grow. They are perennial in their native habitat but are treated as annuals where frosts occur in winter.

Leaves and flowers of nasturtiums may be eaten in salads and sandwiches and have a flavour rather like cress. Young leaves are to be preferred as older leaves may be leathery. The flowers contain honey in their long spurs and taste sweeter. The seedpods may be pickled and used as a substitute for capers but contain oxalic acid, so should not be used too often or in too great a quantity. Always remove pistil and stamens, which taste bitter, from the flowers, wash the flowers and pat them dry with paper towels because little bugs sometimes hide among the petals.

Nasturtium Cigarettes

Spread washed, dried, tender nasturtium leaves with a mixture of savoury fish, or cream or cottage cheese to taste. Finely chopped chives, raisins or nuts may be added. Roll leaves up and tie with a long-stemmed nasturtium flower or fasten with a toothpick.

Nasturtium Butter

Mince or chop finely young leaves, stems and flowers of nasturtium and mix into softened butter using about 1 tbs to each 50 g butter. Leave about 30 minutes in a covered container and use to spread on biscuits or bread.

Cottage or Cream Cheese with Nasturtium

Remove pistil and stamens from flowers and stuff with cottage or cream cheese to taste. Raisins, nuts or finely chopped herbs may be added to cheese.

Nasturtium Flowers Stuffed with Fish

Blend together a little flaked tuna, chopped parsley and mayonnaise. Remove pistil and stamens from flowers and stuff each with 1 tsp of the fish mixture.

Stuffed Nasturtium Flowers

Blend well together:

mashed pulp of 2 ripe avocados
2 cloves garlic, minced
2 tbs lemon juice

6 small tomatoes, chopped
2 tbs finely chopped onion
1 tbs fresh oregano
pinch cayenne pepper

Stuff nasturtium flowers with mixture and serve with lettuce salad, cold meat and/or bread and butter.

Nasturtium Sandwiches

8 thin slices bread
small carton cream cheese

12 nasturtium flowers
12 nasturtium leaves

Spread 4 slices bread with cream cheese and sprinkle with 8 finely chopped nasturtium flowers, without pistil and stamens, and 12 finely chopped leaves. Top with 4 slices bread spread with more cream cheese. Place a whole flower on each sandwich and serve.

or

nasturtium flowers or young leaves

buttered brown bread
mayonnaise

Wash and lightly dry flowers on paper towels. Remove petals and arrange on slices of buttered brown bread which have been spread with a little mayonnaise. Cover with another slice of brown bread and serve. Young leaves may be used instead, but they are more like cress in flavour. They go well with white bread and marmite too.

Chilled Peaches with Nasturtium

3 cups ripe, sliced peaches
1 cup orange juice
½ cup lemon juice

sugar to taste
nasturtium flowers

Arrange sliced peaches in a dish and pour over orange and lemon juice mixed together. Sprinkle with sugar to taste, and chill. Serve garnished with nasturtium blossoms.

Fresh Pear and Nasturtium Fruit Salad

1½ cups cold syrup
4 ripe pears
4-6 nasturtium flowers

chopped, crystallised ginger
(optional)

Pour syrup into a serving dish and peel and slice ripe pears into it. Chill in refrigerator, and before serving arrange nasturtium flowers among the pears. Chopped ginger may be added.

Nasturtium in Salads

Flowers and leaves may be chopped and added to any salad to taste and flowers may be used as a garnish for any salad. Stuffed flowers may also be dressed with French dressing and served as a salad.

With apple

Combine finely sliced apples, chopped walnuts and torn nasturtium flowers. Toss with a little French dressing and serve.

With cucumber

Marinate peeled, sliced cucumber in French dressing for ½ hour and decorated with nasturtium flowers and a few small nasturtium leaves arranged round the cucumber.

With flowers

Arrange different coloured nasturtium flowers in a salad bowl. Sprinkle with 1-2 tbs finely chopped chervil, a pinch of salt and 2-3 tbs olive oil combined with juice of 1 lemon. Toss salad in the bowl gently until flowers are well coated and serve.

With lettuce

1 lettuce
4-6 nasturtium leaves
½ cup pineapple pieces

nasturtium flowers
French dressing

Wash, dry and tear lettuce into bite-sized pieces. Wash, dry and finely chop nasturtium leaves, and combine with lettuce and pineapple in a bowl and toss. Garnish with nasturtium flowers and serve with French dressing.

With plum

Combine in a salad bowl:
1-1½ cups sliced nasturtium
  leaves
4-5 cups torn lettuce
1 cup thinly sliced celery
8-12 sliced, firm, ripe plums

Shake in a screw-top jar:
½ cup safflower oil
4 tbs tarragon vinegar
½ cup lime juice
¼ cup honey
pinch nutmeg
1 beaten egg yolk (optional)

Toss salad in dressing and garnish with nasturtium flowers.

Nasturtium and Apple Jelly

Make apple or crab apple jelly as usual and add 2 crushed nasturtium leaves and 1 cup sugar to every ½ litre liquid. Stir and boil until jelly sets when tested on a saucer. Remove leaves and pour jelly into small jars, each containing a fresh nasturtium leaf.

Nasturtium Sauce

1 litre vinegar
6 peeled shallots
6 cloves
1 tsp salt

½ tsp pepper
1 litre nasturtium flowers
1 cup soya sauce

Boil together vinegar, shallots and seasonings for 10 minutes. Pour over flowers, cover and leave 1-2 months. Add soya sauce and strain into bottles.

Pickled Nasturtium Seedpods

Always use green seeds — do not leave them until they are yellow. When pickled they may be used as a caper substitute but taste different.

Combine and bring to the boil:
½ litre white wine vinegar
2 tsp salt
10 black peppercorns

4 cloves
½ tsp mace
1 crushed garlic clove

Allow liquid to cool and add nasturtium pods as they ripen. Store in a covered jar in a cool place.

or

1 cup small green nasturtium
  seedpods
1 cup water
1 tbs rock salt
1 tbs chopped onion

1 cup white vinegar
½ tsp salt
3 peppercorns
pinch each nutmeg and chilli
  powder

Wash seedpods, drain and place in a bowl. Cover with brine made from 1 cup water and 1 tbs rock salt. Leave 3 days, draining and covering with a fresh brine each day. Drain well and arrange in layers with chopped onion in a jar. Combine vinegar, salt, peppercorns and spices in a saucepan and boil for 10 minutes. Strain liquid over seedpods. Cover when cold with a plastic lid and store in a cool place. Ready to use in a week, but seedpods improve with keeping.

Nasturtium Soup

1 cup nasturtium flowers fried   *4 cups chicken stock*
  in a little butter   *salt and pepper to taste*

Heat chicken stock and add fried blossoms. Season to taste with salt and pepper and serve.

Oregano

The flavor is more pronounced when the herb is dry than when it is fresh. Gertrude B. Foster

Oregano is a flavour which is obtained from several cultivars of *Origanum vulgare* and also from some other plants. The *Origanum vulgare* cultivars, *prismaticum* and *Viride*, are the herbs which I grow and use. They are perennial, native to Greece, and grow as downy, green, mat-forming plants which have spikes of white flowers with green calyces, whereas wild marjoram, *O. vulgare*, has pink flowers and reddish bracts. Oregano may be grown from seed or root division and seems quite hardy in a sunny, well-drained situation. The leaves may be used fresh or dried, but the flavour is stronger dried. To dry oregano, the long flower stalks should be cut just as the flowers form, tied in bundles and hung in large, brown paper bags until quite crisp. Hang the bags in a shady, but warm and airy place, and when the leaves are crisp, strip them into dark glass containers. Do not dry the herb in too hot or sunny a place or the colour and flavour will not be good.

Oregano, finely chopped if fresh and crumbled if dry, is used with many different meat dishes, with tomatoes, courgettes and other vegetables, and is an essential ingredient in pizza. Because the flavour is strong, use it with a light hand and do not cook it for too long or the essential oils evaporate and leave a bitter taste.

278

Grilled Garlic Bread with Oregano

1 crushed clove garlic
1 tbs chopped oregano
2 tbs oil

pinch salt and pepper
6 thin slices bread

Crush garlic and oregano in a mortar with a pestle and gradually add oil, drop by drop, to make a thick sauce. Season with salt and pepper. Paint onto slices of bread with a brush and grill until warm and lightly brown.

Cooking Meat with Oregano

Chicken:

1 frying chicken
1-2 tbs each butter and oil
2 ripe, skinned, chopped
   tomatoes

2 cloves chopped garlic
1 tbs chopped parsley
1 tbs chopped oregano
salt and pepper to taste

Cut up chicken into small pieces and brown in butter and oil. Add rest of ingredients, cover and simmer until tender, and serve in the sauce.

Veal:

Slice meat thin and saute in a small amount of butter and oil. Add remaining ingredients and continue as above.

Steak:

Slice steak into thin strips and proceed as above.

Whole Steaks:

Brown steaks in hot oil quickly on both sides. Season with salt and pepper, remove from the pan and keep warm. Add garlic and tomato to pan and cook quickly until well blended. Return steaks to pan, sprinkle with oregano and cook a minute or two longer, according to taste, on both sides. Serve on warm plates with the sauce poured over and garnish with parsley.

Marinated Olives

500 g olives
1 cup oil
1 tsp each thyme and
    peppercorns

3 tsp oregano

Prick olives and pack into a jar with other ingredients. Cover, shake well and leave in refrigerator for 2 days before eating.

Oregano Dumplings

1 cup flour
1½ tsp baking powder
pinch salt

2 tbs butter
1 tbs finely chopped oregano
2 tbs water

Sift flour, salt and baking powder into a basin. Rub in butter until mixture is like breadcrumbs and add oregano. Mix to a soft dough with water and roll into small balls. Roll in flour, or use well-floured hands to shape them. Drop dumplings into a boiling stew or casserole, cover and cook 20 minutes. Serve with stews.

Grilled Steak with Oregano

Before grilling, rub steak with a cut clove of garlic. Combine and blend well 50 g softened butter, 1-2 tsp finely chopped oregano and a squeeze of lemon juice. Allow to chill 30 minutes in refrigerator for flavours to blend before using. Spread steak thinly with oregano butter and grill, or grill as usual and serve with a knob of oregano butter melting on each steak.

or

For each fillet steak use:
2 tbs olive oil
2-3 cloves crushed garlic

1 tsp oregano

Put oil in a dish with crushed garlic and leave one hour. Remove garlic, brush both sides of meat with oil and sprinkle with finely chopped oregano. Wrap in greaseproof paper and leave overnight in the refrigerator. Next day brush off herbs and grill steak. Serve with salt and pepper.

Liver with Oregano

Cook small pieces of liver for about 10 minutes in very hot oil or butter to seal in the meat juices. Drain and sprinkle with salt, pepper and 1 tsp finely chopped oregano.

Meatballs with Oregano-Tomato Sauce

350 g minced meat
150 g pork sausage meat
¼ cup raw rice
½ minced onion

salt and pepper
flour
3 tbs oil

Combine meat, rice and onion and mix well. Form into about 8 balls, roll in seasoned flour and fry until brown in hot oil. Remove to a sheet of brown paper and drain.

½ minced onion
1 clove crushed garlic
2 cups tomato puree
½ cup dry white wine

pinch nutmeg
½ tsp each oregano and
thyme

Add onion and garlic to oil in pan and fry gently for 10 minutes. Add liquids, nutmeg and herbs, and bring to the boil. Pour this sauce over meatballs in a heavy saucepan and cook slowly over a low heat for about 30 minutes. Serve with rice or mashed potatoes.

Tamale Pie

1 onion
1 tbs butter or lard
1 cup corn
1 cup skinned, chopped
   tomatoes
½ chopped green pepper

½ cup yellow cornmeal
½ cup cooked, minced meat
1 beaten egg
1 tsp oregano
salt and cayenne pepper to
taste

Cook minced onion in butter until soft, and add corn, tomatoes and green pepper. When this mixture boils, gradually stir in cornmeal and cook for 20 minutes, stirring often. Mix in meat and allow to cool. Add beaten egg, finely chopped oregano and salt and pepper to taste. Pour into a buttered ovenproof dish and bake at 180°C for 30-45 minutes.

Pizza and Spaghetti Sauce

For the pizza dough:
2 cups flour
1 tsp sugar
1 tbs dried yeast

½ cup water
1 tsp salt
5 tbs oil

For the filling:
1 peeled, sliced onion
oil for frying
1 crushed clove garlic
500 g skinned, chopped
   tomatoes

1 bay leaf
1 tsp each salt and sugar
1 tsp oregano
pepper to taste
grated cheese for topping

Sift 1 cup flour into a basin, add sugar, stir in dried yeast and mix well. Pour in ½ cup lukewarm water and mix thoroughly. Leave until mixture begins to bubble a little, then add remaining flour, salt and oil. Mix well and knead lightly until dough is soft and elastic. Leave to rise in a basin covered with a cloth, for about an hour. Knead dough again, place on a floured surface and flatten with your hands. Make a circle 25-30cm across, place on a greased, floured baking tray, and cover with filling.

Make the filling by frying sliced onion in hot oil until transparent. Add garlic and fry for one more minute. Add remaining ingredients and simmer gently, stirring often, for about an hour until thick. Cool before spreading on the dough, and leave pizza to prove for 30 minutes before topping with grated cheese and baking at 220 °C for 30 minutes, fairly low in the oven. If you make the filling while the dough is rising in the basin, it is generally cool enough to spread when the dough has been finally shaped.

Spaghetti Sauce

500 g minced steak
1 finely chopped clove garlic
1 peeled, chopped onion
2 tbs oil
500 g skinned, chopped
   tomatoes

salt and pepper
1 tbs finely, chopped oregano
1 cup beef stock

Fry together steak, garlic and onion in hot oil in a heavy pan. When it is evenly browned add tomatoes, seasonings and stock. Cover and simmer gently for 30 minutes. This is sufficient to serve with

flowers and pat them dry with paper towels because little
bugs sometimes hide among the petals.

Nasturtium Cigarettes

Spread washed, dried, tender nasturtium leaves with a mixture of
savoury fish, or cream or cottage cheese to taste. Finely chopped
chives, raisins or nuts may be added. Roll leaves up and tie with a
long-stemmed nasturtium flower or fasten with a toothpick.

Nasturtium Butter

Mince or chop finely young leaves, stems and flowers of nasturtium
and mix into softened butter using about 1 tbs to each 50 g butter.
Leave about 30 minutes in a covered container and use to spread on
biscuits or bread.

Cottage or Cream Cheese with Nasturtium

Remove pistil and stamens from flowers and stuff with cottage or
cream cheese to taste. Raisins, nuts or finely chopped herbs may be
added to cheese.

Nasturtium Flowers Stuffed with Fish

Blend together a little flaked tuna, chopped parsley and
mayonnaise. Remove pistil and stamens from flowers and stuff
each with 1 tsp of the fish mixture.

Stuffed Nasturtium Flowers

Blend well together:
mashed pulp of 2 ripe   6 small tomatoes, chopped
  avocados   2 tbs finely chopped onion
2 cloves garlic, minced   1 tbs fresh oregano
2 tbs lemon juice   pinch cayenne pepper

Stuff nasturtium flowers with mixture and serve with lettuce salad,
cold meat and/or bread and butter.

Nasturtium Sandwiches

8 thin slices bread
small carton cream cheese

12 nasturtium flowers
12 nasturtium leaves

Spread 4 slices bread with cream cheese and sprinkle with 8 finely chopped nasturtium flowers, without pistil and stamens, and 12 finely chopped leaves. Top with 4 slices bread spread with more cream cheese. Place a whole flower on each sandwich and serve.

or

nasturtium flowers or young
leaves

buttered brown bread
mayonnaise

Wash and lightly dry flowers on paper towels. Remove petals and arrange on slices of buttered brown bread which have been spread with a little mayonnaise. Cover with another slice of brown bread and serve. Young leaves may be used instead, but they are more like cress in flavour. They go well with white bread and marmite too.

Chilled Peaches with Nasturtium

3 cups ripe, sliced peaches
1 cup orange juice
½ cup lemon juice

sugar to taste
nasturtium flowers

Arrange sliced peaches in a dish and pour over orange and lemon juice mixed together. Sprinkle with sugar to taste, and chill. Serve garnished with nasturtium blossoms.

Fresh Pear and Nasturtium Fruit Salad

1½ cups cold syrup
4 ripe pears
4-6 nasturtium flowers

chopped, crystallised ginger
(optional)

Pour syrup into a serving dish and peel and slice ripe pears into it. Chill in refrigerator, and before serving arrange nasturtium flowers among the pears. Chopped ginger may be added.

250 g raw spaghetti cooked in boiling water and may be garnished with grated cheese, fried bacon and parsley to taste.

Courgette and Oregano Salad

1 kg small courgettes
boiling water
1-2 capsicums
4 tbs chopped shallots or
  1 onion
2 tbs finely chopped parsley
1 tbs finely chopped oregano

½ cup safflower oil
3 tbs cider or wine vinegar
2 tsp honey
1 tsp salt
freshly milled pepper
stoned olives to garnish

Slice courgettes in rounds and blanch in boiling water for 2 minutes. Drain and when cold place in a serving bowl with de-seeded and chopped capsicums (red if possible for contrast), chopped shallots or finely sliced onion, and the herbs. Combine oil, vinegar, honey, salt and pepper in a screw-top jar and shake well. Pour over salad and toss. Chill and serve garnished with olives.

Tomato and Oregano Salad

500 g firm, ripe tomatoes
2 white onions
1 tsp sugar
2 tsp finely chopped oregano
1 tsp salt
pepper to taste

2 tbs dry white wine
2 tbs oil
finely chopped parsley
asparagus spears (optional)
olives (optional)

Layer sliced tomatoes and peeled, sliced onions in a serving dish. Combine seasonings, wine and oil, and mix well. Pour over tomatoes and leave to marinate 2 hours in the refrigerator. Sprinkle with parsley before serving, and garnish with asparagus and olives.

Oregano Courgettes

Slice courgettes in 2cm thick slices and dip in beaten egg. Then roll in a mixture of fine breadcrumbs, salt and pepper with 1 tsp of crumbled oregano added. Fry in oil or butter until tender.

Stuffed Eggplant with Oregano

2 large eggplants
2 tbs oil
1 sliced onion
2 chopped cloves garlic
750 g minced meat

500 g skinned, chopped
  tomatoes
2 tbs finely chopped oregano
salt and pepper to taste
grated cheese

Halve eggplants longways and fry in hot oil for 5 minutes each side. Drain on brown paper. Add sliced onion and garlic to oil and when soft, add meat and cook until lightly browned. Add tomatoes, oregano and seasoning. Scoop pulp out of eggplants and leave the shells intact. Add pulp to the ingredients in frying pan and cook mixture until it is well blended. When thoroughly cooked, pile mixture into eggplant shells and bake in a moderate oven, 180 °C, until shells are tender and cheese is well melted. Any extra filling can be cooked in an ovenproof dish, topped with cheese in the same way.

Vegetable Stew with Oregano

3 peeled, sliced onions
1 minced clove garlic
4 tbs oil
5 large green peppers

3 skinned, chopped tomatoes
salt and pepper
1-3 tsp oregano
2 peeled, diced potatoes

Cook onions and garlic in hot oil, gently, for about 20 minutes but do not allow to brown. Add deseeded and sliced pepper and chopped tomatoes and stir well. Season with salt and pepper, add oregano and cook, covered, for 20 minutes. Finally add potatoes, stir, cover and cook slowly for about an hour, stirring. Taste and season as necessary and serve with slices of fresh bread and a green salad.

Cabbage with Oregano

1 medium cabbage, shredded
3 tbs butter
1 chopped onion
1 chopped green pepper
6-8 skinned tomatoes

1½-2 tsp oregano
2 tsp salt
1 tsp sugar
2 tsp lemon juice

Cook shredded cabbage very gently in a little boiling water in a covered saucepan for 8-10 minutes. Drain. Melt butter and saute chopped onion and green pepper until soft, add tomatoes and simmer gently for about 12 minutes. Pour tomato mixture over the cabbage, add remaining ingredients and reheat, stirring until heated through.

Corn and Oregano Pie

3 minced onions
1 minced clove garlic
1 deseeded, minced green
 pepper
3 tbs oil
1 kg minced, cooked meat
1 cup seedless raisins
½ cup stock or vegetable
 water

salt, pepper and nutmeg to
 taste
3 tsp finely chopped oregano
3 tins whole kernel corn
4 hard-boiled eggs
paprika

Fry onions, garlic and green pepper in oil until soft. Add meat, raisins and stock and heat through. Add seasonings and herbs, stirring well. Drain corn from tins and use 2 tinsful to line a large ovenproof or meat dish. Fill the centre with meat mixture and add slices of hard-boiled egg. Cover with remaining corn and sprinkle with a little paprika. Bake 30 minutes at 180°C.

Courgette Frittata with Oregano

2 peeled, halved cloves garlic
5 tbs oil
1 peeled, sliced onion
9 eggs
1 cup toasted breadcrumbs

salt and pepper
¼ cup chopped parsley
1-2 tsp oregano
½ cup grated cheese
500 g cold cooked courgettes

Cook garlic halves speared on toothpicks in 2 tbs oil until brown. Add onion and cook until transparent. Remove and discard garlic. Beat eggs and combine with all ingredients in a basin including the slightly cooled onion and oil mixture from the pan. Blend well and return to the pan. Cover and cook over a low heat until sides of the frittata come away from the sides of the pan and the centre is set. Finish cooking by placing the pan under a grill to brown the top. Serve in slices.

Parsley

The leaves are pleasant in sauces and broth, in which beside that they give a pleasant taste, they be also singular good to take away stoppings and to provoke urine...   John Gerard

Parsley, *Petroselinum crispum,* is an annual or biennial, native to the Mediterranean. It is probably the best known and most used of all herbs and is rich in vitamins and minerals. It is grown from seed which is slow to germinate. Plants, if set about 20-30cm apart in good soil and kept well watered in hot weather, will produce lots of leaves for use in the kitchen. Parsley stalks should always be picked around the outside of the plant — if you pick the small stalks from the middle, the plant can not grow. In its second year parsley will go to seed and then the leaves do not taste so good. However, if 1-2 plants are left to self-sow there are usually plenty of seedlings for transplanting later.

The leaves of parsley are usually served finely chopped as a garnish, or in sauces, salads, soups, with eggs, meat and fish to taste. The stalks are used as part of a bouquet garni to give flavour to dishes that are cooked longer. Plain-leaved and curly parsley are equally good to use, and the roots of Hamburg parsley are used like carrots. Parsley may be frozen in ice cubes in the same way as basil. It is an important plant in our diet for it contains iron and vitamin C in balance so that iron may be absorbed. Parsley is best used fresh but tastes excellent cooked. However if drunk as a tea it should only be taken in moderation because it is a diuretic.

Parsley Cheese Ball

100 g blue vein cheese
100 g cheddar cheese
75 g cream cheese
2 tbs evaporated milk

2 tsp Worcestershire sauce
¼ onion, grated
½ cup chopped walnuts
½ cup chopped parsley

Allow cheese to warm to room temperature, then grate and mix with cream cheese. Blend in milk, sauce and grated onion. Combine chopped walnuts and parsley on a sheet of greaseproof paper, form cheese into a ball and roll it in the walnut-parsley mixture, to coat all sides. Wrap in foil and leave to allow flavours to blend before serving with crackers.

Egg, Prawn and Parsley Entree

4 hard-boiled eggs
small tin prawns
1 tbs French mustard
salt and pepper to taste
1 tbs finely chopped parsley

½ cup cream
4 tbs grated cheese
4 tbs breadcrumbs
25 g butter

Chop eggs finely and mix in drained prawns. Add mustard, seasoning, parsley and cream and mix well. Place in buttered ramekins and sprinkle with a mixture of grated cheese and breadcrumbs. Dot with a little butter and brown in the oven at 180 °C until heated through.

Tahini and Parsley Dip

1 cup tahini
1 cup lemon juice
4 minced cloves garlic

1 tsp salt
1 cup finely chopped parsley
½ cup finely chopped mint

Blend all together well, season to taste and add more lemon juice if too thick. Serve with bread, biscuits or chips.

Parsley Pancakes

½ cup flour
pinch salt
1 beaten egg
¾ cup milk

¼ cup finely chopped parsley
25-50 g chive butter
pepper to taste

Sift flour and salt together into a bowl, make a well in centre of mixture and add combined beaten egg and milk, a little at a time, to make a smooth batter. Add parsley and mix well. Leave to stand 30 minutes. Melt a small amount of butter in a small pan, coating surface all over. Stir batter and pour a little into the pan, spreading evenly over the whole surface. Cook pancake until bubbly on top and brown underneath, turn and cook the other side. Continue until all the mixture is used. Spread with chive butter and eat as a hot savoury with, or without, vegetables and/or salad, or allow to cool, spread with chive butter, season to taste, and roll up before cutting into slices to serve as a cocktail savoury.

Parsley, Chive and Bean Sprout Biscuits

4 tbs butter
2 cups flour
2 tsp baking powder
1 tsp salt

¼ cup mung bean sprouts
2 tbs chopped parsley
2 tbs chopped chives
⅔ cup buttermilk

Mix butter into flour, baking powder and salt until mixture is crumbly. Stir in chopped sprouts and herbs and mix to a soft dough with buttermilk. Knead, roll out and cut into rounds or fingers. Bake at 215 °C for 15 minutes.

Parsley Drop Scones

2 cups flour
4 tsp baking powder
½ tsp salt
2 tsp sugar

2 tbs butter
1 cup chopped parsley
¾-1 cup milk

Sift together flour, baking powder and salt and mix in sugar. Rub in butter to form a crumbly mixture, add parsley and mix well. Make a well in the centre and gradually stir in milk to make a dough that will drop easily by spoonfuls into greased patty tins. Bake at 200 °C for 10-15 minutes until light, puffy and brown. Serve as a potato substitute, or with hot soup.

Cheese Muffins

Sift together 1½ cups flour, 2 tsp baking powder and ¼ tsp salt. Add 1 chopped spring onion, some parsley and 100 g grated cheese. Mix together with ⅔ cup milk and 1 beaten egg. Bake at 200 °C for 15-20 minutes in greased muffin tins.

Maitre d'Hotel Butter

Blend well together:
½ cup softened butter
2 tbs lemon juice

2½ tbs finely chopped parsley
pinch salt and pepper

When thoroughly blended, chill until butter can be placed on a piece of greaseproof paper and rolled into a cylinder about 2½ cm in diameter. Chill roll until firm and store in the refrigerator. To serve, cut roll into 1cm thick slices and place a slice on hot steak immediately before serving.

Parsley Butter for Snails

1 clove garlic
1 small, finely chopped onion

2 tbs finely chopped parsley
75 g butter

Crush garlic and mix with onion and parsley into softened butter with a fork. Put cleaned, cooked snails back in their shells using the handle of a teaspoon to press them in, and fill snail shell with parsley butter. Put a fairly thick layer of plain salt in a baking dish, set the snail shells upright so butter does not run out, and cook for 5 minutes at 200 °C. The butter runs down into the snails and they taste delicious.

Green Sauce for Vegetables

1 large handful parsley
1 tbs capers
1-2 cloves crushed garlic
1-2 anchovy fillets

4 tbs oil
1 slice white bread
1 tbs lemon juice
salt and pepper

Chop parsley without stalks and blend with capers, crushed garlic and anchovies. Soak bread without crusts in oil, add to parsley mixture and pound all together. Add lemon juice and season to taste. Serve as a thick sauce with vegetables.

Parsley Sauce

To serve with boiled chicken, eggs, fish or ham. Infuse 1 bay leaf, 1 blade mace, 6 peppercorns and stalks of 2 handfuls of parsley in 2 cups of hot milk. Boil leafy sprigs of parsley in a little water for 5 minutes, drain and rub through a sieve to make 1 dessertspoon of parsley puree. Melt 40 g butter in a pan, remove from the heat and stir in 2 tbs flour. Blend in strained milk and return to the stove. Stir until boiling, season with salt and pepper and simmer for 2-3 minutes before stirring in parsley.

Persillade Sauce

1 hard-boiled egg
3 tbs French dressing

6 tbs finely chopped, fresh parsley

Mash hard-boiled egg and mix in other ingredients. Spoon into a dish, cover and leave 30 minutes to develop flavour.

Parsley Cocktail

Liquidise together:
2 cups shredded spinach
1 cup each parsley and watercress

3 cups orange juice

Parsley Lemonade

To each ¼ litre boiling water use 2 handfuls chopped parsley and 1 chunky cut lemon. Put parsley and lemon in a bowl and pour on boiling water. Stand 15 minutes, squeeze out juice and strain into a jug. Chill before drinking.

Parsley Wine

500 g parsley
5 litres water

juice 2 lemons
1 tsp strong tea

1½ kg sugar   *pkt yeast and nutrient*

Put parsley in a large saucepan with water and bring to the boil. Simmer about 5 minutes, cover and allow to cool a little before straining onto the sugar. Stir well to dissolve sugar and when it is lukewarm add tea, strained lemon juice and the wine yeast and nutrient. Stir well, cover and leave to ferment vigorously for 1-2 days in a large container before pouring into containers fitted with airlocks to continue fermentation. When this ceases siphon into clean, dry bottles and cork. Leave 6 months before drinking.

Baked Oysters

3 dozen oysters   *4-5 drops tabasco sauce*
2 cups spinach, washed and   *½ cup breadcrumbs*
  dried   *½ cup butter*
1 cup chopped parsley   *salt and pepper*
1 cup spring onions

For 6 people, arrange 6 oysters each in 6 ramekins and add about 1 tbs water to each. Puree spinach, parsley and spring onions, add tabasco sauce, breadcrumbs, butter and seasoning and work to a paste with a wooden spoon. Put oysters in a hot oven, 200-220 °C and cook until edges of oysters begin to curl. Remove from the oven and cover oysters with a generous dollop of the green paste. Return to the oven and bake until the dish is heated through but do not allow to burn — about 5 more minutes.

Fish Fillets with Parsley

500 g filleted fish   *100 g butter*
seasoned flour   *lime or lemon juice*
oil for frying   *1-3 tbs finely chopped parsley*

Cut fish into convenient pieces and roll in seasoned flour to coat both sides. Fry until tender, browning both sides. Drain fish on brown paper and place in a warm serving dish. Pour oil away, melt butter in pan and pour browned butter over fish. Sprinkle with lime or lemon juice and finely chopped parsley and serve.

Fish Pie

⅓ cup rice
salt
water
100 g butter
1 onion
50 g mushrooms (optional)

300-400 g puff pastry
2 tbs finely chopped parsley
200 g tin salmon
2 hard-boiled eggs
salt and pepper to taste

Cook rice in boiling salted water for 10-15 minutes and drain. Melt 50 g butter in a pan and fry sliced onion and mushrooms for 5 minutes. Divide pastry in half and roll out into 2 rectangles, 30 x 15cm. Lay one piece of pastry on a baking tray and arrange rice in a wide strip down the middle. Spread with onion, parsley and mushrooms. Flake salmon on top, and finally add sliced, hard-boiled eggs. Season each layer with salt and pepper to taste. Damp edges of pastry and lay the second piece of pastry over the filling. Press edges together, slit the top in several places to allow the steam to escape, and bake in a hot oven, 220 °C, for about 30 minutes. Melt remaining 50 g butter and pour into the pie through the slits just before serving.

Sauteed Paua

2 beaten eggs
¼ cup grated cheese
¼ tsp thyme
1 tbs finely chopped parsley
salt and pepper

6 paua, beaten flat
breadcrumbs
oil
lemon slices

Mix beaten egg with cheese, thyme, parsley and seasoning. Dip paua in this mixture and then in breadcrumbs and fry in hot oil in a moderately hot pan. Turn when light brown, and fry other side. When fish feels tender, remove and serve with lemon slices.

Parsley Jelly

Wash about 50 stalks of parsley, put them in a pan with lemon peel and cover with water. Cover and simmer about an hour. Strain liquid and discard parsley. Add 1 cup sugar to every cup of liquid and juice of 2-3 lemons. Return to the pan, bring to the boil, stirring to dissolve sugar, and boil until it sets when tested on a saucer. Pour into warm jars and seal when cold. Serve with chicken or fish, or on herb scones.

Parsley Stuffing for Fish or Fowl

Mix in a basin:
1½ cups soft breadcrumbs
1 cup chopped parsley
1 small onion, grated
2 tsp fresh sage, chopped
salt and pepper to taste

Bind with:
juice ½ lemon
1 tsp soya sauce
2 tbs melted butter

Chicken Fricassee

1 young hen
seasoned flour
3 tbs oil
boiling water
½ bay leaf
5 freshly ground peppercorns
1 tsp summer savory

2 whole shallots
4 tbs butter
4 tbs flour
1 egg or 2 egg yolks
1 cup hot milk or cream
1 cup finely chopped parsley

Skin and cut up hen and roll pieces in seasoned flour. Heat oil in a deep saucepan and brown pieces on all sides. Add boiling water to cover, and bay, pepper, summer savory, chopped shallots and their green tops. Cover and simmer until meat is tender. Remove chicken from stock and keep warm. Make up quantity of the liquid to 3 cups if necessary. In another saucepan melt butter, stir in flour and gradually add 1 cup hot stock, stirring to prevent lumps forming. Let this cook slowly for several minutes to cook flour, then stir in remaining stock and simmer 10 minutes. Beat egg or egg yolks in a basin and stir in hot cream or milk. Remove gravy from heat and gradually stir in egg mixture. Taste and season with more salt if necessary. Add chicken and parsley and reheat but do not boil.

Cooked leftover chicken may be combined with a white sauce and fresh parsley and reheated in an ovenproof dish topped with breadcrumbs and dotted with butter if a less elaborate fricassee is wanted.

Kidney and Mushroom with Parsley

4 prepared lamb kidneys	1 tsp chopped summer savory
1 tbs butter	6 large mushrooms
½ peeled sliced onion	¼ cup stock
1 tbs flour	1 tbs finely chopped parsley
salt and pepper	

Prepare kidneys by skinning them, slicing and removing membranes. Blanch them by dropping into boiling water, and drain. Melt butter and brown onion, add kidneys and sautee them to brown both sides. Sprinkle with flour, season to taste, and add savory. Cook gently for 5 minutes on each side. Add peeled, sliced mushrooms and stock and cook 5-8 more minutes until all is tender and sauce thick. Serve with parsley sprinkled over mixture and a big plate of hot buttered toast.

Veal and Parsley Sauce

4 pieces veal schnitzel	2 peeled, cored, sliced pears
2 tbs butter	½ cup chicken stock
2 tsp grated root ginger	2 tbs each cream and brandy
3-4 tbs finely chopped parsley	salt and pepper

Cut veal into bite-sized pieces and cook in melted butter in a frying pan with ginger and 3 tbs parsley. Cook until meat is browned on both sides, then add pears and stock. Cover and simmer until meat and pears are tender, about 15 minutes. Remove meat and pears with a slotted spoon to a warmed serving dish. Boil pan liquid down to ½ cup and stir in cream and brandy. Season to taste, and pour over meat. Sprinkle with remaining parsley and serve.

Parsley Steak

1 onion, sliced	1 kg stewing steak
6 tbs finely chopped parsley	1½ cups stock
½ tsp dried mixed herbs	salt and pepper
4 tbs butter	1 tbs brown sugar

Combine chopped onion and parsley with mixed herbs. Melt butter and cut meat into 2cm cubes. Roll these in melted butter, then in herb-onion mixture and brown in remaining butter in a frying pan. Pour into a casserole, add stock and seasoning to taste, and cook about 2 hours at 180 °C.

Parsley Water Ice

1 lemon	*2 tbs finely chopped parsley*
1 cup water	*1 tbs dry sherry*
100 g sugar	*1 stiffly beaten egg white*

Peel lemon rind off in thin strips and put it, lemon juice, water and sugar in a saucepan and bring to the boil, stirring to dissolve sugar. Add parsley and simmer 5 minutes. Cool, remove lemon peel, add sherry and pour into an ice-cream tray and freeze. When mixture is semi-set, take it out, pour into a basin and beat in stiffly beaten egg white. Return to the tray and freeze until set. Serve on a bed of ice.

Broad Bean Salad with Parsley

Cook broad beans in usual way and while warm cover with this dressing. Mix well together:

1 tbs tarragon vinegar	*1 crushed clove garlic*
3 tbs oil	*salt and freshly ground pepper*
1 tsp mustard powder	*to taste*
1 tsp paprika	*1 tbs finely chopped parsley*

Pour over warm beans and allow to cool before serving.

Green Mayonnaise

Place in an electric blender and puree at high speed:

1½ cups mayonnaise	*1 tbs chopped chives*
¼ cup parsley sprigs	*2 tbs dry white wine*
¼ cup watercress leaves (no stems)	

Tip into a container and store, covered, in the refrigerator overnight. ½-1 cup torn, tender spinach may be added. If you have no blender, mince or mouli the greens twice, and mix well with mayonnaise and wine afterwards.

Tabuli

2 cups raw cracked wheat
1 cup warm water
1 cup lemon juice (or less)
½ cup finely chopped onion
salt and pepper to taste

1 cup finely chopped parsley
  or dandelion
2 sliced tomatoes, or grated
  carrot, or cabbage
fresh herbs to garnish

Soak wheat in water until water is absorbed. Add remaining ingredients, garnish with finely chopped fresh herbs — mint is nice — and store in a cool place until served.

Tomato and Parsley Salad

Cut top off individual tomatoes, loosen pulp with a teaspoon, sprinkle with a little salt and turn upside down to drain. Pound together a mixture of 2 cloves garlic, 2 or more sprigs of parsley, a pinch of salt and a little oil. Put a small spoonful of mixture into each drained tomato and leave 2 hours to absorb flavour before serving.

Parsley Soup

3 peeled, diced potatoes
1 peeled, sliced onion
1½ cups chopped parsley

1-2 tsp salt
pepper to taste
6 cups chicken stock or water

Combine all ingredients in a saucepan, cover and bring to the boil. Simmer 30-45 minutes until vegetables are soft. Blend or mouli to make a puree and return to the saucepan. Taste and add more salt or pepper if necessary. Reheat but do not boil and serve garnished with more finely chopped parsley.

or

1 tbs butter
1 tbs flour
pinch salt and pepper
2 cups milk
1 cup water

1 sliced onion
1 beaten egg
½ cup cream
½ cup finely chopped parsley

Melt butter in a saucepan and stir in flour. Gradually add

seasoning, milk and water, and sliced onion. Bring to the boil, stirring, and simmer gently for 10-15 minutes. Strain out onion. Combine beaten egg with cream, stir into the strained liquid and cook, stirring until thick. Just before serving add finely chopped parsley, taste and adjust seasoning.

Plum and Parsley Soup

12 large red plums
1 clove of garlic (optional)
½ tsp salt

4-5 tbs chopped parsley
1½ cups water
pepper and sugar to taste

Stone plums and chop them finely. Crush garlic with salt and combine all ingredients in a saucepan. Heat gently, stirring, until plums are pulpy but do not let mixture boil. Serve warm or very cold. Sugar and/or pepper may be added to taste.

Baked Asparagus

500 g cooked, drained
   asparagus
1-2 hard-boiled eggs
3 tbs finely chopped parsley

juice ½ lemon
2 tbs butter
1 cup breadcrumbs

Place asparagus in a buttered ovenproof dish and cover with a mixture of sieved hard-boiled egg and parsley. Squeeze over a little lemon juice and top with breadcrumbs previously sauteed in butter. Place in a moderate oven, 180 °C, until heated through.

Cauliflower Sauteed with Parsley

1 tbs butter
3 tbs oil
1 crushed clove garlic
1 cauliflower cooked and
   broken into florets

salt and pepper
1-2 tbs finely chopped parsley

Heat butter and oil together and fry crushed garlic. Add cauliflower florets and turn until each piece is coated with oil. Season, stir again, then cover and cook gently about 5 minutes. Turn into a serving dish and gently toss parsley through it.

Artichokes and Peas

12 baby artichokes
500 g green peas
1 tbs oil
1 clove garlic
1 sliced onion
500 g skinned, chopped
 tomatoes

1 cup mushrooms
½ tsp rosemary
1 cup chopped parsley
salt and pepper

Wash artichokes and peel off tough outer leaves. Cut off tops and halve artichokes. Put in a saucepan of boiling water, add shelled peas and cook 15 minutes. Heat oil in another pan, add garlic cut in half with a toothpick in each piece. Add onion and cook gently 10 minutes. Add tomatoes, peeled, sliced mushrooms and rosemary, and cook slowly for 30 minutes. Remove and discard garlic, add parsley, taste and season. Add drained vegetables to the sauce and pour into a buttered casserole. Bake at 160 °C for about an hour.

Vichy Carrots

8-10 baby carrots
1½ tbs butter
4 tbs boiling water

½ tsp salt
2 tbs finely chopped parsley

Scrub carrots and slice into thin rounds or strips. Put in a heavy-bottomed saucepan with butter, water and salt, cover and cook at a low heat until liquid is absorbed and carrots tender. Toss in parsley and serve hot.

Stuffed Eggplant with Parsley

4 eggplants
salt
4 tbs oil
1 small onion
1 small red pepper
2 cloves crushed garlic

250 g minced meat
2 tbs chopped parsley
2 tbs pine nuts
¾ cup fresh breadcrumbs
freshly ground black pepper

Cut eggplants in half lengthways and score pulp with a knife. Sprinkle with salt and leave 20-30 minutes, then drain. Brush with oil and grill slowly until tender, about 20 minutes. Remove pulp from skins and chop finely. Heat 1 tbs oil and fry sliced onion, red pepper and crushed garlic for 5 minutes. Tip into a bowl with eggplant pulp, meat, parsley, nuts and breadcrumbs. Season to taste. Blend well, then put back into eggplant skins. Place in a greased ovenproof dish, sprinkle with a little oil and bake in a moderate oven, 190 °C for 20-30 minutes.

Frittata with Parsley

Make as for *Frittata with Oregano*, adding ⅓ cup finely chopped parsley. Other cooked vegetables can be substituted for cooked courgettes, e.g. asparagus or beans, and the whole may be cooked in a baking dish in the oven at 180 °C until frittata is set and brown on top.

Hamburg Parsley

The roots may be used grated raw into salads, or boiled or steamed, whole or sliced, and served with butter, salt, pepper and a garnish of chervil. The cooked roots may also be served in a casserole in white sauce containing eggs, whole, or beaten into sauce, topped with grated cheese and/or slices of bacon and grilled in the oven.

Mushrooms with Chives and Parsley

500 g mushrooms
oil or butter for frying
salt and pepper

1 tbs finely chopped parsley
1 tsp chives

Peel and slice mushrooms and their stems and cook gently in oil with salt and pepper, parsley and chives until they are just tender. Serve in their sauce.

Baked Tomatoes

Arrange 6 tomatoes cut in half horizontally in a shallow ovenproof dish with their cut sides up. Sprinkle with salt and pepper and top with a mixture of 1 cup fresh breadcrumbs, 2 tbs chopped parsley and 1 crushed clove garlic. Dot with butter and bake at 180 °C for 15-20 minutes.

Rose

*The fruit when it is ripe maketh most pleasant
meates and banqueting dishes, as tarts and such-
like.*
John Gerard

There are thousands of different roses but those which were originally used for food and medicine were *Rosa gallica officinalis,* the Apothecary's rose, *Rosa centifolia,* the cabbage rose and *Rosa damascena,* the damask rose. The roses used for hips were *Rosa canina,* the dog rose, *Rosa rubiginosa,* the eglantine and nowadays the rugosa roses, all of which have a much higher vitamin C content than citrus fruit. No rose is poisonous, however, and all scented rose petals may be used in cooking, though the red rose is traditionally preferred.

To use rose petals: Gather whole scented roses which are dry of dew and rain, carefully strip off their petals and cut off the slightly bitter white base to the petal. Rose petals are used to make butters, jams, drinks or rose water, but do not use roses which are too full-blown because their scent, flavour and texture are not so delicate.

To prepare rose hips: Snip off plump, ripe, well-coloured hips and trim off the blossom end with scissors. Always use stainless steel knives, wooden spoons and glass, stainless steel or enamel basins and saucepans — never aluminium which has a detrimental effect on the vitamin C. Cook rapidly in a covered pan and cook quickly to preserve vitamin C. Strain

300

out hairs and seeds or rub through a sieve if the hairs and seeds have not been scooped out first. Store in dark glass containers, or away from light and heat, to preserve the vitamin C. Rose hips may also be dried and used for teas or drinks. *Rosa rugosa* 'Frau Dagmar Hastrup' gives quantities of large hips which may be eaten raw — nibble the sweet pulp around the outside and leave the hairs and seeds in the middle.

Rose Petal Butter

Line a dish with fragrant rose petals. Add butter and cover with more rose petals. Cover the dish and leave overnight for butter to absorb rose flavour. Use to butter bread for afternoon tea, or rose petal sandwiches, or scones.

Rose Sugar Cookies

1 cup butter
1 cup rose sugar
2 beaten eggs
2¾ cups sifted flour
2-3 tsp baking powder

2 tbs rose water or 1 tsp rose syrup
2 tbs anise or caraway seeds
sultanas or raisins to garnish
rose sugar

Cream butter and sugar and beat in eggs. Mix well and add sifted flour and baking powder alternately with rose water or syrup, and seeds. Stir until well combined then drop small spoonfuls on greased baking trays and press a raisin or sultana in centre of each. Sprinkle with a little more rose sugar and bake at 190 °C until lightly browned, about 15-20 minutes.

Rose Petal Sandwiches

Spread brown bread with butter and/or cream cheese, add a sprinkle of sugar and/or ground cinnamon and lay rose petals on top. Close sandwich with more buttered bread. Rose butter and rose sugar may be used in the sandwiches.

Rose Brandy

Add 2 cups rose petals to every 1 litre brandy, and infuse for a month. Then make a syrup of 2 cups sugar to 3 cups water and bring to the boil, stirring to dissolve sugar. Add 2 cups rose petals, cover, remove from the heat and stand an hour. Strain syrup and brandy, discard rose petals and bottle the liqueur.

Rossolio

8 litres scented rose petals
boiling water
vodka

cinnamon and water
sugar syrup or orange blossom
    syrup to taste

Pour rose petals into a very large pyrex or china container and cover with boiling water. Infuse overnight. Strain, measure the liquid and discard the rose petals. To every 2 cups liquid add 1 cup vodka which has been flavoured with 1 tsp cinnamon dissolved in 1 tbs hot water and strained. Sweeten to taste with syrup or orange blossom syrup, then bottle and cork.

Rose Petal Ice Blocks

Half fill an ice block tray with water and freeze it hard. Tip out the half blocks and lay a rose petal in each section. Replace the half block and fill the tray up with water. The half block will hold the rose petal under so that it is set in the centre of the block. Float the rose petal ice blocks in summer drinks.

Rose and Pineapple Punch

6 red or pink roses
2 litres cold water
¼ cup lemon juice

450 g crushed pineapple
sugar to taste

Cover rose petals with cold water and stand in a cold place (but not the refrigerator), for 4-6 hours. Strain out roses and add strained lemon juice and chilled crushed pineapple. Mix well and add sugar. Pour into glasses and float a rose petal in each.

Rose Petal Wine

4 litres water   juice 1 lemon
2 litres rose petals   wine yeast and nutrient
5 cups sugar

Bring water to the boil and pour over rose petals and sugar and stir well. When lukewarm, add lemon juice, stir again and then add wine yeast and nutrient. Cover and leave to ferment in a warm place for a week, stirring daily. Strain into a container fitted with an airlock and leave to ferment. Rack off when a deposit has formed and siphon into clean bottles when fermentation ceases. Cork and leave 6 months before drinking.

Rose Petal Conserve

5 cups rose petals   strained juice 1 large lemon
1 litre water   1 kg sugar

Simmer rose petals in water gently for 5 minutes in a large saucepan. Strain out and reserve the petals. Return liquid to the saucepan and add lemon juice and sugar. Stir to dissolve sugar, add rose petals and bring to the boil. Boil fast 5 minutes, remove from the heat and bottle. Seal when cold. This conserve is not thick and is suitable for using to flavour desserts.

Crystallised Rose Petals

Combine equal quantities of gum arabic, or acacia powder (from the chemist) and water, e.g. 4 tbs acacia powder and 4 tbs water. Leave 24 hours and add 1 tbs sugar. Strain into a clean jar and paint this solution onto heeled rose petals with a fine paintbrush. Dip each petal into castor sugar and set aside to dry on waxed paper. When quite dry store in an air-tight container between layers of waxed paper.

or

Lightly beat the white of an egg and paint this onto rose petals. Dip into castor sugar and proceed as above.

Rose Petal Honey

1 litre honey   ½ litre rose petals

Heat honey nearly to the boil. Add rose petals and stand, covered, for 3-4 hours. Reheat honey and rose petals, then strain out petals and pour honey into jars.

Rose Petal Jam

1 cup sugar   2 tbs strained lemon juice
3 tbs water   1¼ cups fragrant rose petals

Put sugar, water and lemon juice in a saucepan and bring to the boil, stirring to dissolve sugar. Strip rose petals from their stems and stamens and add to syrup. Cook gently for 20-30 minutes, stirring often. Pour into little pots and seal when cold.

Rose Petal and Strawberry Jam

2½ cups fragrant rose petals   1½ cups strawberries
1 cup water   2 tbs lemon juice
2 cups sugar   pinch cream of tartar

Trim and discard white bases off petals and put petals in a saucepan with water and sugar. Wash, hull and halve strawberries, add them and rest of ingredients to the saucepan. Heat slowly, stirring to dissolve the sugar, then boil rapidly until a little dropped on a saucer will wrinkle when cool. Pour into clean hot jars and seal when cold.

Rose Petal Jelly

Make as for any herb jelly adding as many rose petals as mixture of sugar and apple juice will hold and boil 5 minutes. Test for setting and boil longer if necessary. Add a pinch of cream of tartar to prevent any bitterness, and strain into warm dry jars over 1 fresh rose petal in each jar.

Rose Sugar

To every 1 cup sugar add ¼ cup minced or finely chopped rose petals and pound them together with a pestle and mortar or a potato masher. Keep in a closed container for a week before using. Sift out rose petals if wished.

or

Pound sugar with double its weight of rose petals until they are thoroughly blended. Or pack sugar and rose petals in alternate layers in a jar. Keep tightly closed and use to flavour special puddings and cream.

Rose Petal Syrup

1 litre rose petals
4 cups water

4 cups sugar to every 1 litre of liquid

Place rose petals and water in a saucepan, bring to the boil and simmer 20 minutes. Cover and leave to infuse overnight. Next day strain out liquid and squeeze out petals.

Measure liquid and add 4 cups sugar to every litre. Put in a saucepan and bring to the boil, stirring to dissolve sugar, and boil 10 minutes. Skim any froth off the top, overflow and seal with Perfit seals, or leave to cool and keep in the refrigerator.

Rose Petal and Rhubarb Syrup

500 g rhubarb
½ litre water

1½ cups sugar
1 cup heeled rose petals

Cut rhubarb into pieces and simmer in water until pulped. Strain through a fine sieve and pour liquid back into saucepan, add sugar and rose petals and stir well. Bring to the boil, simmer 15 minutes and strain. Bring to the boil again and continue to boil until syrup is a good red. Pour into warmed dry jars, overflow and seal with Perfit seals.

Rose Vinegar

Pack rose petals loosely into a wide-mouthed glass jar and fill with white wine, red wine or cider vinegar. Cover and stand 2-3 weeks shaking daily. Strain into clean bottles when flavour is strong enough.

Rose Bavarian Cream

25 g rose petals
½ litre water
500 g sugar or rose sugar
25 g gelatine to every ½ litre
   liquid

juice ½ lemon
whipped cream
crystallised or chocolate rose
   petals

Put petals in water with sugar in a saucepan. Bring to the boil, stirring, and simmer 20 minutes. Strain and allow to cool slightly. Measure and allow 25 g (3 tsp) gelatine to every ½ litre of liquid. Soften gelatine in lemon juice, add to the warm syrup and stir until completely dissolved. When cool, beat with an electric beater until frothy, and fold in 1 cup whipped cream to every 2 cups of jelly. Pour into a mould or set in individual glass dishes and decorate with crystallised or chocolate rose petals.

or

2 cups milk
50 g rose petals
4 egg yolks
125 g sugar

1 tbs gelatine softened in a
   little cold water
2 cups whipped cream

Bring milk to the boil in a saucepan, add rose petals, cover and infuse 2 hours. Beat egg yolks with sugar in a basin, then cook in a double boiler with milk and roses, stirring without boiling until custard coats the back of a metal spoon. Add softened gelatine and stir to blend thoroughly. Strain into a basin, stand basin in a bowl of ice and stir until mixture begins to set. Fold in whipped cream, pour into a serving dish and set in the refrigerator. This may be set in a wet mould and unmoulded to serve. It should not be too cold.

Rose Petal Custard Tarts

¾ cup milk
½ cup finely minced rose
   petals

1 egg
2 tbs rose sugar
9 pre-cooked tart shells

Combine milk and rose petals in a saucepan and heat until almost boiling. Beat egg and sugar together until frothy and gradually beat in hot milk. Divide mixture among tart shells and bake at 180 °C until custard is set, about 20 minutes. Serve hot or cold and decorate with fresh rose petals.

Damask Cream

½ litre milk
1 tsp rennet
2 tsp rosewater
2 tbs castor sugar

4 tbs cream
1 tsp rosewater
1 tbs castor sugar
1-2 red or pink roses

Warm milk and stir in rennet, 2 tsp rosewater and 2 tbs castor sugar. Stir for about a minute and leave to set in a cool place. Just before serving pour over a mixture of lightly whipped cream, rosewater and castor sugar and decorate with fresh rose petals. Nutmeg may be added to taste.

Rose Petal Fritters

Dip rose petals in brandy or sherry, then in batter. Fry in hot oil quickly, drain and dust with a little castor sugar and serve.

Rose Petal Parfait

Combine ½ cup rose conserve, 3 tbs rose brandy and ½ litre whipped cream. Fold all together until well mixed and serve in glass dishes with tiny sponge cakes.

Rose Petal Souffle

4 egg whites
5 tbs rose petal conserve

1 tbs brandy or sherry

Beat egg whites until stiff and fold in rose conserve and brandy. Pour into a greased souffle dish and bake at 190 °C for 10 minutes.

Rose and Strawberry Ice Cream

1 cup crushed strawberries
1½ cups whipped cream

6 tbs rose petal conserve

Combine all ingredients by folding gently. Pour into a tray and freeze until just set. Serve with rose petal syrup. More cream may be added.

Rose Petal Surprise

finely chopped dates soaked in
orange juice to taste
sliced banana and/or
pineapple, or fruit in season

rose petal conserve
rose petals
whipped cream

Line tall glasses or glass dishes with a layer of red rose petals and
then add alternate layers of dates soaked in orange juice, bananas,
rose conserve until the glasses are nearly full. Top with a dollop of
whipped cream and a red rose petal.

Rose Syullabub

1½ cups whipped cream
1 tbs brandy

5 tbs rose petal conserve

Whip cream lightly, add brandy and whip until soft but firm. Fold
in rose petal conserve, put into wine glasses and chill slightly before
serving.

Rose Petal Conserve Tart

2 cups flour
pinch salt
100 g butter
water to mix

6 tbs rose petal conserve
1 tbs strained lemon juice
¼ tsp each ground cinnamon
and ginger

Sift flour and salt into a basin and cut in butter until mixture
resembles fine breadcrumbs. Add cold water, about 4 tbs, and mix
to a soft dough. Knead until smooth and rest in a plastic bag in the
refrigerator for 15 minutes. Combine conserve, lemon juice and
spices, and blend well with a spoon. Roll out pastry on a floured
surface until ½ cm thick and use to line a well-buttered, 20cm pie
plate. Pour in filling, using any leftover pieces of pastry cut in thin
strips and twisted, to form a lattice pattern over the top. Bake at
190°C in the centre of the oven for 20 minutes, reduce heat to
170°C and cook 15 minutes more. Serve hot with cream.

Rose Trifle

Soak sponge cake in rose wine and cover with custard. Add some crushed pineapple, finely sliced peaches or cherries, slivered almonds and whipped cream. Decorate with crystallised rose petals.

Rose Water

Fill a saucepan with red rose petals and cover with water. Bring just about to the boil, but do not boil, cover and maintain this heat for an hour. Strain out rose petals and add fresh ones, cover, and repeat the process until water has a strong enough flavour. When cool store in the refrigerator.

Rose Water Jelly

Soften 3 tsp gelatine in a little cold water for every 2 cups hot rose water. Add 1 tbs maraschino or rose brandy and stir well to dissolve gelatine thoroughly. Strain into small glass moulds over 1-3 red or pink rose petals and when cool place in the refrigerator to set. A little red food colouring may be added.

This jelly may be set in a pre-baked pie shell or a biscuit and butter pie shell and decorated with whipped cream and crystallised rose petals when set.

Khoshaf

Take equal quantities of dried apricots, figs, prunes and 1 cup sultanas, place in a bowl and cover with water. Leave 2 days. An hour before serving chop fruit into bite-sized pieces, add rose water to taste and chopped blanched almonds. Mix well and serve just chilled.

Rose Drops

25 g red rose petals　　　　　*lemon juice*
2 cups castor or icing sugar

Mince rose petals very finely, combine with castor or icing sugar and mix together well. Add enough lemon juice to make a stiff paste, put into a stainless steel saucepan over a slow heat and stir well. When it is boiling all over drop small drops off a spoon onto waxed paper and keep in a warm, dry place until set and dry.

Rose Petal Salad

Arrange in a salad bowl:

2 cups diced, cooked potatoes   2 cups rose petals
2 cups finely chopped
   dandelion and plantain
   leaves

Toss with a dressing made by combining and shaking well:
¼ cup lemon juice   1 tsp finely chopped tarragon
½ cup salad oil   ½ tsp salt
1 crushed clove garlic   pinch cayenne pepper

Garnish with 2-3 hard-boiled eggs cut in slices.

Chocolate Roses

8 fresh pink roses   Grand Marnier or other
200 g dark chocolate   liqueur
50 g copha butter

Separate petals of 4 roses carefully so as not to bruise them. Melt chocolate in a double boiler over just simmering water and add copha butter little by little. Stir and mix thoroughly, remove from the heat and add a dash of Grand Marnier or some other liqueur. Allow to cool until just warm, then dip base of each rose petal in the chocolate mixture. Turn some paper patty cases upside down on waxed paper and rest dipped petals against them to dry, or put a tray of them arranged like this in the refrigerator. When chocolate is completely set, arrange petals base down in small glass dishes in the shape of a rose and place a fresh rose in the centre. A few dark green rose leaves may be used to surround the rose petals.

Chocolate Rose Leaves

Melt dark chocolate in a double boiler over simmering water and when it is liquid pour small quantities of chocolate onto large, perfect rose leaves, turned upside down, and leave to set. When chocolate is firm the leaves may be peeled off and a leaf-shaped chocolate will be left.

Rose Hip Paste

3 cups ripe rose hips   1 tsp grated lemon rind
2 tsp lemon juice   sugar and water

Chill hips, halve them and scoop out seeds and furry lining. Cover seeds with water and simmer for 10 minutes. Measure hips, cover with an equal measure of water and simmer in another pan for 15 minutes. Strain, keep both liquids and discard seeds. Mince hips and add them to the liquid with lemon rind and juice. Measure this and add an equal quantity of sugar. Place all in a heavy-bottomed pan and cook, stirring, over a low heat until thick. Cool slightly and beat to a paste with a wooden spoon. Pour into a wax paper-lined tin and refrigerate for 24 hours. Cut into slices and eat as a sweetmeat. Store in foil.

Rose Hip and Semolina Paste

2 cups rose hips   75 g butter
water   ¼ cup blanched almonds
¾ cup sugar   ½ cup semolina
juice 1 lemon   1 tbs rosewater

Top and tail hips, halve them and scrape out seeds and tiny hairs. Wash under running water. Put hips in a saucepan and cover with water. Cover, cook over a gentle heat until hips are soft, about 30 minutes, and strain. Make juice up to 2 cups and add strained lemon juice and sugar. Bring to the boil and cook, stirring, 3-5 minutes. Sieve rose hips and add pulp to syrup. Melt butter in a frying pan and add chopped almonds and semolina and fry gently until brown. Add rose hip mixture, reduce the heat and simmer until it thickens. Remove from the heat and stir in the rose water. Pour into shallow dishes and cool before serving or pour into a shallow dish and cut into fingers when cold.

Rose Hip Puree

Stew 1 kg topped and tailed rose hips gently in 1 litre water until tender, about 20-30 minutes. Sieve to remove seeds and keep in a covered container in the refrigerator. Add spoonfuls to soups, juices, fruit salads and sauces to give extra vitamin C.
N.B. Rose hips should be scarlet; orange rose hips are under-ripe.

Rose Hip Jam

500 g rose hips   sugar
1 cup water

Simmer rose hips in water until very tender, then rub through a sieve to remove seeds and fine hairs. Weigh pulp and add an equal weight of sugar. Return to the heat and stir, while simmering, until thick. Pour into small hot jars and seal when cold.

Rose Hip and Crab Apple Jelly

¾ kg rose hips   2 cups sugar to every 2½ cups
½ kg crab apples   juice
water

Wash fruit, put in a pan and cover with water. Cook gently until soft, mashing occasionally, then tip into a jelly bag and leave to drip overnight. Next day measure liquid and pour into a saucepan. Bring to the boil, add sugar and stir until dissolved. Boil fast for about 10 minutes or until mixture will jell when a little is dropped on a saucer. Remove from the heat, pour into warm, dry jelly jars and cover when cold.

Rose Hip Marmalade

1 litre rose hips   1½ cups sugar
1 cup water   2 tbs fresh root ginger, minced
rind of 1 orange and 1 lemon
   cut in thin strips

Chill hips, halve them and scoop out seeds. Cover seeds with water and cook for about 10 minutes. Strain liquid over hips, orange and lemon rinds and sugar in a heavy pan. Stir well and bring to the boil. Add ginger and simmer until rinds are transparent and mixture has thickened enough to spread. Pour into small jars and seal when cold.

Rose Hip Sauce

75 g rose hip puree   lemon juice to taste

1 cup water or apple or grape juice	1 tsp lemon balm or sweet cicely
75 g sugar	

Combine rose hip puree, liquid and sugar and bring to the boil, stirring. Taste and add lemon juice and finely chopped lemon balm or sweet cicely leaves until flavour is right.

Rose Hip Soup

3 cups ripe rose hips	2 tsp lemon juice
6 cups water	½ tsp grated lemon rind
½ cup sugar	½ tsp ground ginger
1 tbs cornflour	4 tbs cream
1 tbs cold water	

Top and tail and wash hips, scoop out seeds, and boil gently in water for 25 minutes. Cool and mince hips, mix with liquid, and add sugar. Bring to the boil, stirring. Combine cornflour and cold water and slowly stir into hip syrup. Boil until mixture thickens. Remove from the heat, add lemon juice, rind and ginger and mix well. Cool and refrigerate. Serve chilled, topped with a little fresh or sour cream.

or

½ kg topped and tailed rose hips	½ litre water

Combine in a saucepan and boil for about an hour, mashing hips with a wooden spoon. Strain through a jelly bag or a double thickness of muslin to prevent any little hairs getting into the liquid and leave to drip overnight. This is a concentrated puree and must be diluted to make soup. Keep in a screw-top jar in the refrigerator.

1 tbs butter	1 cup rose hip liquid
1 peeled sliced onion	1 tsp Worcestershire sauce
3½ cups chicken stock	salt and pepper to taste

Melt butter in a pan and gently fry onion. Stir in chicken stock and rose hip liquid and season with Worcestershire sauce and salt and pepper. Cover and simmer about 15-20 minutes. The soup may be blended or put through a mouli. Serve hot with sippets.

This may be varied by adding grated carrot and/or nutmeg to ingredients.

Rose Hip Syrup

4 cups rose hips
6 cups water

1 cup sugar

Top and tail rose hips and mince them. Bring water to the boil in a large saucepan and add minced hips. Stir and simmer 5 minutes then draw the pan off the heat, cover and stand for 10 minutes. Strain liquid through a double layer of muslin, without squeezing it. Return liquid to saucepan with 1 cup sugar and stir. Boil 5 minutes and skim. Pour into warm dry jars, overflow and seal with Perfit seals.

Rose Hip Tart

1½ cups deseeded rose hips
¾ cup water
2-3 tbs sugar
½ tsp each cinnamon and
  ginger

1 tsp grated lemon rind and/
  or a squeeze lemon juice
200 g shortcrust pastry

Top, tail and halve the hips. Scrape out seeds and wash hips to remove all the tiny hairs in a basin of water first, and then under running water. Put them in a saucepan with the water, bring to the boil and simmer 15 minutes. Add sugar, spices and lemon rind. Stir well and cook, stirring, 5 minutes. Remove from the heat and cool.

Roll out the pastry into 2 circles and line a greased pie plate with one. Fill with cooled hip mixture. Damp the edges of the pastry, cover with the other circle and seal edges with the back of a fork to make a pattern. Prick the top to allow steam to escape. Bake in the centre of a hot oven, 200 °C, for 20-25 minutes, remove and sprinkle with sugar and return to the oven for a further 5 minutes. Eat hot or cold with cream.

Rose Hip Wine

1 kg rose hips
1 kg sugar
1 lemon

4 litres boiling water
pectic enzyme
yeast and nutrient

Wash rose hips and chop, or crush them with a rolling pin. Put them in a plastic bucket with sugar and thinly peeled lemon rind and pour boiling water over them. Stir to dissolve the sugar. Add strained lemon juice and allow to cool. Add pectic enzyme, yeast and nutrient. Cover and stand in a warm place, stirring daily for 2 weeks. Strain through a jelly bag into a fermentation jar and fit an airlock. When the wine clears, siphon into a clean jar and leave another 3 months before bottling.

Rose Geranium

There are several rose geraniums but all are properly Pelargoniums *Pelargonium graveolens* is the most vigorous and upright of them but to me does not have the rose scent of *Pelargonium capitatum* and its variety 'Attar of Roses'. There are many other scented pelargoniums of which the lemon and peppermint scented ones are the most useful in cooking after the rose. They are all native to southern Africa and were brought to Europe in the eighteenth century. They are perennial, shrubby or prostrate plants and look and grow like 'geraniums' but are noted for their scented leaves and do not have showy flowers. The leaves are used fresh or dried to flavour fruit desserts, jellies, apple jelly, sponge cakes, herb teas and other drinks. They are also used in herb butters and sugar, and leaves and flowers may be used to garnish dishes. One, *P. crispum minor,* with lemony scented leaves was used to scent the water in fingerbowls.

The scented pelargoniums will grow anywhere other pelargoniums thrive and are very adaptable provided they are pruned back occasionally and do not get too wet when they are resting during the winter. They need protection from frost but are otherwise hardy, and may be grown from cuttings or from seed, though they do not necessarily come true from seed. They make good pot plants and may be dried for pot-pourri as well as used in cooking.

The lemon-scented pelagoniums may be used in place of the rose-scented in any of the following recipes.

Peppermint pelargonium recipes are listed under Peppermint.

Rose Geranium and Apple Jelly

Make apple jelly in usual way by roughly chopping whole, unpeeled apples into a pan and covering with water. Bring this to the boil and simmer until the fruit is soft and liquid a good colour. Tip into a jelly bag and allow to drain overnight. Next day measure liquid, return to the pan and bring to the boil. Add 1 cup sugar for every cup of apple liquid and stir until it dissolves. Add 10 rose geranium leaves to each 2 cups liquid, or to taste, and boil rapidly until jelly sets when tested. Strain into warm dry jars over a fresh scented geranium leaf in each jar. Cover when cold.

Rose Geranium Apple Sauce

Fresh apple sauce may be flavoured with rose geranium by cooking 1 leaf in the pot. It may then be served in a bowl decorated with fresh rose geranium leaves.

Rose Geranium Butter

Blend ½ tsp minced rose geranium leaf into 50 g softened butter and chill in the refrigerator for 2-3 hours before using. This may be used to butter bread for rose petal sandwiches.

Rose Geranium Cakes

100 g butter
½ cup sugar
1 beaten egg
1 cup flour
1 tsp baking powder
milk to mix
½ tsp vanilla
rose geranium leaves

Cream butter and sugar and beat in egg. Sift in flour and baking powder alternately with milk and beat to a medium stiff batter. Add a little vanilla to taste. Put a small rose geranium leaf in the bottom of each buttered patty pan, add 1 spoonful of mixture and bake at 180°C for 8-10 minutes.

Rose Geranium Scones

2 cups flour
2-3 tsp baking powder
1 tsp salt
2-3 tbs rose geranium sugar
milk to mix
4 tbs butter

Sift flour, baking powder and salt into a basin and stir in sugar. Cut in butter and mix until like breadcrumbs. Add milk, about ½ cup, and mix well and quickly. Pat dough out on a floured surface to about 1cm thick. Cut with a floured cutter or glass and bake on a tray at 220°C for about 10 minutes.

Geranium Sponge

Line a greased, floured cake tin with rose, lemon or peppermint scented geranium leaves.

125 g flour	*3 eggs*
pinch salt	*125 g castor sugar*

Sift flour and salt together into a basin. Combine eggs and sugar in a bowl and stand in a pan of hot water. Beat egg and sugar mixture with a whisk until light and thick. Fold in the flour and pour carefully over scented geranium leaves in pan. Bake at 170 °C for 45 minutes. Cool on a wire rack. When cold, split and fill with rose flavoured or other jam or jelly, or cream, or icing, to blend with whatever scented geranium has been used. The top may also be iced or dusted with icing sugar.

Rose Geranium Sugared Cookies

1 cup butter	*2½ tsp baking powder*
1 cup sugar	*2 tbs rose geranium water*
2 beaten eggs	*2 tbs aniseed*
2¾ cups flour	*rose geranium sugar*

Cream butter and sugar and stir in beaten eggs. Sift in flour and baking powder and finally add rose geranium water and aniseed. Drop spoonfuls on a greased baking tray and sprinkle with rose geranium sugar, pressing each cookie down a little with the bottom of a glass. Bake at 190 °C about 25 minutes, until lightly browned. Cool on a wire rack.

Chicken Casserole with Rose Geranium

1 raw chicken, jointed	*1 crushed clove garlic*
seasoned flour	*1-2 sliced onions*
2-4 tbs oil	*2 rose geranium leaves or to*
2 cups chicken stock	*taste*
1 cup claret or light red wine	
3-4 sprigs chopped parsley	
and tarragon	

Shake chicken pieces in a bag containing a little seasoned flour until they are well coated and fry in hot oil in a heavy pan until golden brown on both sides. Drain and place in a casserole. Cover with stock and wine and sprinkle remaining ingredients over chicken. Cover and cook gently at 170 °C until tender, 2-3 hours.

Rose Geranium Cream Cheese for Fruit

1 cup cream
4 tbs sugar
2 rose geranium leaves

250 g Philadelphia cream cheese

Combine cream, sugar and leaves in the top of a double boiler and heat but do not boil. Stir to dissolve sugar completely and allow leaves to infuse until mixture is cool. Stir cream mixture into the cream cheese until thoroughly blended and chill in the refrigerator for 12 hours. Remove leaves and serve with strawberries, raspberries or any other fruit.

Creamed Rice and Rose Geranium

2 tbs rice
2 cups milk

1½-2 tbs sugar
3-5 rose geranium leaves

Simmer rice in milk until thick and creamy, taking care not to burn. Add geranium leaves and infuse until flavour seems strong enough, and sweeten to taste. Remove leaves and serve warm or cool.

Rose Geranium Sponge Pudding

1 tbs butter
1 tbs hot water
5 tbs rose sugar
3 eggs

1½ tbs flour
1 cup milk
grated rind and juice 1 lemon
4 rose geranium leaves

Cream butter, hot water and sugar until light and fluffy. Separate eggs and add beaten yolks, then sifted flour, milk, lemon rind and juice. Fold in stiffly beaten egg whites and geranium leaves. Pour into an ovenproof dish and stand in a pan of cold water in the oven. Bake at 180 °C for 45 minutes.

Rose Geranium Custard

3 eggs
2 tbs rose sugar
2 cups milk

1-2 rose geranium leaves
knob butter

Beat eggs in an overproof dish and stir and beat in sugar. Gradually beat in milk, blending well, add leaves and dot with a little butter. Place in a water bath and bake at 180 °C for 45 minutes. Lemon or peppermint geranium leaves may be used in the same way.

Rose Geranium and Red Fruits

Cook gently together:
2 cups each raspberries, red
    currants and cherries

5 cm cinnamon stick
2 rose geranium leaves

When tender remove cinnamon and leaves, and sieve.

Rose Geranium Sorbet

12 scented geranium leaves
1 ¼ cups water
6 tbs sugar

juice 1 lemon
1 stiffly beaten egg white
leaves and flowers to garnish

Wash leaves, shake dry and put in a saucepan with water and sugar. Bring to the boil, stirring to dissolve sugar, cover, remove from heat and infuse 20 minutes. Taste and if flavour is not strong enough bring to the boil again, cover and infuse a further 15 minutes. Strain into a bowl and add strained lemon juice. Leave to cool, then pour into an ice-cream tray and freeze until mushy. Remove from freezer and fold in stiffly beaten egg white. Freeze again for about an hour and serve in glasses decorated with small geranium leaves and/or flowers.

Punch with Rose Geranium

1 cup sugar
½ cup water
6 rose geranium leaves

1 litre apple juice
4 limes
ice

Combine sugar and water and bring to the boil, stirring to dissolve sugar. Add geranium leaves and boil 5 minutes. Cool, strain and combine with apple juice and sliced limes. Pour into glasses half filled with crushed ice and garnish with rose geranium flowers.

Herb and Rose Geranium Punch

2 sprigs each lemon verbena,
  mint and sage
1 small sprig rosemary
6 rose geranium leaves
1 bottle chilled dry white wine
3 tbs honey or castor sugar

2 cups strawberries
1 bottle sparkling white wine,
  chilled
1 bottle fizzy lemonade
borage and geranium flowers

Place herbs in a jug and bruise them with a wooden spoon. Add dry white wine and infuse, covered, overnight. Warm honey and sprinkle over hulled, washed and dried strawberries (or use sugar) and chill one hour. Pour into a punch bowl and strain dry white wine over them. Just before serving add chilled sparkling wine and lemonade and float borage and geranium flowers among the strawberries.

Rose Geranium Honey

2 cups rose geranium leaves
2½ cups liquid honey

1 cup rose geranium flowers

Place leaves in the top of a double boiler and add honey. Heat over boiling water until just about boiling. Remove from heat and cool. Put geranium flowers into a clean jar and strain honey over them. Cover and leave to thicken a little before using.

Yoghurt and Geranium Dressing

1 cup plain yoghurt
½-1 tsp honey
pinch paprika

2 leaves rose or lemon
  geranium, finely chopped

Combine all ingredients and mix well. Cover and chill overnight and serve with any salad to taste.

Potato Salad

2 cups cooked, diced potatoes
½ cup finely chopped celery
1 tbs finely chopped parsley
2 tbs tarragon vinegar

3 tbs oil
salt and pepper
finely chopped rose or lemon
geranium leaves

Combine potatoes, celery and parsley in a salad bowl. Combine vinegar, oil and seasonings in a jar and shake well. Add finely chopped geranium leaves to salad, pour over dressing, toss and serve.

Sandwich Spread with Geranium

Combine 250 g cottage or cream cheese, 1 tbs finely chopped, scented geranium leaves and ½ cup finely chopped walnuts or blanched almonds. Spread on buttered bread, scones or biscuits.

Rose Geranium Sugar

Layer 12 rose geranium leaves through 2 cups sugar and keep in an airtight container. Leave at least one week before using. The leaves must be quite dry from rain or dew before added to sugar.

Rosemary

Rosemary is almost of as great use as Bayes, or as any other herbe both for inward and outward remedies... for civill uses, at weddings, funerals, & to bestowe among friends...   John Parkinson

Rosemary, *Rosmarinus officinalis,* is a perennial, evergreen shrub which likes well-drained soil and a situation in full sun. It may be grown from seed but this takes a long time, so it is mostly grown from cuttings or layers. Many cultivars exist with different habits of growth, prostrate or upright, narrow or broad leaves and flower colours of pale to deep blue and even pink and white. All plants have the beautiful rosemary fragrance and all may be used in cooking or for household purposes.

In cooking, rosemary may be used fresh, the young leaves stripped from their stems and finely chopped, for otherwise they may be chewy. If whole sprigs are used to flavour a dish the leaves will drop off and may need to be strained out before the dish is served. Rosemary may also be dried and then finely crumbled before use. It has a strong flavour so use it lightly.

Traditionally rosemary is used with sheep meat but it also tastes very good in scones, breads and biscuits as well as with chicken and fish. It combines well with oranges and is used in some soups and vegetable dishes as well as in drinks, jelly and conserve.

Rosemary Biscuits

120 g butter
60 g sugar
1½ cups sifted flour

1-2 tbs finely chopped
rosemary

Cream butter and sugar, add flour and rosemary and mix well. Roll into small balls, place on a tray, and press with a fork. Bake at 200 °C for 10-15 minutes. Cool on a rack.

Rosemary Bread

1 cup white flour
1 tbs dried yeast
1 cup warm water
1 tsp honey or sugar

1-2 tbs oil
2-3 cups flour, white or brown
1 tbs finely chopped rosemary
1 tsp salt

Mix 1 cup flour with yeast. Combine warm water and honey, mix well and stir into flour-yeast mixture to make a batter. Leave 5-10 minutes until frothing. Stir in oil, and gradually add 2-3 cups flour with rosemary and salt to make a soft dough. Knead on a lightly floured surface until smooth and elastic. Place in a basin, cover with a cloth and leave to rise in a warm place until double in bulk. Knock back, knead a little and shape into a loaf. Place in an oiled bread tin, leave to rise, then brush top with water and sprinkle with finely chopped rosemary over the top. Bake at 200 °C for 30-45 minutes, until well browned. Cool on a rack.

Rosemary Fruit Cake

125 g butter
½ cup sugar
2 beaten eggs
1 cup flour
1 tsp baking powder

1 cup mixed dried fruit and
peel
1 tsp finely chopped fresh
rosemary
½ cup ground almonds

Cream butter and sugar and beat in eggs. Sift in flour and baking powder and use a little of this to coat dried fruit. Blend all together and add rosemary and ground almonds. Pour into a lined tin and bake at 160 °C for about 1-1¼ hours. Cool in the tin.

Rosemary Scones

2 cups flour
2 tsp baking powder
½ tsp salt
1 tsp sugar

25 g butter
1 tbs finely chopped rosemary
milk to mix

Sift flour, baking powder, salt and sugar together into a basin. Cut in butter and rub in until it resembles fine breadcrumbs. Add rosemary, stir well and mix to a soft dough with milk. Pat out on a floured board, cut into squares and bake at 200-210 °C for 10-12 minutes. Parsley, sage and thyme may be added to taste with rosemary.

Walnut Sables

75 g each butter, flour and
   grated cheese
salt and pepper
1 beaten egg

coarsely chopped walnuts
finely chopped rosemary
rock salt

Rub butter into flour, add cheese and seasonings and knead into a paste. Roll out thinly and cut into strips about 2 inches wide. Brush with beaten egg and sprinkle with walnuts and rosemary. Grind a little salt over this and cut each strip into triangles. Bake in a tin lined with grease-proof paper in a moderately hot oven until golden brown, about 10 minutes.

Wholemeal Shortbread with Rosemary

2 cups wholemeal flour
1 tsp rosemary, finely chopped
½ tsp salt

50 g raw sugar
125 g butter
1 egg

Rub butter into dry ingredients, add egg and mix well. Roll out, cut into fingers and bake at 200 °C for 8-10 minutes.

Rosemary Ice Blocks

Half fill ice-cube trays with water and allow to freeze. Remove half blocks, put several rosemary flowers in each division, return ice blocks and fill with water. Return to freezer until set.

Gin and Rosemary Punch

small sprig rosemary
4 cups pineapple juice
1 cup lemon juice
2 tbs sugar

1 bottle gin
lemon slices stuck with cloves
ice or rosemary ice blocks

Put rosemary and 1 cup pineapple juice in a saucepan and bring to the boil. Cover and cool. Strain out rosemary and add remaining pineapple juice, lemon juice, sugar and gin and mix well. Float a few lemon slices stuck with cloves on top to garnish and serve with ice or rosemary ice blocks.

Mulled Cider with Rosemary

Combine and bring to the boil:
1 cup water
½ cup sugar
4-5 cm cinnamon stick

1 small sliced lemon or orange
3 cloves
1 sprig rosemary

Boil 5 minutes, add 1 cup cider and reheat but do not boil. Strain and drink hot.

Rosemary Orange Fizz

1 handful rosemary sprigs
1 tbs honey or 3 tbs sugar
1 cup water

½ litre ginger ale, chilled
½ litre orange juice, chilled
ice cubes

Combine rosemary, honey or sugar and water in a saucepan and bring to the boil, stirring. Simmer 5 minutes, cover and allow to cool. When cold combine with ginger ale and orange juice and pour into glasses half full of ice cubes. Apricot or lime juice may be used in place of orange.

Wassail Bowl

Heat some cider gently with 3-6 cloves, 5cm stick cinnamon, 2½cm crushed root ginger and 1-2 sprigs rosemary but do not boil. When steaming hot, pour into a warmed bowl, add 2 cups brandy and serve, surrounding the bowl with sprays of holly, ivy, rosemary and bay. Strain into hot mugs.

Rosemary Wine

1 tbs chopped rosemary to every 1-2 cups white wine or cider. Leave to infuse 3 days, chill and strain before drinking.

Fish Fillets with Herb Butter

4 fish fillets
salt and pepper
1 tsp each finely chopped
  parsley, rosemary and lemon
  thyme

50 g butter

Place each fish fillet on a piece of foil big enough to wrap it completely. Season with salt and pepper. Combine herbs and butter, divide mixture in four and spread a quarter on each fillet. Wrap them up tightly and bake at 180°C for 30-40 minutes. Serve with lemon slices.

Beef Casserole with Rosemary

Make a marinade by combining in a shallow dish:
2 sliced onions
2 peeled, sliced carrots
2 cloves garlic, crushed
1 bay leaf
2 cloves

3 sprigs rosemary
1 sprig parsley
rind of ½ orange
2 cups red wine
1 tbs wine vinegar

Add 1 kg chuck steak, cut into cubes and leave to marinate for 12-24 hours in a cool place, turning now and then. Drain meat and keep marinade. Cook 2 slices bacon and 2 sliced onions gently in a pan, add meat and brown both sides. Add 4 tbs flour and cook gently to brown flour before stirring in strained liquid from marinade. Pour into a casserole, cover and cook at 170°C for about 2½ hours. Carrot from marinade may be added. Taste and season as necessary before serving.

Rosemary Chicken

1½-2 kg whole chicken
4 10 cm rosemary sprigs

1 sliced lemon
salt and pepper

Rinse chicken inside and out and pat dry. Arrange sprigs of rosemary on top of slices of lemon inside chicken cavity and season with salt and pepper. Place in an oven bag, or meat dish with a well-fitting lid, and cook at 180 °C for 1-1½ hours. When tender remove lemon and rosemary and serve hot or cold. Lemon thyme, marjoram or tarragon may be used in the same way.

Chicken Casserole with Rosemary

1 chicken, jointed
seasoned flour
2 tbs butter
4 tbs oil
1-2 cloves garlic

1 tbs finely chopped rosemary
1 tsp salt
2 tbs white wine vinegar
1 cup chicken stock

Shake chicken pieces in a paperbag with seasoned flour. Heat butter and oil in a frying pan and fry chicken lightly until brown on all sides. Add garlic cloves, cut in half and spiked on toothpicks, and rosemary, salt, vinegar and stock. Bring all to the boil. Remove garlic and transfer the rest to a casserole and cook 30-45 minutes at 180 °C.

Rosemary Marinade

¾ cup salad oil
¼ cup vinegar
2 tsp salt

2 tsp finely chopped rosemary
½ tsp pepper
½ cup sliced onion

Combine ingredients and use to marinate lamb or chicken.

Rosemary with Roasts

Rosemary is traditionally used to flavour roast lamb in this country, particularly 'lamb on the spit'. The sprigs of rosemary are placed on top of the meat and underneath, or slits are made in the skin of the joint and small pieces pressed in — garlic cloves may be added. Beef, pork or veal may be flavoured in the same way. Chicken is best first rubbed with butter, then sprinkled with chopped rosemary.

Rosemary Crumb Topping for Roast Lamb

1 leg lamb
1 tsp finely chopped rosemary

1½ cups soft breadcrumbs
2 tbs melted butter

Remove fine layer of outer skin from lamb, place in a baking dish and cook at 180°C for 1½-2 hours. Mix together rosemary, breadcrumbs and butter. Remove lamb from the oven and spread breadcrumb mixture over the meat, pressing in firmly. Return to the oven and bake a further hour until meat is tender and topping crisp and golden.

Rosemary Lamb

1 leg lamb
2 cloves garlic

12-15 rosemary leaves
salt and pepper

Cut slits in the fat of lamb, insert slivers of garlic and rosemary leaves, and season. Cook in a hot oven for 30 minutes, reduce heat to 160°C and cook for a further 2-2½ hours for a leg weighing 2½ kg. Baste with the hot fat from time to time. Serve garnished with a sprig of fresh rosemary.

Lamb and Rosemary Turnovers

For 8 lean lamb cutlets use:
4 tbs butter
2 tsp finely chopped rosemary
1 crushed clove garlic
  (optional)

salt and pepper
250 g puff pastry
1 beaten egg

Cream butter with rosemary, garlic and seasonings, and spread on one side of each cutlet. Grill cutlets until tender, browning both sides and basting with the butter. Allow to cool and spread with remaining butter. Roll out pastry and divide into 8 pieces big enough to cover the individual cutlets. Place a cutlet in the centre of each piece, brush the edges with beaten egg and fold pastry over. Place turnovers on a baking tray, brush tops with egg and bake at 210°C, about 20 minutes.

Rosemary Mustard

2 tbs mustard powder
2 tbs white flour
½ tsp salt

2 tsp sugar
wine vinegar to mix
1 tbs finely chopped rosemary

Combine all ingredients and mix to desired consistency with wine vinegar. Keep in a sealed jar 2-4 weeks before using.

Rosemary and Prune Stuffing

1 tbs butter
1 peeled sliced onion
6 prunes, soaked in water
1 cup breadcrumbs

1 tsp finely chopped rosemary
salt and pepper
1 beaten egg

Melt butter in a pan and gently cook onion until tender but do not allow to brown. Remove stones from soaked prunes, chop them and add to onions. Add breadcrumbs, rosemary, salt and pepper and combine well. Bind all together with beaten egg. Use to stuff pork or poultry.

Rosemary and Rice Stuffing

Cook 6 tbs rice in water until tender. Drain and combine with:

4 chopped rashers bacon
50 g sultanas
1 tsp finely chopped rosemary

½-1 tsp grated lemon rind
salt and pepper
1 beaten egg

Mix all together well and use to stuff lamb, mutton, poultry or veal.

Veal and Ham with Rosemary

1 kg veal steak
4 tbs seasoned flour
2 tbs butter
1 peeled sliced onion
500 g chopped bacon or
  cooked ham

1 tsp finely chopped rosemary
3-4 cups water
seasoning to taste

Cut veal into small cubes and roll them in seasoned flour. Heat butter in a saucepan and brown meat on both sides. Add onion and continue to fry gently until tender. Add bacon, rosemary and water. Stir well and bring to the boil. Turn down heat and simmer about 30 minutes until meat is tender and gravy thick. If ham is used, add at end of the cooking. Taste and season if necessary with salt and pepper. Serve hot with mashed potatoes. This stew may be cooled and made into a pie by topping with pastry and cooking in a hot oven 200-220 °C until pastry is crisp and brown.

Turkey Souffle with Rosemary

Make as for Chervil Souffle, using 4 eggs and substituting 1½ cups minced cooked turkey for cheese and ½-1 tsp minced rosemary for chervil. Add lemon juice to taste.

Rosemary Conserve

½ litre rosemary sprigs *juice 1 lemon*
½ litre water *2 cups sugar*

Combine rosemary and water and bring to the boil. Simmer 5 minutes, remove from heat, cover and allow to cool. When cold, strain back into the saucepan, add strained lemon juice and sugar and bring to the boil, stirring to dissolve sugar. Boil fast about 10 minutes until mixture begins to thicken. Pour into warm jars and seal when cold.

Rosemary Conserve with Fruit Puree

1 tbs sugar *½ cup whipped cream*
2 tbs rosemary flowers
2 cups pureed soft fruit e.g.
strawberries

Pound flowers and sugar together in a mortar until well combined. Fold into fruit puree with whipped cream, and serve chilled with sweet biscuits or sponge fingers.

Rosemary Jelly

Make apple or crab apple jelly in the usual way as for Mint Jelly, but add ½ cup rosemary leaves for every 3 cups liquid strained from the jelly bag. When jelly is ready to set strain out rosemary and discard. Pour jelly over a tiny sprig of fresh rosemary in each jelly jar.

Apple Mould with Rosemary

6 apples, peeled and quartered
1-1½ cups sugar
2 cups grape juice
rind 1 lemon
1 sprig rosemary finely
   chopped

3-4 tsp gelatine
½ cup sherry
1 cup whipped cream

Cook apples in a pan with sugar, grape juice, lemon rind and rosemary, simmering until fruit is soft. Strain, reserve liquid and puree apples. Soften gelatine in sherry and melt in a basin over hot water. Combine with syrup, mix well with apple pulp and chill. When mixture begins to thicken fold in whipped cream and pour into a rinsed mould. Chill until firm. Serve unmoulded with cream or custard.

Orange Compote with Rosemary

3 15cm long rosemary sprigs
1½ cups water

½ cup honey or 1 cup sugar
6 oranges

Combine rosemary, water and sweetener and bring to the boil, stirring all the time. Boil 5 minutes, cover and allow to cool. Peel oranges and slice into thin rounds, removing pips and pith. Arrange in a glass dish, strain syrup over fruit and chill before serving.

Rosemary Syllabub

2 lemons

pinch freshly grated nutmeg

100 g castor sugar
4 tbs sherry
1 tbs brandy

1 sprig rosemary, bruised
2 cups whipped cream

Combine juice and grated rind of lemon with sugar, sherry, brandy, nutmeg and rosemary in a bowl, cover and stand overnight. Strain and fold in whipped cream. Serve in glasses.

Chicken and Rosemary Soup

1 litre chicken stock
1 cup minced leftover chicken
1 onion or 12 spring onions
1 sprig thyme
1 sprig finely chopped
   rosemary leaves

salt and pepper
2 tbs cornflour
¼ cup cold water
3 beaten eggs

Combine in a saucepan and bring to the boil the chicken stock, minced chicken, finely chopped onion or spring onions, thyme, chopped rosemary and seasonings. Mix cornflour with cold water in a cup. Stir in a little of the hot soup to mix to a smooth paste and gradually add to the soup, stirring all the time. Taste and adjust seasonings if necessary. Whisk in beaten eggs, allowing to fall into soup in a thin stream so that it cooks in thin strips as it meets the hot liquid. Remove from the heat and serve.

Golden Soup

500 g pumpkin
sprig each thyme and
   rosemary
1 cup water

salt and pepper
1 tbs butter
2 cups milk
1-2 tbs grated cheese

Cook pumpkin until soft with thyme and rosemary in water. Remove herb stalks and sieve or mouli pumpkin pulp (if pumpkin has been cooked in its skin remove pulp from skin first). Season to taste, add butter and milk, reheat but do not boil, and serve topped with cheese.

Rosemary Soup

1 lettuce
1 cup sorrel
1 cup watercress
1½ litres chicken stock

1 tbs rosemary
1 beaten egg
½ cup top milk or cream
salt to taste

Wash and finely chop the greens and cook gently in chicken stock with finely minced rosemary for 30 minutes. Beat egg with cream and stir into soup just before serving. Add salt to taste.

Green Beans with Rosemary

1 kg green beans
salt and pepper
½ tsp finely chopped
   rosemary

a little boiling water

String and slice beans, season with salt and pepper and rosemary, add a little boiling water, cover and cook until tender.

Stuffed Courgettes with Rosemary

4-5 courgettes
¾ cup sliced onion
1 clove garlic
1 tbs oil
250 g mince
salt and pepper

1 tsp rosemary
3 slices bread
½ cup milk
2 tbs chopped parsley
3 tbs grated cheese

Cook courgettes whole in boiling water for 10 minutes, drain, cut in half lengthways and remove pulp. Cook onion and garlic gently in oil until soft, add mince, seasonings and finely chopped rosemary, and cook 15 minutes. Soak bread in milk and add to mince. Add courgette pulp and parsley and mix well. Spoon mixture into courgette halves, top with grated cheese and arrange in a baking dish. Bake at 170 °C for about 30 minutes.

Mushroom Pie with Rosemary

1 kg mushrooms

1 tsp finely chopped rosemary

100 g butter
3 tbs flour
1 cup chicken stock

¼ cup cream
¾ cup sherry or madeira
flaky pastry to cover

Peel and slice mushrooms and fry gently in butter until tender. Drain and arrange in a pie dish. Stir flour into remaining butter in pan, add chicken stock and stir until thick. Add rosemary, cream, sherry or madeira, and blend well. Pour over mushrooms, cover with flakey pastry and bake in a very hot oven, 220 °C, for about 10 minutes.

Rosemary Baked Potatoes

Wash old potatoes and cut in half without peeling. Sprinkle cut surface with salt and finely chopped rosemary and place cut side-down on an oiled baking tray. Bake 30-40 minutes or until soft, at 200 °C, and serve with butter.

Potato Pie with Rosemary

1 kg peeled, sliced, raw
  potatoes
½ kg peeled, sliced onions
salt and pepper

2 tsp finely chopped rosemary
  leaves
1¼ cups milk
50-75 g butter

Layer vegetables in a greased casserole sprinkling each layer with salt, pepper and rosemary. Pour in milk, dot with butter, cover and cook at 180 °C for about 1½ hours, until vegetables are cooked and milk absorbed.

Silverbeet or Spinach with Rosemary

Wash and chop 1 kg silverbeet or spinach, and mix with finely chopped parsley, spring onions and 1 tsp finely chopped rosemary. Heat 1 tbs butter in a heavy saucepan and add wet vegetables. Cover, turn the heat very low, and cook gently until tender. Serve as a vegetable or with bacon and/or eggs.

Tomato and Rosemary Flan

4 tbs oil	salt and pepper
2 sliced onions	2-4 tbs grated cheese
500 g skinned, chopped	1 pre-cooked pastry case to
tomatoes	line a 20cm flan case
2 crushed cloves garlic	
1½ tsp finely chopped	
rosemary	

Heat oil in a pan and fry onions gently, add tomatoes, seasonings and herbs, cover and simmer about 20 minutes. Remove lid and cook 10 minutes, stirring mixture to thicken. Spread half the cheese over bottom of flan case and cover with tomato mixture. Sprinkle top with remaining cheese. Bake in a moderate oven, 180°C, for about 20-30 minutes until heated through.

or

Use less cheese and cover top with halved anchovy fillets and black olives.

Vegetable Casserole with Rosemary

1 medium eggplant or 3-4	2 tsp finely chopped rosemary
courgettes	1 tbs finely chopped parsley
2 skinned, sliced tomatoes	salt and pepper
1 peeled, sliced onion	1 tbs butter
2-3 sliced cloves garlic	

Arrange sliced vegetables in layers in a casserole, sprinkling each layer with herbs and seasonings. Dot with butter, cover and cook for about an hour at 180°C until done.

Sage

He who would live for aye must eat sage in May.

Sage, *Salvia officinalis*, is a perennial and grows as a small, shrubby bush with grey-green, pebbly leaves and beautiful blue flowers. There is also a purple or red-leafed sage and several variegated forms which may be used in cooking too, but the grey and the purple are considered to have the best flavour. Sage may be grown from seed, cutting or root division and needs a sunny, well-drained situation. However, sage is not a long lived perennial like thyme and often dies after a wet winter.

The leaves are the part used and have a strong flavour. They aid the digestion of rich and fatty foods and are traditionally served in stuffings and with pork. Sage is also used with onions, cheese and bread, and may be drunk as a tea or eaten on bread and butter as a tonic. Sage should be used lightly, especially when dried, because it can taste bitter. However it is a delicious and healthful herb when properly used.

Sage and Cottage Cheese Filling

Combine and blend into a smooth paste:
250 g cottage or cream cheese   *1-3 tsp finely chopped sage*
1 tsp mixed mustard   *milk or cream*
salt and pepper

337

Sage Bread

Make as for Rosemary Bread using 1½ tbs finely chopped sage instead of rosemary. 1 tsp celery seed may be added or celery salt substituted for salt.

or

sage leaves
butter

French bread

Finely chop washed, dried fresh sage leaves and mix with softened butter. Slice a long French loaf diagonally every 3cm without cutting it right through. Spread soft sage butter onto every slice, wrap whole loaf in aluminium foil and bake in a hot oven until crisp and heated through. Serve hot.

Cheese Straws with Sage

1 cup flour
pinch each salt and cayenne
  pepper
½ tsp mustard powder

75 g butter
½ cup grated cheese
2 tsp chopped sage
water to mix

Sift flour and seasonings, and cut in butter until the mixture is like breadcrumbs. Stir in grated cheese and sage, and mix to a medium dry dough with cold water. Roll out very thin on a floured board and cut into thin strips. Place on a cold oven tray and bake at 200 °C for 8-10 minutes until crisp and golden brown.

Sage Fingers

1½ cups flour
2 tsp baking powder
½ tsp salt

50 g butter
1½ tbs finely chopped sage
milk to mix

Sift together flour, baking powder and salt. Rub in butter, add sage and mix to a light dough with milk. Knead lightly, roll out on a floured board and cut into fingers. Brush with milk, place on a greased tray and bake at 210 °C until brown, about 5 minutes. Serve with soup.

Cheese Fondue with Sage

1 cup dry white wine or cider

2-3 tbs finely chopped sage

338

500 g coarsely grated cheese
1 tbs cornflour
1 tbs lemon juice

pepper to taste
squares or small chunks of
    white bread for dipping

Pour wine or cider into fondue pot and bring to the boil. Remove from heat and add cheese. Return to the heat and stir until cheese melts and bubbles. Blend cornflour and lemon juice until smooth, stir into the fondue and continue to stir until it thickens. Add sage and pepper to taste, lower the heat but keep the fondue bubbling gently all the time. Eat by dipping squares of bread into the fondue on long forks and twirling them round.

Sage and Cheese Quiche

200-250 g pastry
1 cup creamy milk
2 beaten eggs

75 g grated cheese
3-4 finely chopped sage leaves
salt and pepper

Line an 18cm buttered pie plate with pastry. Combine milk and beaten eggs and stir in cheese and sage. Season with salt and pepper and pour into the pastry case. Cook at 190 °C for 30-35 minutes and serve very hot or cold.

Sage and Cheese Souffle

1¼ cups milk
2 eggs, separated
¾ cup soft white breadcrumbs
125 g grated cheese

1 tbs grated onion
2 tsp finely chopped sage
salt and pepper

Warm milk and stir in beaten egg yolks and all other ingredients except egg whites. Stand an hour, then fold in stiffly beaten egg whites and pour into a buttered ovenproof dish. Bake at 180 °C for about 30 minutes.

Welsh Rarebit with Sage

1 cup beer
250 g grated cheese
2 tsp finely chopped sage

salt and pepper
½ tsp mustard

Warm beer in a saucepan, add cheese gradually, stirring all the time. Season and continue to stir until the cheese has melted and the rarebit thickened and heated through. Serve poured over hot buttered toast.

Roast Dumplings with Sage

4 cups fresh, white
   breadcrumbs
1½ tbs finely chopped sage
2 peeled, sliced onions

salt and pepper
1 beaten egg
25 g melted butter

Combine first four ingredients and mix well. Bind with egg and melted butter, mixing with a fork. With wet or floured hands divide into about 12-14 pieces, roll into balls and coat with a little flour. Bake 30-35 minutes in hot dripping round a roast or fry in hot oil 10 minutes each side. Serve with any beef, veal, pork or poultry.

Eel with Sage

Make a marinade by combining:
3 tbs lemon juice
6 tbs oil
1 sliced onion

salt and pepper
1 tsp each chopped parsley,
   dill leaves and tarragon

Cut eels into about 6 medium-sized pieces and marinate for 2-4 hours, turning from time to time. Drain eel, reserving marinade, and wrap each piece in a slice of bacon, enclosing a sage leaf or two. Tie with thin string and place pieces in a casserole. Pour strained marinade over and cook uncovered for about 30 minutes at 180 °C until eels are tender.

Kidney and Mushrooms with Sage

6 lambs' kidneys
salt and pepper
2 tbs oil or lard
1 sliced rasher bacon

1-2 tbs flour
1½ cups stock and wine
50 g sliced mushrooms
1-2 tbs chopped sage

Skin and slice kidneys and remove the cores. Season with salt and pepper and fry in a pan in hot oil or lard for about 5 minutes, browning both sides gently. Lift kidneys out with a slotted spoon and keep them hot. Fry bacon, lift out when just cooked, and stir in flour. Cook gently for 2-3 minutes, stir in stock, or mixture of stock and wine, and bring to the boil. Add mushrooms and return kidneys and bacon to the pan, taste and add more salt and pepper if necessary. Finally stir in sage and simmer until meat is reheated and the whole dish flavoured. Serve on hot toast, or with rice, or mashed potatoes.

Sage with Lamb

Five hours before cooking make several slits in the skin of a leg of lamb or hogget. Rub finely chopped sage into the slits and a little garlic. Place in a baking dish and pour ½ cup red wine over the meat, sprinkle with salt and leave to marinate. Cook in the usual way, basting meat with wine and pan juices about every 30 minutes.

Pork and Sage Casserole

2 tbs lard or oil
750 g pork pieces or 375 g
    each pork pieces and pork
    liver
2 chopped onions
2 chopped carrots

2 chopped sticks celery
4 tbs flour
2 cups stock or water
1 tbs finely chopped sage
salt and pepper to taste

Heat lard in a large frying pan and brown sliced pork and/or pork liver on both sides for about 5 minutes altogether. Remove to a casserole and fry vegetables in lard for about 10 minutes. Stir in flour, continue to fry a further 3 minutes before gradually adding stock or water and bring to the boil stirring all the time. Add sage and seasoning and pour over the meat in the casserole. Mix well, cover and cook at 180 °C until meat is quite tender, about 1½ hours.

Pork Fingers with Sage

potatoes
pork fingers
1 beaten egg
1 onion

breadcrumbs
sage
salt and pepper

Peel, cut and bring potatoes to the boil, and boil one minute while preparing meat. Cut skin and excess fat off meat, and dip pork in beaten egg. Mix sage, salt and pepper with breadcrumbs and roll meat in the mixture. Chop onion, place on one side of a large roasting pan and lay pork fingers on top of onions. Drain potatoes and place on other side of the pan. Cook in a moderate oven, 180 °C, for about an hour. Baste potatoes occasionally.

Rabbit Stew with Sage

1 rabbit, jointed into serving
  pieces
½ cup flour
pepper and salt
1 tbs finely chopped sage
4 tbs oil or butter

4 slices chopped bacon
1½-2 cups stock, or 1 cup red
  wine and 1 cup stock
250 g mushrooms
parsley to garnish

Toss pieces of rabbit in a mixture of flour, seasoning and sage and
fry in hot oil with bacon until well browned. Remove to a casserole
and heat stock, or stock and wine, before pouring over meat. Cover
and cook at 170 °C for 2 hours, then add mushrooms and cook a
further 30 minutes. Garnish with chopped parsley before serving.

Sage and Sausage Loaf

1 kg sausagemeat, or minced
  ham or pork
1 minced onion
2 tsp fresh, or 1 tsp dried,
  sage

salt and pepper
¼ cup cream
1 beaten egg
strips of bacon

Thoroughly mix meat, onion, sage and seasonings and bind with
cream and beaten egg. Form into a roll, and arrange strips of bacon
along it. Tie it up in a floured cloth and simmer in a large saucepan
of water, to which 1 tbs vinegar has been added, for about 2-3
hours. Serve cold, sliced with salad or as a sandwich filling.

Veal and Ham with Sage

8 very thin slices of veal
8 thin slices ham or bacon
8 fresh sage leaves
salt and pepper to taste

4 tbs butter
1 tbs oil
4-5 tbs white wine

On each slice of veal arrange a slice of ham or bacon and a sage
leaf. Season to taste with salt and pepper, turn in the sides and roll
each slice up securing it with a toothpick. Heat combined butter
and oil in a pan and cook veal rolls until light brown on all sides.
Add wine, cover and cook gently until meat is tender, about 10-15
minutes.

Veal and Ham Pie

500 g veal steak
250 g ham or bacon
3 tbs oil or butter
1 sliced onion
1 sliced carrot

1 tbs flour
1 cup stock or water
salt and pepper to taste
1 tbs finely chopped sage
100-150g puff pastry

Trim meat, cut into small pieces and cook gently in hot oil or butter to brown all sides. Add sliced onion and carrot and cook, stirring, for several minutes. Add flour, cook and stir for two more minutes, stir in stock or water and bring to the boil. Season to taste and add sage. Pour into a shallow pie dish and cover with thin pastry. Use trimmings to decorate the pie top, brush with milk and bake in a hot oven, 210 °C, for 30-40 minutes.

Sage Jelly

1 tbs gelatine softened in a
   little cold water
½ cup boiling water
¼ cup castor sugar

1 tbs lemon juice
½ cup wine vinegar
½ cup finely chopped sage

Pour boiling water onto softened gelatine and sugar, and stir to dissolve, add strained lemon juice, vinegar and finely chopped sage. Pour into small moulds or a flattish dish and allow to set. Serve, either unmoulded or cut into small squares with hot or cold roast meat, especially pork. Use more or less sage to taste.

Sage and Onion Stuffing for Pork

3 onions, finely sliced
50 g butter
150 g fresh white breadcrumbs
2 tsp dried or 3 tsp fresh sage

1 tsp finely chopped parsley
salt and pepper
1 beaten egg or milk to mix

Boil onions for 15-20 minutes in a little salted water and drain them. Add butter, breadcrumbs and herbs and season to taste. Bind with beaten egg or milk. Use to stuff a joint or cook separately in a small ovenproof dish, basting with 1 tbs dripping and cooking for about 30 minutes at 200 °C.

Sage and Ginger Topping for Roast Pork

Mix together:

½ tsp salt

¼ tsp ground ginger

3 tsp finely minced sage

pepper

Rub into skin before roasting in the usual way. Use only 2 tsp dried sage if no fresh sage is available.

Sage Sauce

25 g butter

1 peeled, sliced onion

1 tbs finely chopped sage

1 tsp flour

1 tsp sage vinegar

1 cup gravy or stock

salt and pepper

Melt butter in a saucepan and gently cook onion and sage for about 10 minutes, sprinkled with 1 tsp flour. Stir in vinegar and gravy and season to taste. Reheat and cook 5-10 minutes. If stock is used instead of gravy, use 1 tbs flour. Serve with pork.

Sage and Apple Sauce

250 g peeled, sliced apple

2-3 finely chopped sage leaves

sugar to taste

water

Place apple, sage, sugar and a little water to prevent fruit from sticking, in a saucepan, and cook gently for 5-10 minutes. Serve with pork or duck and use hot or cold.

Sage and Lemon Sauce

25 g butter

1 small, peeled, sliced onion

1 tbs flour

1 tbs finely chopped sage

½ cup stock

1 tsp grated lemon rind

1 tsp lemon juice

salt and pepper

Melt butter in a saucepan and gently cook onion for 10 minutes. Stir in flour and sage and gradually add stock, stirring to keep sauce smooth. Add lemon rind and juice and season to taste. Cook gently 10-15 minutes, adding more stock or water if necessary. Serve with boiled bacon or ham, duck, goose or pork.

Sage and Leek Pie

1½ cups flour	½ cup top milk
75 g butter	1 beaten egg
pinch salt	salt and pepper to taste
2-3 tbs cold water	3-4 sage leave
6 leeks	strips of bacon
25 g butter	grated cheese

Make a pastry by rubbing butter into flour and salt until crumbly and then adding cold water to make a soft dough. Roll this out and line a greased pie plate. Cook washed, sliced leeks in 25 g butter on a low heat until soft. Combine milk and beaten egg and pour over leeks filling the pie dish. Add pepper and salt to taste, sprinkle with chopped fresh sage and top with strips of bacon and/or grated cheese. Bake at 210°C for 20 minutes, reduce heat to 190°C and cook for a further 20 minutes. Onions may be used instead of leeks.

Baked Onions Stuffed with Sage

4 large, firm onions	8 finely chopped sage leaves
boiling water	¼ tsp ground nutmeg
⅓ cup fresh breadcrumbs	salt and pepper
½ cup grated tasty cheese	1 cup cream or sour cream

Peel onions and cook in boiling water until almost tender but still firm. Drain and remove most of inside of onions with a sharp knife. Chop this onion finely and combine with breadcrumbs, cheese and sage, nutmeg and seasoning. Bind with a little cream or sour cream and pile stuffing back into onion shells. Stand in a baking dish and pour rest of cream round them. Bake about 40 minutes at 200°C.

Savoury Pancake Filling with Sage

1 cup stewed apple	salt and pepper to taste
1 tbs minced onion	pinch ground nutmeg
2-3 finely chopped sage leaves	1-2 tbs wine
250 g minced, cooked pork	

Combine all ingredients and simmer until well heated through and blended. Use to fill hot pancakes.

White Beans and Sage

½ kg cooked haricot beans   2 tbs tomato puree
2-4 finely chopped sage leaves   salt and pepper
4 tbs oil

Cook beans in hot oil with finely chopped sage, stirring and cooking gently until oil is absorbed. Add tomato puree and season to taste. Serve as a hot vegetable or cold as a salad.

Salad Burnet

They put it also into cool Tankards like Borage.
Sir John Hill

Salad burnet, *Poterium sanguisorba*, is an attractive perennial, native to Europe and Britain. It grows as a pretty, low clump of stems with pairs of small, fresh, green, toothed leaflets growing up them. The flowers grow in thimble-shaped heads on taller stems and are greenish-red. Grown from seed, salad burnet is wind-pollinated and self-sows readily. It is hardy, preferring a slightly dry soil, and should not be allowed to become too wet in winter or it will rot at the base. The leaves of salad burnet were, as the name suggests, important as a salad herb in the past because they were available all year round. The leaves, which taste faintly of cucumber, are cooling and pleasant in any mixed salad, and are also used in spreads and dips, sauces, drinks and vinegar. Salad burnet should be picked in whole leaves from around the outside of the plant like parsley, and the tiny leaves may then be stripped off the stems. It may be added at the begining of cooking, to asparagus, bean, celery or mushroom soups and is part of the classic ravigote and chivry butters.

347

Chivry Butter

50 g creamed butter

1 tsp each salad burnet, chives, parsley, shallots and tarragon, all finely chopped

Blend well and keep in a covered container in the refrigerator. A little lemon juice may be added.

Ravigote Butter

equal quantities of the following herbs, finely chopped: burnet, chervil, chives, cress and tarragon

a few capers
1 clove garlic, crushed

Weigh herbs and add twice their weight in butter. Mix them together until completely blended, adding a little salt and cayenne pepper. If mixture is too stiff, add a few drops of olive oil.

These herbs may be added in the same proportions to mayonnaise and served with crab or other cold seafood.

Salad Burnet Dip

Combine 250 g cream cheese and 1 handful salad burnet leaves stripped from their stems and chopped. Add freshly ground pepper and salt and thin with a little milk, cream or yoghurt to the desired consistency, or leave thick and use as a spread.

Herb and Cream Cheese Spread

250 g cream cheese
1 tsp grated horseradish
2 tbs finely chopped parsley
2 tbs finely chopped burnet
2 tbs minced chives
1 minced shallot

Combine all ingredients and blend well. Store in a covered container in the refrigerator at least 12 hours to chill and allow flavours to blend. Garnish with a sprig of salad burnet.

Burnet and Sour Cream Dip

Use ½ cup finely chopped salad burnet leaves to every 2 cups sour cream. Mix well and store in a covered container in the refrigerator overnight to allow flavours to blend. Serve with crackers, chips or as a salad dressing, or with baked jacket potatoes.

Burnet and Claret Cup

24 sprigs salad burnet
2 litres claret
2 cups orange juice
6 ripe peaches

1 cup sugar
2 bunches white, 1 bunch
    purple grapes, separated

Marinate burnet in claret and orange juice for 4 hours. Slice peaches, add sugar and separated grapes and combine in a punch bowl. Pour liquid over and add ice to taste. Burnet may be strained out.

Salad Burnet and Mint Sauce

To each 100 g butter use 2 tbs each finely chopped salad burnet and mint leaves. Melt butter and heat leaves gently for 10 minutes. Pour over grilled fish and add salt and pepper to taste.

Asparagus and Burnet Soup

500 g fresh asparagus
bunch salad burnet
1 peeled, sliced onion
1 peeled, diced potato
2 cups chicken stock

2 tbs butter
½ cup cream
½ cup milk
salt, pepper and nutmeg
burnet to garnish

Chop asparagus, strip burnet leaves from stems and cook with onion and potato in the chicken stock until vegetables are tender. Remove from heat and blend, or put through a mouli, and return to the saucepan. Add butter chopped in small pieces, cream and milk, and reheat but do not boil. Taste and season with salt, pepper and a little freshly ground nutmeg. Garnish with fresh burnet leaves.

Savory

Sommer Savourie is not full so hot as Winter Savorie ... it maketh thin and doth marvellously prevaile against winde: therefore it is with good successe boiled and eaten with beanes, peason, and other windie pulses ...   John Gerard

Summer savory, *Satureja hortensis*, and winter savory, *Satureja montana*, are the two savories commonly used in cooking. However, I have also used the creeping savory, *Satureja repanda*, because it grows so well for me, and I find the flavour quite as good as winter savory though the leaves are less tender than those of summer savory. Summer savory, which is an annual, is grown from seed, and germinates more quickly if the seeds are soaked for a short time in hot water before sowing. It is delicious with peas and beans so it should be sown early to be ready at the same time as these vegetables. Winter savory is perennial but the leaves are more chewy, so it is only used when summer savory is not available. Winter savory may be grown from seed, cuttings or root divison. All savories like an open, sunny situation and a light soil. Summer savory is picked by hand, whole leafy sprigs at a time, but care should be taken to pick so as to encourage bushy growth, then the plants may last longer. As well as its traditional use with peas and beans, savory tastes good with courgettes, beetroot and other vegetables, and may be used in recipes in place of hys-

350

sop, thyme or sage. Because of its flavour it may be used as a substitute for salt, so always taste food flavoured with savory before adding other seasonings.

Prawn Cocktail with Savory

1 cup plain yoghurt or sour cream	squeeze lemon juice or a little lemon rind
2 tbs tomato puree	salt and pepper to taste
2 tsp finely chopped savory	250 g peeled prawns

Combine all ingredients except prawns and mix well. Chill, and just before serving fold in prawns. Serve in individual glasses with thin bread and butter.

Savory Meat Loaf

500 g minced beef	2 tsp chopped chives
250 g pork sausagemeat or minced bacon	2 tsp chopped savory
¾ cup fresh breadcrumbs	2 tsp Worcestershire sauce
1 grated onion	salt and pepper
1 tbs chopped parsley	2 beaten eggs

Combine all ingredients and mix well. Form into a loaf shape, tip into a greased 1 kg loaf tin and stand in a pan containing 3 cm cold water. Place in the oven and bake at 180 °C for 1½ hours. Serve hot, or if serving cold, cover with foil and press with weights while cooling.

Savory Stuffing for Fish

50 g butter	2-3 tsp finely chopped savory
½ finely chopped onion	salt and pepper
1 cup fresh breadcrumbs	1 beaten egg
grated rind and juice 1 small lemon	

Melt butter in a pan and gently fry onion until soft but not brown. Combine in a basin with breadcrumbs, lemon rind and juice and savory. Season with salt and pepper to taste and bind with beaten egg.

Veal and Savory Terrine

Line bottom and sides of a rectangular ovenproof dish with slices of bacon. Mince together:

750 g each calves' liver and
    veal

1 onion

Add:

2 cloves crushed garlic
1-2 tbs tomato paste
1 tbs chopped savory

2 tsp chopped oregano
½ cup soft butter
½ cup red wine

Mix well together, seasoning with salt and pepper to taste. Transfer this mixture into the dish on top of bacon slices, lay 4 bay leaves on top and cover with more slices of bacon. Cover dish and cook in a pan of water in a moderate oven, about 180 °C, for about 2½ hours. Remove from oven, take off the lid and cover the top with a piece of foil and weights to press down while it cools. Keep 2-3 days in a cool place to allow flavours to infuse before serving.

Savory Stuffing for Meat

1 cup fresh breadcrumbs
1 tbs finely chopped savory
1 tbs minced onion
1 clove crushed garlic

1-2 tbs butter chopped in
    small pieces
salt and pepper

Combine all ingredients, stuff into a boned joint and cook as usual. This is nice with lamb, hogget or beef.

Rice and Savory Stuffing

6-8 tbs cooked rice
1 tbs finely chopped savory

2 tbs finely chopped parsley
1 beaten egg

Combine all ingredients and mix well. If egg is not sufficient to bind the mixture, add a little milk or stock. This should be enough for a 2 kg chicken. Increase quantity as necessary for larger birds.

Fresh Tomato Sauce with Savory

500 g skinned, chopped
    tomatoes

1 cup water
salt and pepper

1 peeled, minced onion   *50 g butter*
1 tbs finely chopped savory   *1 tbs flour*

Combine first four ingredients and cook gently until soft. Rub through a sieve, taste and add salt and pepper. Melt butter in a saucepan, stir in flour and then gradually add tomato mixture, stirring all the time. Bring to the boil and simmer 3 minutes, until sufficiently thick. Serve hot or cold with grilled meat, fritters, meat balls, etc.

Savory Tripe

1 tbs oil   *250 g mushrooms*
1 chopped onion   *1¼ cups stock*
2 cloves garlic   *1 tbs fresh, finely chopped*
1 kg cooked tripe   *savory*
flour

Cook onion and garlic gently in oil. Roll cubed tripe in flour and fry until golden brown. Tip into a casserole, add mushrooms and stock and cook gently at 160 °C for about an hour. Add finely chopped savory, stir well and stand 5 minutes before serving.

Grape Jelly with Savory

Make a jelly by covering grapes with water and boiling until liquid is a good colour. Strain overnight through a jelly bag. In the morning measure the liquid and add a cup of sugar for every cup of liquid, and the juice of a lemon. Bring to the boil, stirring, and boil until a little liquid will jell on a saucer. Add a good handful of finely chopped summer savory, boil 2 minutes and bottle.

Baked Beans with Savory

In a casserole layer white beans, chopped onion, finely chopped savory and sliced tomatoes. Cover and cook in the oven at 160 °C for 2 hours or until beans are tender. Savory may also be added to taste to canned baked beans to improve the flavour.

Broad Beans with Savory

1 finely chopped, small onion	*2 cups water*
1 clove garlic	*1 kg podded broad beans*
25 g butter	*1-2 tsp chopped savory*

Cook onion and garlic in butter until tender. Add water and beans, cover and cook until done. Drain, add a little butter, and shake finely chopped savory through the beans.

or

Cook broad beans in the usual way and serve with following sauce: Melt 25 g butter and stir in 1½ tbs flour. Gradually stir in 400 ml milk and cook until it thickens. Add salt and pepper to taste, a pinch of nutmeg and 1-2 tbs freshly chopped savory, and stir well. Remove from the heat and add 1-2 tbs cream. Pour over the hot beans and serve.

Bean Stew with Savory

250 g dried beans, soaked	*1 clove garlic, crushed*
* overnight*	*½ cup tomato puree*
3 cups boiling water	*2 cups stock*
1 tsp salt	*1 tsp chopped savory*
2 tbs oil	*1 tsp chopped marjoram*
2-3 peeled, sliced onions	*1 cup chopped cabbage*

Drain soaked beans, simmer in boiling water with salt until tender, about 2 hours. Heat oil in a pan and fry onions and garlic about 10 minutes. Add tomato puree, stock and herbs and cook 10 minutes. Drain beans and add to sauce in a large saucepan, cover and cook slowly for about 2 more hours. Add cabbage after the first hour, and taste and season before serving.

Carrots with Savory

12 young carrots	*1 tsp savory vinegar*
boiling water	*salt and pepper to taste*
1 tbs butter	*1-2 tsp finely chopped savory*
2 tsp honey	

Slice carrots lengthways in 2-4 pieces and cook until tender in a little boiling water. Melt butter in a pan, add all other ingredients except savory and shake carrots to coat them in the glaze. Sprinkle in savory, shake again and serve hot.

Green Beans or Peas with Savory

Top, tail and slice fresh green beans and cook in a little boiling water until tender. Drain and add a knob of butter and finely chopped summer savory to taste. Put the lid on the saucepan and shake to mix butter and savory through the beans. Leave 2 minutes for flavours to blend, pour into a dish and serve. This gives more flavour than cooking savory with the beans. Fresh or frozen green peas may be seasoned in the same way.

Green Bean Salad with Savory

Mix cold, cooked green beans with a little finely chopped chicory or torn lettuce and 2 shallots or spring onions, finely chopped. Add 2 finely chopped sprigs savory and dress with oil and vinegar. Garnish with nasturtium flowers.

Onion Soup with Savory

4 tbs butter
500 g peeled, sliced onions
4 tbs flour

4 cups beef or chicken stock
2 tsp savory
salt and pepper to taste

Melt butter and fry finely sliced onion until tender but only just brown. Stir in flour and brown, stirring all the time. Continue to stir, adding stock and bring to the boil. Add savory, cover and simmer gently 15-20 minutes. Taste and season before serving.

Savory Zucchini

Cook sliced zucchini and finely chopped onion together in a little oil or butter until tender. Serve garnished with finely chopped summer savory.

Savory Stuffed Peppers

4 large green peppers
1 tbs butter or oil
1 sliced onion
250 g minced meat
1 slice white bread

1 beaten egg
salt and pepper
1 tbs finely chopped savory
1 tbs finely chopped parsley
3 tbs water

Cut stalk end out of peppers with a sharp knife and remove seeds but keep the tops. Blanch peppers in boiling salted water for 3 minutes and leave to drain upside down. Heat butter and fry onion for about 5 minutes before adding meat and cooking until brown on all sides. Remove from the heat. Place bread in a bowl and pour beaten egg over it. When egg is absorbed, mash bread and add to meat mixture with seasoning and herbs. Blend well, then spoon into the peppers. Replace their tops, stand them in a dish and add water. Cover and bake at 190 °C for ½ hour. Serve with tomatoes.

Sorrel

At the present day, English cookery is not much indebted to this plant (Rumex acetosa), *although the French make use of it to a considerable extent.*

Isabella Beeton

There are two kinds of sorrel used in cooking — garden sorrel, *Rumex acetosa*, and French sorrel, *Rumex scutatus*. Both are perennial and grow wild in Europe. Garden sorrel is better known and is a larger and taller plant. Its leaves lack flavour in the very early spring but this develops as the weather warms, and it may be used raw in salads or cooked in sauces, soups and many other dishes most of the year. Garden sorrel prefers a dampish situation and thrives in acid soil. French sorrel, which is better known on the Continent, likes a drier soil and an open situation. Its leaves, which are about as long as they are broad, have a milder and more consistent flavour. French sorrel has a beautiful lemony taste, and is used in the same way as garden sorrel. To prepare, fold each leaf in half lengthways, and cut out stalk before chopping.

Sorrrel leaves, finely chopped, give a slightly lemony, acid taste to any green salad and may also be used in potato salads dressed with mayonnaise. They are used in soups of many sorts and as a puree may be added to sauces, omelettes and egg tarts. They make rich food more digestible. Always scald milk or cream before adding them to sorrel or the milk will

357

curdle. Stainless steel, glass or enamel dishes should be used as sorrel will react with aluminium or other metals.

Cottage Cheese with Sorrel

Mix finely chopped sorrel leaves into cottage or cream cheese to taste, add a little melted butter or lemon juice and mix well. Use as a spread on biscuits or bread.

Smoked Fish and Sorrel Pate

4 smoked fish fillets	10-15 sorrel leaves
50 g butter	1 thinly sliced lemon

Remove skin and bones from fish, flake into a bowl and mash until smooth. Melt butter in a frying pan, add finely chopped sorrel (without stalks) and cook gently until it wilts. Beat this into the fish, press into a dish and chill until firm. Serve, garnished with slices of lemon, as a spread on biscuits or toast.

Herb Beer

1 litre sorrel leaves	¼ litre fresh currants
½ litre horehound leaves	25 g root ginger
½ litre dandelion roots	1 kg brown sugar
4 sliced lemons	4 litres water

Place washed leaves and scrubbed dandelion roots in a saucepan with other ingredients. Stir to dissolve sugar and boil gently for 1½ hours. Strain through cheese cloth. When lukewarm add 1 tsp cream of tartar and 1 cake yeast dissolved in a little warm water. Cover and stand in a warm place for 3 days. Skim, bottle and seal. Ready to drink in 2 weeks.

Egg and Cheese Roll

125 g cottage cheese	2-3 tbs chopped parsley
4 eggs, separated	1 tsp mustard powder
4 chopped sorrel leaves	75 g grated mild cheese

Sieve cottage cheese into a basin and beat in egg yolks. Beat in finely chopped sorrel and parsley and sieved mustard powder. Beat egg whites stiff and fold them into the mixture. Line a Swiss roll tin with buttered paper and pour in mixture. Bake at 200 °C for about 20 minutes until mixture is set and the top brown. Remove from the oven and sprinkle with grated cheese. Take hold of one of the narrow ends of the butter paper and roll up like a Swiss roll. Slip onto a warmed plate, cut into slices and serve.

Sorrel Omelette

Use a handful of sorrel leaves to a 6-egg omelette. Wash and dry the leaves and chop them finely without their stalks. Make an omelette in the usual way, adding a little finely chopped parsley or chervil and crushed garlic. When omelette is nearly cooked spread the raw sorrel over it and fold in half. The heat will only warm the sorrel so that it will have a refreshing taste.

Poached Eggs with Sorrel

500 g young sorrel leaves *knob butter*
a little water *4 poached eggs*
salt and pepper

Cook sorrel gently in a little water in a covered pot. Season, chop leaves, add butter and cook 5 more minutes. Dish up onto hot plates and serve with a poached egg on each portion.

Sorrel Souffle

3 tbs butter *60 g grated gruyere cheese*
4 tbs flour *1 cup sorrel puree*
1 cup milk *3 eggs, separated*
salt, pepper and nutmeg

Melt butter and stir in flour and milk, and bring to the boil, stirring all the time to avoid lumps. Remove from the heat and season with salt, pepper and freshly ground nutmeg. Add grated cheese and sorrel puree and beat in egg yolks. Beat egg whites until quite stiff and fold them into the mixture. Pour into a buttered souffle dish and bake at 180 °C for about 30 minutes. Take straight from the oven to the table or the souffle will sink.

Eggs Stuffed with Sorrel

¾ *cup sorrel*
2 tbs butter
salt and pepper
8 hard-boiled eggs

3 tbs cream cheese
1 tbs grated cheese
pinch nutmeg

Wash sorrel, cut off stalks and cook gently in butter, with pepper and salt to taste, in a covered pan. When tender put through a mouli or sieve. Halve eggs, remove yolks and put them through a sieve. Combine yolks with sorrel and cheeses, add a pinch of nutmeg and blend well. Pile stuffing into egg whites and serve with watercress or lettuce.

Fish with Sorrel

Poach a piece of fish in court-bouillon with onion, herbs and some lemon peel. Wash and cook sorrel until tender and put it through a sieve or mouli. Mix in some finely chopped tarragon. Serve fish on this bed of sorrel, either hot or cold, and garnish with slices of lemon and/or hard-boiled egg.

or

Brush small, cleaned fish or fish fillets with oil and season with salt and pepper. Wrap each in large sorrel leaves to completely cover and place in a casserole. Cover and cook at 190 °C until fish are tender, about 20-30 minutes. Remove and discard sorrel before serving.

or

4 medium-sized fish
6 tbs butter
¾ *cup white breadcrumbs*

4 tbs chopped sorrel
salt and pepper
2 tbs lemon juice

Fillet fish and lay skin side down on a board. Melt 4 tbs butter and blend with breadcrumbs, sorrel, pepper and salt. Divide this stuffing among the fish fillets and roll them up, starting with the head end. Place stuffed fish close together in a casserole, dot with 2 tbs butter and pour the lemon juice over. Cover and cook at 190 °C for 30-40 minutes.

Sorrel Salad

500 g young sorrel leaves
6 chopped, pickled walnuts
1 tbs lemon juice

3 tbs oil
salt and pepper

Finely chop sorrel leaves and mix in walnuts. Dress with a mixture of seasoned lemon juice and oil and toss.

Sorrel and Dandelion Salad

Wash and dry equal quantities of sorrel and blanched dandelion leaves and tear them into bite-sized pieces. Arrange in a salad bowl and pour over a dressing made by combining and shaking well 3 tbs oil, 1½ tbs lemon juice and a pinch each of salt, sugar and pepper. Toss and serve.

Sorrel and Lettuce Salad

Combine washed lettuce torn into bite-sized pieces, diced cucumber, finely chopped spring onions or shallots and 4-6 leaves finely chopped sorrel. Dress with oil and lemon juice shaken together. Corn salad may be added.

Sorrel and Potato Salad

750 g peeled, sliced potatoes
1 grated onion
1 apple, sliced
2 tbs lemon juice

1 tbs chopped lovage
4 tbs oil
pepper and salt
sorrel leaves

Cook potatoes gently in boiling water until tender. Drain and combine with onion, apple tossed in lemon juice, finely chopped lovage, oil and pepper and salt to taste. Toss well and leave to cool. Wash and dry sorrel leaves, removing their stems and arrange in a salad bowl. Pile cold potato salad into the middle and serve.

Gooseberry and Sorrel Sauce

1 cup green gooseberries
water
1 glass sherry

1-2 tsp sugar
½ cup sorrel puree
25 g butter

Cook gooseberries gently in a little water and when tender rub them through a sieve. Combine with other ingredients, simmer for 3-4 minutes and serve very hot with young goose or duck.

Sorrel Sauce

1 litre sorrel leaves
butter

pepper

Wash and chop sorrel leaves, put them wet into a saucepan and cook carefully 5 minutes. Drain and return to the pan with butter and freshly ground pepper. Beat to a puree with a betel or wooden spoon and serve hot with pork or duck.

Creamy Sorrel Sauce

125 g sorrel leaves
25 g butter
1 tbs flour

1 cup stock
1 beaten egg yolk
1 tbs cream

Wash and chop sorrel finely and cook gently in a saucepan with melted butter until tender. Stir in flour and blend in stock, stirring until it is smooth and thick. Season to taste with salt and pepper, remove from the heat and stir in beaten egg yolk and cream. Serve with fish, eggs or meat.

Sorrel Soup

50 g butter
250 g washed, chopped sorrel
3 cups chicken stock

salt and pepper
2 egg yolks
½ cup cream

Melt butter in a saucepan, add sorrel and cook gently for about 5 minutes. Add chicken stock, bring to the boil, cover and reduce heat. Allow soup to simmer 20-25 minutes. Put soup through a sieve, mouli or blender, return to the saucepan and reheat. Season with salt and pepper to taste. Beat egg yolks and cream together lightly and add 1 ladle of soup. Pour this into the soup allowing it to curdle. Reheat but do not boil, and serve. 2 tbs finely chopped chervil may be added to vary the flavour.

Sorrel and Lentil Soup

1 handful sorrel
1 tbs butter
1½ litres chicken stock

150 g cooked lentils
salt and pepper
3-4 tbs cream

Cook chopped sorrel in butter, stirring, for about 5 minutes. Add stock and sieved, cooked lentils, bring to the boil and cook, stirring 10 minutes. Add pepper and salt to taste and, before serving, 3-4 tbs cream.

Sorrel and Lettuce Soup

125 g finely shredded sorrel
* leaves*
1 small finely shredded lettuce
1 tbs finely chopped chervil

1 tbs lard or butter
1 litre stock
1 egg

Cook sorrel, lettuce and chervil gently in lard or butter for about 5 minutes, stirring. Add stock, cover and simmer for about 15 minutes. Season with pepper and salt to taste and pour in lightly beaten egg, holding the basin high and letting it form a thin stream to set as it meets the hot soup. Serve garnished with more chervil.

Braised Sorrel

1 kg sorrel
2 cups water
4 tbs butter
2 tbs flour
3 cups chicken stock

pinch salt and castor sugar
3 eggs
½ cup scalded cream
150 g butter

Wash sorrel, remove stalks and cook in water over a low heat until it wilts. Drain. In another saucepan melt butter and stir in flour, mix well and gradually add stock, stirring all the time. Bring to the boil and cook gently for 3 minutes. Season with salt and sugar and add sorrel. Transfer to a casserole and cook at 180 °C for about an hour. Sieve the mixture, add beaten eggs and cream and blend in butter. Stir well and serve.

Chiffonade

Chop finely ½ lettuce and an equal quantity of sorrel leaves. Cook gently in 25 g butter until soft. Add a little stock or water and 1 tbs rice and simmer until rice is cooked.

Sorrel Puree

500 g sorrel
1 tbs butter
½ cup scalded top milk or
  cream

2 egg yolks or 1 egg
1 tbs chopped parsley
salt and pepper

Wash and drain sorrel and cook very gently in butter in a covered pan until tender. Chop finely, then stir in milk and egg beaten together. Add chopped parsley and season to taste.

Stinging Nettle

To Mrs Symons, and there we did eat some Nettle
porridge, which was made on purpose today, and
was very good.   Samuel Pepys

Stinging nettle, *Urtica dioica*, is a weed, naturalised over much of the world. A perennial with a creeping rootstock, stinging nettle also self-sows so it spreads quickly if unchecked. The whole plant is covered with coarse stinging hairs, which are hollow and sharp, with a swollen poison sac at the base. Once dried or cooked, however, the 'sting' disappears. For centuries the stinging nettles has been enjoyed as a pot herb, or vegetable, in soups and stuffings, puddings and drinks. The young tops, which must be picked with gloves on or plastic bags covering hands and wrists to avoid the stings, are generally used only in spring for, as the plants grow towards flowering, the silica crystals in them taste gritty and unpleasant. Stinging nettles are a valuable food containing minerals and vitamins and are used commercially to make chlorophyll and in green food colourings. When young shoots are 15-20 cm long cut them and use to make some of the traditional spring dishes, and in this way you may keep a patch of nettles under control. Stinging nettles are excellent in the compost heap and dried in hay or poultry food too.

Nettle Beer

2 kg young nettle tops
4 handfuls each dandelion and
   goosegrass leaves
50 g bruised root ginger

8 litres water
1½ kg sugar
25 g dried yeast

Boil plants in water for 10 minutes, then strain liquid onto sugar in a bucket. Stir to dissolve sugar and when it has cooled to lukewarm, add yeast. Cover and leave in a warm place for 3-5 days. Siphon into clean bottles and leave until clear. It should be ready to drink in about a week.

Nettle Cooler

Boil gently for an hour, 1 kg nettle tops in 2 litres water. Strain and add 500 g sugar to each ½ litre of liquid. Stir well and simmer ½ hour. Cool and dilute with soda water. Less sugar may be used and lemonade added instead of soda water.

Nettle Wine

4 litres nettle tops
10 cm ginger root
zest and juice 2 lemons

4 litres water
2 kg raw sugar
yeast and nutrient

Wash nettle tops and put in a large pan with ginger and lemon zest. Cover with water and simmer about an hour. Strain and add more boiled water to make up to 4 litres. Stir in sugar and when liquid is hot add yeast and nutrient and lemon juice. Stir well and cover. After 4-5 days pour into jars fitted with airlocks and allow to ferment until clear and still. Then bottle and seal.

Nettle Pudding

1 small cup barley
6 handfuls nettle tops

sprig each mint and thyme
1 peeled chopped onion

1 handful dandelion leaves
small bunch sorrel leaves
small bunch watercress

salt and pepper
1 tbs butter
1 beaten egg

Boil barley in water until soft, and drain. Wash and chop the greens and mix into the barley with salt and pepper to taste, and 1 tbs butter. Bind with beaten egg and put into a greased pudding basin. Cover and steam 1½ hours in a saucepan of water. Serve hot with sauce or gravy.

Nettle and Rice Pudding

1 basin nettle tops
¾ cup raw rice
boiling water
3 leeks or 2 onions, sliced

25 g butter
2 tsp marjoram, chopped
salt and pepper

Wash and chop nettles. Wash rice, cook for 5 minutes in boiling water and drain. Cook sliced leeks or onions in melted butter for 5 minutes, add nettles and marjoram and season to taste. Cover and cook gently over a low heat for 5 minutes. Butter a pudding basin and put a layer of mixed vegetables in the bottom and cover with a layer of rice. Continue until all is used. Dot with a little extra butter and cover. Steam in a large saucepan of water for about 1 hour. The water should boil briskly, add more as it boils down. Serve with melted butter, sauce or gravy.

Nettle and Suet Pudding

1 basin nettle tops
2 peeled, sliced onions
25 g butter
50 g grated suet

2 cups breadcrumbs
salt and pepper
1-2 tsp thyme or marjoram
water to mix

Wash and chop nettles. Fry sliced onions in butter, add nettles, cover and allow to cook gently 5 minutes. Mix suet with breadcrumbs, seasonings and thyme or marjoram and add water to bring to a dropping consistency. Layer nettle mixture alternately with suet mixture in a greased pudding basin. Cover and boil in a saucepan as above for 2 hours.

Nettle Souffle

2 tbs butter
2 tbs flour
¼ cup water

4 eggs, separated
1½ cups cooked, sieved or
    blended nettles

Heat butter in a saucepan and stir in flour. Remove from the heat and blend in water until mixture is smooth. Add egg yolks, stir well, then add blended nettles. Add salt and pepper to taste. Finally beat egg whites stiff and fold them into the mixture. Pour into a buttered, floured straight-sided ovenproof dish and bake at 180°C for 30-45 minutes when the souffle should be puffed up and lightly browned. Remove from the oven to the table — if not served at once it will sink.

Nettle Soup

Wash young nettles, chop finely and cook until tender in a little water. Add some milk and butter and season to taste. Thicken with mashed potatoes or a little cornflour mixed with cold water, stirred in and cooked for about 3 minutes.

or

25 g butter
1 sliced onion
2 peeled cubed potatoes
500 g chopped nettle tops

1 litre liquid — ½ milk,
    ½ stock or water
salt and pepper

Melt butter and gently cook onions until golden. Add nettles and potatoes and cook, stirring, for 2-3 minutes. Add stock, cover and cook gently until vegetables are soft. Blend or put through a mouli, add milk, taste and season and reheat but do not boil.

Creamed Nettles

500 g young nettle tops
25 g butter
pinch thyme

salt and pepper
2 tbs water

Cook nettles gently in butter and water with salt, pepper and thyme, until tender. Drain and serve over crumbled fresh bread or hot mashed potato in a warm bowl.

Nettle Haggis

nettles
boiling water
salt and pepper

2-3 tbs oatmeal
rashers of bacon

Cook nettles as above, strain and chop them. Remove rind from bacon and fry it. Remove bacon and keep hot, pour the bacon fat onto the chopped nettles and mix well. Add 1 cup nettle water to the frying pan and add oatmeal when water boils. Stir all the time to make a porridge and season to taste. When oatmeal is properly cooked, stir in nettles and serve with fried bacon.

Nettle and Potato Bake

1 basin nettle tops
50 g butter
1 sliced onion
3 peeled, sliced potatoes

salt and pepper
1 tsp grated nutmeg
1 tsp ground ginger
½-1 cup milk

Wash nettles and cook with sliced onion very gently, covered, for 10 minutes in melted butter. Arrange sliced potatoes in a well-buttered ovenproof dish and season with salt and pepper. Cover with a layer of nettle and onion mixture seasoned with a little nutmeg and ginger. Repeat layers and seasoning and top with a layer of sliced potato. Pour in enough milk to come halfway up the vegetables and dot with butter. Bake at 180 °C for about an hour until milk is absorbed, and potatoes crisp on top.

Nettle Pottage

50 g butter
50 g oatmeal
1 litre stock, milk or water
    salt, pepper

6 heaped tbs finely
chopped nettle tops

Fry oatmeal in butter until brown. Stir in stock and nettles, bring to the boil, stirring, and simmer 10-15 minutes with lid on the pot. Serve hot.

369

Sauteed Nettles

butter	*salt and pepper*
onion	*minced garlic*
nettles	*white sauce*

Melt butter and gently cook peeled, sliced onion. Add washed, chopped nettle tops and saute until green and tender. Season with salt and pepper and a little minced or crushed garlic, and add a spoon or two of water or beer. Serve with a white sauce and mashed potatoes.

or

Wash nettles, chop finely and cook in a little boiling water for a few minutes. Heat some butter in a frying pan and lightly saute a sliced onion before adding some breadcrumbs, salt, pepper and some cooking liquid from the nettles. Add nettles, stir and cook quickly until soft. Mix in a little grated nutmeg.

Westmorland Nettles

Bring ½ litre water to the boil in a large saucepan and add nettle tops. Press them down so that water covers them and boil with the lid off the pot for about 10 minutes. Strain, keep the water for soup, and chop nettles. Put them back in the pan with a little salt and pepper and butter or cream. Stir and reheat quickly until heated through and serve.

Nettle and Oatmeal Stuffing

small basin of nettle tops	*2 tsp chopped tarragon*
3 rashers bacon	*salt and pepper*
1 cup oatmeal	*1 crushed clove garlic*
2 tsp marjoram	*50 g melted butter*

Wash and drain nettles and chop finely. Cut rind off bacon, slice into small pieces and fry gently until brown. Pour nettles, bacon and bacon fat into a bowl and add oatmeal, chopped herbs, salt and pepper, and crushed garlic. Mix well and finally stir in melted butter. Pack stuffing into a 2 kg chicken and fasten the tail skin together with a skewer or sew it. Roast as usual.

Nettle Champ

500 g hot, cooked, mashed   *250 g hot, cooked, chopped*
  potatoes   *nettles*

Mix well and add salt and pepper to taste. Serve very hot in bowls
making a hollow in the centre of each serving to hold a knob of
butter. Dip each spoonful in butter as you eat it.

Tansy

In the Spring time are made with the leaves hereof newly sprung up, and with egs, cakes or tansies, which be pleasant in taste and good for the stomacke.
John Gerard

Tansy, *Tanacetum vulgare*, is a creeping perennial native to Europe and Britain. It dies back in winter but shoots early in spring and the leaves were used, as Gerard describes, as an Easter tonic to purify the system. It grows 60 cm-1 metre high in flower and has bright, dark green, fern-like leaves and clusters of yellow button flowers without rays growing on stiff stems. It is easily propagated by division of the creeping rootstock, as long as it is kept watered, and sometimes becomes very invasive in the garden.

Tansy leaves, which are the part used, were thought to taste slightly of ginger. They should be used only in small quantities because they taste unpleasant in large amounts. The whole leaf should be picked and the leaflets stripped from the stalks and finely chopped before using. Tansy may be used with eggs, cakes, puddings, fish and meat, but it should only be used in small quantities and not eaten too often. It is at its best in spring and summer.

Tansy Biscuits

---

500 g flour   *1 tbs finely chopped tansy*

1 tsp baking powder
pinch salt

1 beaten egg
½ cup milk

Sift flour, baking powder and salt together, then mix in tansy. Combine beaten egg and milk and pour into a well in the centre of the flour mixture. Make into a dough, roll out, cut into rounds and bake 8-10 minutes at 200 °C.

or

¼ cup honey
½ cup butter
1 beaten egg
1 tsp vanilla

2 cups wholemeal flour
2 tsp baking powder
1½ tsp tansy, finely chopped
1 tbs yoghurt

Cream honey and butter, add beaten egg and vanilla. Gradually mix in flour, baking powder and tansy, adding yoghurt to make a dough. Roll out, cut into shapes and bake at 190 °C for about 10 minutes.

Tansy Cake

2 cups flour
2 tsp baking powder
2 tsp finely chopped tansy

1 cup sugar
¾ cup softened butter
4 eggs

Sift together flour and baking powder, add tansy and sugar and mix well. Add softened butter and lightly beaten eggs and beat with a wooden spoon until well mixed. Pour mixture into a lined, greased tin and bake at 180 °C for 30 minutes. Lower temperature to 170 °C and continue baking until cake is cooked, about another 15-30 minutes. Cool on a rack.

Soused Fish with Tansy

For 4 medium-sized fish: Place a tansy leaf inside each gutted fish after cutting off their heads and tails and washing well inside and out. Arrange in a casserole and add:

¾ cup vinegar
¾ cup water
8 peppercorns

pinch salt
pinch freshly ground nutmeg
1 peeled onion, sliced in rings

Cook at 170 °C for an hour and leave to cool in the liquid. Remove tansy and serve with bread and butter.

Tansy Stuffing for Fish

For about 4 medium-sized fish:

4 tbs oatmeal
1-2 tsp grated lemon rind
pinch salt and pepper

2 tsp finely chopped tansy
3 tbs boiling water

Combine oatmeal, lemon rind and seasonings in a bowl, add tansy
and mix well. Pour on boiling water and mix with a fork to bind the
stuffing. Divide into four portions and use to stuff fish which may
then be dipped in seasoned flour and fried in hot butter and oil
until cooked.

Chicken and Tansy Casserole

50 g butter
½ cup flour
2 cups stock
salt and pepper
1 tsp finely chopped tansy
    leaves

1 tsp finely chopped thyme
1½-2 cups cooked, diced
    chicken

Make a sauce by melting butter, stirring in flour and gradually
adding stock, stirring all the time to keep the sauce smooth. Bring
to the boil, season with salt, pepper, tansy and thyme and cook
gently for 3 minutes. Add chicken and combine well. Pour into a
greased casserole, top with buttered breadcrumbs and cook in the
oven at 180 °C until heated through and browned on top.

Tansy with Roast Lamb or Hogget

Make small slits in the skin of the joint before cooking, and insert
about 6 small tansy leaflets into the skin in the same way as
rosemary or garlic is slipped in. Roast as usual.

Tansy Sauce for Cold Chicken or Pork

2 egg yolks
1 cup chicken stock
50 g butter

1 tbs chopped parsley
1 tbs cider vinegar
salt and pepper

1 tsp each finely chopped tansy and tarragon   *1 tsp gelatine soaked in 1 tbs cold water*

Beat egg yolks lightly in the top of a double boiler and stir in stock. Heat over gently boiling water, stirring all the time and adding butter piece by piece, until mixture thickens. Remove from the heat, add chopped herbs and carefully stir in vinegar. Return to the heat, add salt and pepper to taste and stir until sauce is nearly boiling. Add gelatine which has been softened in cold water and stir to blend well. Serve when it is cool or cold, but do not chill.

Tansy Stuffing

Combine in a bowl and mix together well:
1 cup fresh breadcrumbs   *2 tbs chopped parsley*
½ cup shredded suet   *salt and pepper to taste*
1 tsp chopped thyme   *2 tbs grated onion*
1 tsp finely chopped tansy

Bind with 1 beaten egg and use to stuff any meat.

Apple Tansy

500 g apples, peeled and chopped   *2 beaten eggs*
3-4 tbs water   *sugar or honey to taste*
sprig of tansy   *1 cup whipped cream*

Cook apples and tansy gently in water, stirring so that it does not burn. Cool, remove tansy and add beaten eggs and sugar or honey to taste. Cook again slowly, stirring until thick. Fold in whipped cream and serve hot or cold.

Tansy Pudding

Combine in a bowl:
½ cup ground almonds   *freshly grated nutmeg*
1 tbs rose petal syrup   *1 tsp finely chopped tansy*
1 tbs brandy   *¼ cup melted butter*
2 tsp chopped, mixed peel

Add 2 cups boiling milk and when mixture is lukewarm add strained juice of ½ lemon and 4 lightly beaten eggs. Pour into a buttered ovenproof dish and bake at 180 °C for about 45 minutes.

Parsnip and Tansy Wine

2 kg parsnips
4 litres water
1½ kg sugar
1 handful tansy leaves and
   flowers

½ cup cold tea
juice 1 lemon
wine yeast and nutrient

Scrub and slice parsnips and cook until tender in most of the water. Strain hot liquid onto sugar in a bucket and stir well. Put tansy in a little water in a saucepan, bring to the boil and simmer 5 minutes. Strain this with tea and lemon juice onto the sugar and other liquid. When cooled to lukewarm, add yeast and nutrient and pour into a container with an airlock. Allow to work until fermentation ceases, then siphon into bottles and cork.

Tarragon

Tarragon is hot and drie in the third degree, and not to be eaten alone in sallades, but joyned with other herbes, as Lettuce, Purslain, and such like, that it may also temper the coldnes of them ...

John Gerard

There are two types of tarragon, French tarragon, *Artemisia dracunculus* var. *sativa*, and Russian tarragon, *A. dracunculus*. There is also a Mexican marigold, the cloud plant, *Tagetes lucida*, which has a similar flavour to French tarragon and may be used in the same way. French tarragon, which is considered to have the better flavour, rarely flowers and never sets seed, so it must be grown from root division. Tarragon is difficult to grow in climates where it is not cold enough for it to become dormant in winter, so it does not flourish in our mild, wet climate. Growing to ½-1 metre high when full grown, it needs a well-drained open situation with adequate moisture in summer and should be divided and reset often, like chrysanthemums. The leaves, being the part used, have a distinctive flavour with overtones of anise and make the tip of the tongue slightly numb when chewed. Russian tarragon is quite pleasant but in no way comparable in flavour to French tarragon, which is used finely chopped to flavour a variety of chicken and fish dishes, with eggs, salads, meat and in vinegar. It does not dry well but may be frozen like basil in ice cubes. In autumn, cut it back and use the whole stems to flavour vinegar before it dies down.

377

Avocado and Tarragon Appetiser

For each avocado:

3 tbs cold tarragon cream
  sauce
75 g peeled shrimps

finely chopped parsley or
  chervil

Halve avocados and remove stones. Combine sauce and shrimps and pile into middle of each avocado half. Garnish with a little finely chopped parsley or chervil.

Cheese Pate

1 tbs butter
1 tbs flour
½ cup milk
100 g grated cheese
1 tbs mayonnaise
3 small, finely chopped
  gherkins

salt and pepper
1 dessertspoon finely chopped
  tarragon, or chervil, chives
  or lovage

Melt butter, stir in flour and gradually add milk to make a white sauce. Cook, stirring, for 2 minutes. Remove from the heat, add grated cheese and other ingredients and mix well. Turn into a china pot, cool and chill. Serve on biscuits or toast.

Chicken Liver Pate

1 clove garlic
1 onion, finely chopped
25 g butter
250 g chicken liver
1 tsp finely chopped tarragon
  or mint

salt and pepper
75 g creamed butter
1 tbs brandy
clarified butter

Cook crushed garlic and chopped onion in butter until soft. Add chopped liver, herbs, salt and pepper and fry until cooked. Cool, sieve and mix in creamed butter and brandy. Pour into a china pot and serve with biscuits or toast. To store, cover pate with clarified butter.

Chive, Tarragon and Tomato Cocktail

½ litre tomato juice
1 tsp honey
salt and pepper
1 tsp chives, chopped

1 tsp tarragon, chopped
2 tbs each orange and lemon
juice

Warm tomato juice and stir in honey, seasonings and herbs. Stand 2 hours, strain and add fruit juice. Serve chilled.

Pears in Tarragon Cream Appetiser

3 ripe, firm dessert pears
1 tbs tarragon vinegar
¾ cup cream

pepper, salt and sugar
1-2 tsp finely chopped
tarragon

Peel and halve pears and scoop out cores with a teaspoon. Arrange on a plate and brush all surfaces with a little tarragon vinegar to prevent them turning brown. Whip cream with remaining vinegar until thick, season with salt, pepper and sugar to taste, and pour over pears. Garnish with freshly chopped tarragon and chill about 30 minutes before serving.

Tarragon Chicken

Joint chicken and brown in butter. Add 1½ cups white wine, a large sprig of tarragon and a sprinkle of salt and pepper. Cover and cook gently for 30 minutes. Serve with tarragon butter.

or

5 tbs butter
1 tbs tarragon
salt and pepper
1½ kg roasting chicken
1 onion

1 tbs butter
2 tsp flour
½ cup cream
1 tbs finely chopped tarragon

Cream butter with finely chopped tarragon and season with salt and pepper. Spread a little of this over outside of chicken and stuff remainder inside. Slice onion, put with chicken in a roasting pan and cook until tender, about 1½ hours at 180 °C. Remove chicken to serving dish and keep warm. Melt tablespoon of butter with flour and stir into pan juices. Add cream and heat gently but do not boil. Finally add finely chopped tarragon and either pour over chicken or serve sauce separately.

Chicken and Gelatine Mould

1½ tbs gelatine softened in a
    little cold water
1 cup hot chicken stock
250 g minced, cold, cooked
    chicken

2 tsp finely chopped tarragon
salt and pepper
pinch nutmeg
1 hard-boiled egg

Put softened gelatine in a basin and pour on hot chicken stock. Stir until gelatine is dissolved, then strain a little of mixture into a rinsed mould and refrigerate until jelly is set. Combine chicken, tarragon and seasonings with remaining gelatine and stock mixture and stir well. Slice hard-boiled egg and arrange in a pattern on set jelly in mould. Spoon chicken mixture over and allow to set in the refrigerator until firm. Unmould and serve with lettuce salad. Ham or ham and chicken may be used instead.

Chicken, Ham or Rabbit with Tarragon

250 g minced, cooked chicken,
    ham or rabbit
½ cup fresh breadcrumbs
30 g melted butter

2 beaten eggs
¾ cup stock
1 tbs finely chopped tarragon
salt and pepper

Combine all ingredients and mix well. Spoon into 4-6 well-buttered ramekins and place them in a shallow pan of hot water. Bake in the oven at 180 °C for 30-45 minutes until mixture is firm. Remove from the water and allow to stand several minutes before loosening the edges with a knife and turning them out onto a dish. Serve with tarragon sauce.

Chicken and Tarragon Pancake Filling

25 g butter
50 g sliced mushrooms
1-2 tbs flour
½ cup milk
125 g cooked chicken, finely
    chopped

2 chopped, hard-boiled eggs
1 tbs cream
1 tsp chopped tarragon
1 tsp chopped parsley
salt and pepper

Melt butter in a saucepan and gently cook mushrooms until tender. Stir in flour, gradually add milk and bring to the boil. Add remaining ingredients, season to taste, and blend well. Use to fill pancakes and serve hot.

Tarragon Liqueur

1 litre brandy
1 large handful tarragon
1½ cups sugar

water
2 tbs orange flower water

Infuse tarragon in brandy for 5 days. Put sugar in a pan with just enough water to dissolve it and bring to the boil. Cool and combine with strained brandy and orange flower water.

Eggs in Aspic with Tarragon

6 eggs
1 tbs gelatine
¼ cup cold water
1½ cups clear chicken stock

2 tbs sherry, port or madeira
fresh tarragon leaves
1-2 thin slices ham

Hard boil eggs, cool under running water and shell. Soak gelatine in cold water, pour heated chicken stock over and stir until gelatine dissolves. Add wine, and set aspic aside to cool. Spoon a little cold aspic into the bottom of 6 wet moulds, to form a ½cm layer, and leave to set. In each mould make a pattern of 2-4 tarragon leaves and place an egg on top. Spoon more aspic over and cover each egg with a lid of thinly sliced ham. Top with more aspic, chill to set thoroughly, and serve unmoulded with green salad garnished with tomatoes.

Baked Eggs with Tarragon

For each person:
1 egg
2 tbs cream
salt and pepper

¼-½ tsp finely chopped
tarragon

Break an egg into each well-buttered ramekin, add cream and salt and pepper to taste and sprinkle with chopped tarragon. Bake at 200 °C for about 10 minutes until egg whites are set. Remove from the oven and serve at once or egg yolks become hard.

Tarragon and Oysters

1 clove garlic
1 tbs sliced onion
½ cup peeled, sliced
  mushrooms
2 tbs butter
1 tbs each finely chopped
  parsley and tarragon

24 oysters
1 tbs flour
⅓ cup wine or water
parsley and lemon slices to
  garnish

Fry sliced garlic, onion and mushrooms gently in butter until tender but not brown. Add finely chopped herbs and oysters and cook a minute more. Stir in flour, add wine or water, and blend until thick. Cook a further 15 minutes, then pour into a pie dish and brown in the oven for a few minutes. Serve garnished with parsley and slices of lemon.

Tarragon Mince

500 g minced meat
1 minced onion
1 beaten egg

seasoned flour
butter and oil
1 tbs finely chopped tarragon

Combine meat, onion and egg and mix well. Roll into little balls and dip in seasoned flour. Fry in hot butter and oil and when cooked, serve sprinkled with finely chopped tarragon.

Pork Chops with Tarragon

4 tbs oil
4 loin pork chops
salt and pepper

500 g skinned, sliced tomatoes
½-1 tbs finely chopped
  tarragon

Heat oil and brown pork chops quickly on both sides. Season with salt and pepper and transfer to a casserole. Add tomatoes, cover and cook at 190 °C for 1-1½ hours. Remove the lid, add finely chopped tarragon and mix well. Stand covered 5 minutes before serving.

Veal with Tarragon

Use thin slices of veal, dip them in flour and brown them both sides

382

in hot butter in a heavy frying pan. Add 4 sprigs tarragon, a little salt and pepper, ½ cup white wine (or water), cover, and cook gently until tender.

Tarragon Wiener Schnitzel

4 slices wiener schnitzel
½ cup dry red wine
½ onion, finely sliced
½ cup flour

2 tsp finely chopped tarragon
salt and pepper
4 tbs butter
½ cup chicken stock

Place schnitzel in a flat dish and cover with wine and onion. Leave to marinate for 2 hours or more. Drain. Mix together flour, tarragon, salt and pepper and toss schnitzels. Heat butter in a heavy pan and cook meat until crisp and brown on both sides and tender inside. Remove to a serving dish and keep hot. Strain marinade into pan, add chicken stock and bring to the boil, and stir gravy to reduce and concentrate. Pour over schnitzel.

Bearnaise Sauce

1¼ cups white wine vinegar
⅓ cup dry white wine
1 tbs finely chopped shallot
1 tbs finely chopped tarragon

4-6 peppercorns
pinch salt
125 g butter
3 egg yolks

Boil all ingredients except butter and egg yolks over a moderate heat until liquid is reduced to 2 tablespoons. Soften butter. Beat egg yolks until thick in a bowl over simmering hot water. Strain reduced liquid onto egg yolks, whisking all the time, then gradually drop in softened butter a little at a time, combining it thoroughly before adding the next piece. The sauce should become thick and creamy. Remove from the hot water, taste and season with more salt and pepper if necessary. Serve with roast beef.

Tarragon Butter

Cream 25 g soft butter with 1 tsp finely chopped tarragon and 1 tsp lemon juice. Stand an hour in a covered container to let flavour develop before using.

383

Tarragon Cream Sauce

50 g butter
½ cup cream
1-2 tbs finely chopped
  tarragon

1 tbs lemon juice
salt and pepper

Melt butter in a saucepan over a gentle heat and stir in cream. Simmer very gently until sauce is thick. Add tarragon and lemon juice and season to taste. Cover and keep hot for several minutes before serving.

Tarragon Dressing with Cream

1 egg
50 g castor sugar
3 tbs tarragon vinegar

salt and pepper
½ cup cream
1 tsp finely chopped tarragon

Beat egg lightly in a bowl with a fork and stir in sugar and vinegar. Stand the bowl in a pan of boiling water and continue to stir until mixture begins to thicken. Remove from heat and add salt and pepper to taste. Stir well and leave to cool. When cold add lightly whipped cream and finely chopped fresh tarragon.

Gooseberry Sauce with Tarragon

225 g gooseberries
½ cup water
1 tbs sugar
25 g butter

1 tsp lemon juice
pepper and salt
½-1 tsp finely chopped
  tarragon

Top and tail washed gooseberries and cook with water in a saucepan until tender, about 15 minutes. Rub through a sieve to remove skins, return to the heat adding sugar, butter, lemon juice, seasonings and tarragon to taste. Reheat gently and serve as a sauce with fish, pork or poultry.

Remoulade Sauce

1½ cups mayonnaise
2 tsp French mustard

1 tsp each finely chopped
  chervil, parsley and tarragon

2 tsp finely chopped capers

Combine and mix all ingredients well and stand 30 minutes for flavours to infuse.

Tarragon Mayonnaise

4 sprigs parsley
3 sprigs tarragon
3 sprigs chervil
50 g silverbeet or spinach

1½ cups mayonnaise
2 tbs cream
salt and pepper

Cook herbs and spinach, or silverbeet, in a very little water over a low heat until tender, 5-8 minutes. Drain and blend or puree finely through a sieve. Just before serving add puree to mayonnaise with cream, taste and season. Serve with cold fish.

Tarragon Sauce

2 tbs cornflour
1¼ cups milk
3 tbs white wine

5 tbs finely minced tarragon
pinch thyme
pepper and salt

Mix cornflour to a paste with a little cold milk. Bring remaining milk to the boil then stir into cornflour paste. Return to the pan and heat, stirring, until sauce is thick. Add wine, herbs and seasoning to taste, and cook 5 minutes. This sauce may be made in a blender, then cooked for 5 minutes.

Tarragon Sauce Vinaigrette for Cold Asparagus

Mash 1 hard-boiled egg yolk in a bowl and add:
2 finely chopped shallots
2 sprigs each finely chopped
  chervil, parsley and tarragon
½ tsp finely chopped chives

1 tbs finely chopped capers
pinch each salt and paprika
2 tbs tarragon vinegar
4 tbs oil

Mix well, chill and serve.

Orange and Tarragon Salad

4 oranges, peeled and sliced
  in thin rounds
finely chopped tarragon, alone
  or with chervil

French dressing

Combine all ingredients and toss well. Garnish with watercress and serve.

Tomato Salad with Tarragon

Skin tomatoes by putting them in boiling water and peeling off split skins. Drain, slice them and allow to cool. Make a dressing of cream, sour cream or yoghurt containing 1 tbs tarragon or basil and pepper and salt to taste. Pour over tomatoes and serve cold.

Jellied Tarragon Mushrooms

2 cups peeled, sliced
  mushrooms
2 cups chicken stock
1 tbs gelatine softened in 2 tbs
  cold water

juice ½ lemon
2 tsp finely chopped tarragon

Simmer prepared mushrooms in chicken broth until tender. Drain and reserve both mushrooms and stock. Dissolve softened gelatine in a little hot stock, stir well and strain into the rest of the stock. Add lemon juice and tarragon and mix well. Fold in mushrooms and pour into small individual moulds previously rinsed with cold water. Chill until firm. Serve unmoulded on a bed of lettuce, garnished with tomatoes and mayonnaise.

Iced Tomato and Tarragon Soup

2 tbs butter
1 onion, sliced
1 peeled, sliced potato
500 g skinned, chopped
  tomatoes

1 tbs chopped tarragon
1½ cups chicken stock
juice ½ orange
1 tsp grated orange rind
salt, pepper and sugar

Melt butter and gently fry onion and potato about 5 minutes. Add tomatoes and tarragon and mix well before adding stock. Bring to the boil, cover and simmer for 15-20 minutes. Remove from the heat and blend or put through a mouli. Stir in orange juice and rind and season to taste. Chill well before serving sprinkled with a little finely chopped tarragon.

Tarragon Beetroot

Peel hot, cooked beetroot and serve, tossed in the following dressing:

1 tbs oil   *1 tsp sugar*
1 tbs butter   *salt and pepper*
1-2 tsp finely chopped tarragon   *vinegar to taste*

Courgette and Tarragon Fritters

2 cups grated courgettes   *2 tsp finely chopped tarragon*
1 minced onion   *flour to mix (about 5 tbs)*
1 beaten egg   *oil to fry*

Combine courgettes, onion and egg. Stir in tarragon and enough flour to bind. Drop by tablespoonfuls into hot oil and cook and brown both sides. Drain on brown paper and serve.

Thyme

Being eaten with meat it avails for ye dull sighted.
It is good instead of sauce for the use in health.

Dioscorides

Thyme, *Thymus vulgaris*, is a shrubby evergreen perennial, native to the Mediterranean. It comes in two forms: A narrow-leaved French thyme and a broad-leaved English thyme. Both have small aromatic leaves but those of French thyme are narrow and grey whereas those of English thyme are more rounded and dark green. They grow in opposite pairs on upright stems and have pretty pink flowers growing in interrupted whorls at the tops of the branches. There are variegated forms which are also edible but more delicate to grow.

Lemon thyme, *Thymus citriodorus*, is a more mat-forming plant with rounded dark green, or green and gold leaves smelling strongly of lemon. Like common thyme it prefers a limey soil, light and free-draining, and a sunny situation. It spreads into quite large clumps and also has pink flowers. Thyme should be picked in small sprigs all round a bush to make it grow shapely. Thymes may be grown from seed division and cuttings and are used both fresh and dried to flavour meat and fish, soups, stews and sauces. Whole sprigs may be added to food, as the leaves will drop off and the stems may be removed before serving, or the leaves may be stripped off by hand first. Common thyme, which is part of

the bouquet garni, has a strong taste a
lightly.

Lemon thyme may be used in fish pies and sauce
and milk puddings, rice, scrambled eggs, etc. Recipes
lemon balm are suitable for lemon thyme.

Thyme and Pork Pate

2 kg fatty pork
3 sprigs thyme
1 bay leaf

2 cloves crushed garlic
salt and pepper
½ cup water

Remove skin and bones from pork and chop meat into small pieces.
Put all ingredients into a casserole, cover and cook at a low heat,
160 °C, for about 3 hours. Strain and reserve juices. Cut all but the
very fatty pieces of pork up finely so that meat seems mashed.
Press into a bowl and pour strained juices over. The fat will rise to
the top and seal the pate which will keep in the refrigerator for
several weeks.

Vegetable Puree with Thyme

½ cup oil
1 peeled, sliced onion
2 sliced eggplants
2 sliced courgettes
2 large, skinned, chopped
    tomatoes

2 tsp chopped thyme
pinch cayenne pepper
salt to taste

Heat oil in a frying pan and cook onion for 5 minutes. Add
eggplants and courgettes and fry a further 10 minutes over a gentle
heat. Add remaining ingredients, cover and cook gently until
vegetables are all well cooked. Remove the lid and mash mixture
with a fork to mix well. Then cook at a higher heat, uncovered,
stirring to thicken the mixture. Repeat mashing and cooking until
mixture is thick enough. Taste and add more seasoning if
necessary. Pour into a serving dish, cool and chill 3 or more hours
before serving with bread, crackers, or as an hors d'oeuvre.

1 ¼ cups light beer
½ cup water
1 tbs chopped thyme
salt, pepper and sugar

.bes. Heat oil in a pan and brown meat on
.ry onions for about 10 minutes until golden
.ld cook for a minute before stirring in beer
Bring to the boil, stirring all the time, and
.dd browned meat, thyme and some seasoning,
cove. .ntly for 2 hours. Taste and add more seasoning if
needed.

Chicken with Thyme and Rosemary

2 kg chicken, cut into bite-
sized pieces
1 cup flour
3 large eggs beaten with 1 tbs
water

5 cups fresh breadcrumbs
oil for frying
2 cups sour cream
1 tsp each fresh thyme and
rosemary, minced

Dip chicken pieces in flour, then egg and roll in breadcrumbs to
coat all sides. Heat oil, saute chicken until brown on all sides and
remove with a slotted spoon to a casserole. Mix sour cream and
herbs and pour over chicken. Bake at 190 °C until cream is
absorbed. Serve hot or cold as a main dish, or warm as an appetiser
serving with toothpicks.

Chicken with Thyme and Walnuts

1 tbs oil
1 finely chopped onion
1 chopped stick celery
125 g sliced mushrooms
500 g diced, cooked chicken
2 tsp thyme

1 tbs cornflour
½ cup white wine
chicken stock
salt and pepper
75 g chopped walnuts

Heat oil, add onion and celery and cook gently for a few minutes
until soft. Add mushrooms, chicken and thyme, stir and cook
about 10 minutes. Put cornflour in a cup and stir in wine to make a

smooth paste. Add this to the pan with chicken stock to make the right consistency and stir until mixture thickens. Season with salt and pepper, add walnuts and heat through. Serve hot.

Liver and Thyme

500 g calves' liver	*2 tbs butter*
2 tbs flour	*2 tbs oil*
salt and pepper	*juice of an orange*
½-1 tbs chopped thyme	*parsley to garnish*

Slice liver and dip both sides in a mixture of flour, thyme and seasonings. Heat oil and butter together in a frying pan and cook liver gently, browning both sides until tender, about 8-10 minutes. Remove to a hot serving dish and keep warm while stirring orange juice into the pan juices. Simmer this 2-3 minutes, pour over liver and serve garnished with chopped parsley.

Rabbit Casserole with Thyme

1 cleaned, jointed rabbit	*¾ cup water*
pepper and salt	*1¾ cups red wine*
25 g butter	*2 tsp French mustard*
4 slices chopped bacon	*100 g mushrooms*
250 g sliced onions	*3 sprigs thyme*
4 tbs flour	

Season washed, dried rabbit pieces well. Melt butter and fry bacon and onions until onions are browned. Transfer to a casserole with a slotted spoon and fry rabbit until browned on both sides. Add to the casserole and stir flour into the fat in the pan, stirring and cooking until it turns a good brown colour. Stir in water and wine and bring to the boil, stirring continuously. Mix in mustard, blend well and pour over the rabbit in the casserole. Add mushrooms and thyme, cover and cook at 180 °C for 1½ hours or until tender. Remove thyme stalks, taste and adjust seasoning before serving.

Roast Meat with Thyme

Rub chopped thyme into skin of beef or veal before roasting, or place a sprig of two in cavity of a chicken before roasting in usual way.

Meat Loaf

¼ cup breadcrumbs
500 g minced steak
250 g minced bacon
1 minced onion

1 tsp thyme
salt and pepper
1 beaten egg
½ cup milk or stock

Combine breadcrumbs, meat, onion and seasonings and mix well.
Combine egg and milk or stock and stir into meat mixture. Put into
a greased loaf tin, cover with foil and bake at 180 °C for about one
hour, or until firm. Serve hot or cold.

Thyme Stuffing

2 cups fresh white
  breadcrumbs
2 cups peeled, diced, eating
  apples
1 peeled, finely chopped onion
½ cup sultanas

2 tsp thyme, finely chopped
2 tsp lemon thyme, finely
  chopped
salt and pepper
1 beaten egg

Combine all ingredients and mix well, binding with egg. If mixture
is too crumbly add a little lemon juice or water. Use to stuff poultry
or pork.

Thyme and Celery Stuffing

This is sufficient for an average chicken. Double the quantity for a
turkey or adjust to the size of any roasting bird.

1 finely chopped onion
1 finely chopped stick celery
1 tbs chopped fresh parsley
1 tbs chopped fresh thyme or
  1½ tsp dried thyme

1⅓ cups fresh breadcrumbs
pinch salt and pepper
grated rind and juice ½ lemon
1 beaten egg

Combine all ingredients and blend well.

Potato and Thyme Casserole

5 tbs butter

salt and pepper

3 peeled, sliced potatoes
3 peeled, sliced onions

4 sprigs thyme
milk

Butter the casserole with 1 tbs butter and arrange half the potato slices in it covered with half the onion slices. Season with salt and pepper and dot with butter. Repeat with remaining vegetables and seasoning and butter. Pour in enough milk to cover first layer of potatoes and onions, place thyme sprigs evenly on top, cover and bake about 45 minutes at 160 °C. Remove lid and brown the top for 15-20 minutes and serve hot.

Savoury Yorkshire Pudding

Mix together:
1 grated onion
250 g minced beef
1 tsp thyme
salt and pepper

Make a batter by combining:
1 cup flour
½ tsp salt
1 beaten egg
1 ¼ cups milk and water

Divide savoury mixture and put in 12 greased patty tins. Bake at 210 °C for 10 minutes. Then pour some batter on top of each savoury and bake 20 minutes more.

Bean Salad with Thyme

1 ½ cups dried white beans
½ cup oil
1 onion sliced
2 cloves crushed garlic
1 bay leaf

4 sprigs thyme
1 tbs tomato puree
juice of a lemon
salt and pepper
chopped parsley to garnish

Soak beans in cold water overnight. Drain. Heat oil and fry onion gently until golden before adding beans, garlic, bay, thyme and tomato puree. Cook gently for 10 minutes, cover bean mixture with boiling water, cover and simmer for 2 hours or until beans are tender. Add lemon juice, season to taste and leave beans to cool in the liquid. When cold pour into a serving dish and garnish with parsley.

Thyme, Parsnip and Tomato Soup

2 tbs butter
2 peeled, sliced onions
1 peeled, sliced potato
500 g peeled, sliced parsnips
salt and pepper
1½ tbs chopped thyme

4 cups chicken stock or 3½
  cups stock, ½ cup milk
1 bay leaf
400 g skinned, chopped
  tomatoes

Melt butter and fry sliced onion gently for 5 minutes. Add potato and parsnips and stir well. Cook a further 5 minutes. Add salt, pepper and thyme and stir in stock or stock and milk. Add bay leaf and chopped tomatoes. Cook, covered, until all vegetables are tender, 30-40 minutes. Remove bay leaf and puree soup through a mouli or in a blender. Reheat before serving.

Thyme, Carrot and Tomato Soup

250 g grated carrots
400 g skinned, chopped
  tomatoes
1 sliced onion
1 tbs lemon juice

1 bunch of thyme sprigs
1½ litres chicken stock
salt and pepper
paprika
parsley, chervil or chives

Combine all ingredients, except seasoning and herbs, in a large saucepan. Cover, bring to the boil and simmer about 30 minutes. Remove thyme stalks and taste before seasoning with salt, pepper and paprika. Sprinkle with fresh, finely chopped parsley, or chervil, or chives before serving.

Cabbage Casserole with Thyme

12 large savoy cabbage leaves
50 g butter or 4 tbs oil
1 chopped onion
1 chopped green pepper
50 g sliced mushrooms

500 g minced beef and/or veal
2 tbs tomato puree
2 tsp chopped thyme
salt and pepper
25 g butter

Blanch cabbage leaves in boiling water for 2 minutes, drain and dry well. Melt butter in a pan and cook onion and green pepper gently for about 5 minutes. Add mushrooms, meat, tomato puree and thyme, and season to taste. Cook, stirring well, for 5-10 minutes.

394

Line a buttered ovenproof dish with cabbage leaves and spread a layer of meat mixture over it. Continue to layer cabbage and meat alternately until the dish is full, ending with a layer of cabbage. Dot with 25 g butter and bake at 190 °C for 30-45 minutes.

Onion and Thyme Quiche

6 onions
50 g butter
pinch each nutmeg and cloves
½-1 tsp thyme
salt and pepper to taste

2 eggs
½ cup top milk
about 100 g short pastry
3 rashers bacon

Peel and slice onions finely and cook for 5 minutes in a little boiling water. Drain and cook them gently in melted butter in a heavy pan. When they are transparent, but not brown, add a pinch each of nutmeg and cloves and thyme and seasoning. Beat eggs and milk together and stir into onions. Remove the pan from the heat and allow to cool while rolling out pastry and lining a pie plate. Fill the pastry with onion and egg mixture, top with bacon cut into small pieces and bake at 180 °C for about 30-40 minutes until pastry is done and filling is firm.

Tomato and Thyme Flan

175-200 g pastry
400 g skinned, sliced
    tomatoes

1 tbs finely chopped thyme
50 g tasty cheese

Roll out pastry and line a shallow pie dish. Cover with sliced tomato and sprinkle with thyme and grated cheese. Bake at 200 °C for 20-30 minutes. Anchovies and olives may be used to decorate the flan before baking.

Courgettes with Thyme

50 g butter
500 g sliced courgettes

3 sprigs thyme
pepper and salt

Melt butter in a pan, add sliced courgettes, thyme and season to taste. Shake well to prevent courgettes from sticking, cover and cook over a low heat until courgettes are tender, about 15 minutes. Remove thyme stalks before serving.

Green Beans with Thyme

500 g green beans
4 tbs butter
2 tsp chopped thyme

1 clove crushed garlic
salt and pepper
1 tbs grated cheese

Top and tail and slice beans and blanch for 5 minutes in boiling water. Melt butter, add thyme and garlic and cook gently for 5 minutes. Add beans, toss well and cook 5 more minutes. Season and sprinkle with grated cheese just before serving.

Leeks Vinaigrette

leeks
French dressing

thyme

Trim off roots and green parts of leeks, wash well and cook in a little boiling water until just tender. Drain and dress with 3-4 tbs French dressing and chopped thyme to taste. Toss well and serve warm.

Lettuce with Hot Butter and Thyme

1 lettuce
juice ½ lemon
salt, pepper and sugar

2 tsp finely chopped thyme
50-75 g butter

Wash and dry lettuce and tear into bite-sized pieces. Place in a serving dish and pour combined lemon juice, seasonings and thyme mixture over it, tossing well to mix thoroughly. Melt butter just before serving, and when hot and frothy, pour over tossed lettuce.

Violet

The violet, *Viola odorata*, is a creeping perennial whose leaves and flowers grow directly from the rootstock on long stalks. The leaves are evergreen, heart-shaped, slightly wrinkled and toothed along the edges, and the flowers may be purple, lighter blue, white or pink. They are very fragrant and may be single or double.

Violets are propagated by seed or division, and like a rich, moist but well-drained soil and a sunny situation. They grow wild in many places, often at the edges of deciduous woods, and also do quite well in semi-shade though they do not flower so prolifically. Both the leaves and flowers of violets, which contain vitamin C, may be used in small quantities. The leaves are mainly used in salads but the flowers may also be used candied or fresh as a garnish, or in syrups, vinegars and in a variety of desserts. Before serving remove the calyx of each flower carefully, leaving the petals intact.

Violet Delight

Soak fresh pineapple or peaches or pears in a little brandy and arrange in small serving dishes. Top with a little ice cream or whipped cream and fresh or crystallised violets.

397

Violet Jelly

1 cup violet flowers
2 cups boiling syrup
2 tbs fruit juice, orange,
    lemon, pineapple or cherry

3 tsp gelatine softened in a
    little cold water

Put flowers picked from their stems in a bowl and pour over boiling syrup. Cover the basin and allow flowers to infuse until lukewarm. Add strained fruit juice and mix well. Soften gelatine in cold water and heat over boiling water until it dissolves. Stir it into the strained jelly and pour into a wetted mould. Set in the refrigerator and serve unmoulded and decorated with crystallised violets.

or

Make apple jelly in usual way and when it is near setting add 1 cup violets to every 2-4 cups jelly. Bottle, and cover when cold.

Violet Mousse

2 cups milk
2 tbs sugar
3 eggs, separated
4 tsp gelatine, softened in
    cold water

2 tbs violet syrup
½ cup whipped cream
candied violets

Heat milk and sugar together in a saucepan until boiling and pour onto lightly beaten egg yolks, stirring well. Return to the saucepan and cook, stirring until mixture thickens. Add softened gelatine and mix well. Allow to cool and stir in violet syrup. Beat egg whites until stiff and fold them and the whipped cream into the mixture. Pour into a glass dish to set and serve decorated with crystallised or fresh violets.

Violets in Fruit Salad

Fresh violet flowers may be added to fruit salad to taste. They taste very nice with any citrus fruit such as oranges, grapefruit or mandarins, or with pineapple.

To Candy Violet Flowers

Pick violets on a dry day and use a child's paintbrush to coat them both sides with lightly beaten egg white or a mixture of acacia powder and water, as for rose petals. Dip flowers in castor sugar and set to dry on waxed paper or on a tray in a cool oven. When quite dry store in airtight container between layers of waxed paper.

Violet Honey

Add 1 cup violets to 2 cups liquid honey and heat them together in the top of a double boiler over gently boiling water. Do not let the honey boil. Allow to infuse until cool then strain out violets and bottle honey.

Violet Syrup

500 g violets   sugar
1 litre water

Remove calices from flowers, put flowers in the water in a saucepan and bring to the boil. Simmer gently for 30 minutes, pour into a bowl, cover and infuse overnight. Strain and measure and add an equal quantity of sugar. Pour into a saucepan, bring to the boil, stirring, and boil 10 minutes. Overflow and seal in small jars with Perfit seals, or skim and allow to cool before pouring into bottles and storing in the refrigerator.

Salads with Violets

Violet flowers may be added as an edible garnish to any salad, e.g. add ½ cup violets to a salad of diced, cooked potatoes, sliced apple dipped in lemon juice and finely chopped celery. Toss in French dressing to taste and decorate with sliced, hard-boiled egg.

Salmon and Violet Salad

Combine tinned salmon broken into bite-sized pieces with sliced cucumber and a little finely chopped fennel leaves and violet leaves. Garnish with violets and serve with mayonnaise. Cold, cooked chicken may be used in place of salmon.

Violet Salad

Combine equal quantities of endive or chicory leaves and finely chopped celery and sprinkle thickly with finely chopped parsley. Add 40 violet flowers and toss all with a dressing of a combination of olive oil, white vinegar and a little claret. Olives may be added to salad.

Violet Butter

Spread a layer of violet flowers in a dish and add 50-100 g butter or butter balls. Surround and cover with more violet flowers. Cover the container and leave 24 hours.

Violet Sandwiches

Spread rye bread with violet butter and thinly sliced cooked chicken. Dot with violets and cover with another slice of buttered bread. Cut into triangles and serve garnished with violet leaves and flowers.

Mixed Herb Soup

Collect a mixture of herbs such as nettle tops, dandelion, watercress and violet leaves and cook with a ham bone and 2 cloves garlic in a large pan of water. Simmer about 30 minutes, covered, then add 2-3 peeled, chopped potatoes and cook another 30 minutes. Remove the bone, add some of the meat to each plate with a few diced potato pieces and pour the leafy soup over. If you prefer a vegetarian soup omit the ham bone and serve with slices of hard-boiled egg.

Index

402

Meat balls in curry sauce 128
Meat balls (hyssop) 207
Meat balls (lovage) 228
Meat balls (oregano) 281
Meat loaf (horseradish, sage) 202
Meat loaf (thyme) 392
Moussaka 241
Parsley steak 294
Roast beef (caraway) 86
Roast meat with thyme 391
Rosemary with roasts 328
Savory meat loaf 351
Shepherd's pie 242
Steak (bay) 71
Steak (marjoram) 243
Steak (oregano) 279
Stir-fried beef (lemon grass) 220
Tamale pie 281
Tarragon mince 382
Turkish meat balls 257
Lamb, hogget, mutton
Baked chops (coriander) 133
Bay marinade 67
Boiled lamb and dill sauce 156
Breton lamb 68
Devilled mutton 203
Lamajoon 256
Lamb and rice (fennel) 178
Lamb stuffed with mint 255
Lamb and rosemary turnovers 329
Lebanese lamb (coriander) 126
Mint crust for hogget 254
Mint and mutton patties 256
Rosemary crumb topping 329
Rosemary lamb 329
Rosemary marinade 328
Rosemary with roasts 328
Sage and lamb 341
Tansy with roast lamb 374
Liver, kidney, tripe
Basil lamb's fry 52
Fennel seeds with liver/kidney 178
Liver casserole (bay) 70

Liver with marjoram 240
Liver with oregano 281
Liver and thyme 391
Kidney and mushroom (parsley) 294
Kidney and mushrooms (sage) 340
Savory tripe 353
Pork, ham, bacon
Anise pork 45
Baked chops with coriander 133
Fennel with bacon 185
Ham with tarragon 380
Hot dandelion and bacon 149
Pork baked with marjoram 242
Pork chops with tarragon 382
Pork fingers with sage 341
Pork pieces with coriander 127
Pork and sage casserole 341
Potted pork (bay) 70
Sage and ginger topping 344
Thyme and pork pate 389
Veal and ham (rosemary) 330
Veal and ham (sage) 342
Veal and ham pie (sage) 343
Rabbit
Rabbit casserole (thyme) 391
Rabbit stew (bay) 70
Rabbit stew (sage) 342
Rabbit with tarragon 380
Sausages
Basil luncheon sausage 52
Boiled sausage (fennel) 178
Sage and sausage loaf 342
Sauerkraut and frankfurters 90
Sausage casserole (garlic) 194
Veal
Anise veal casserole 45
Rolled schnitzel 242
Tarragon wiener schnitzel 383
Veal and caraway rice 87
Veal and ham (rosemary) 330
Veal and ham (sage) 342
Veal and ham pie 343
Veal and oregano 279
Veal and parsley sauce 294
Veal and savory terrine 352

415

419

425